Tracking
Gobi Grizzlies

[Above] Co-researchers Harry Reynolds (pointing) and Michael Proctor discuss possible bear travel routes while searching for a Gobi grizzly's dropped radio collar. [Opposite] After being captured and radio-collared, the young bear named Altan charges the first sound he hears: the click of a remote camera. The camera did not survive. [Next Spread] Another slope of scattered shrubs, another gravel plain, another range of mountains to cross. Photos: Joe Riis

Tracking Gobi Grizzlies

Surviving
Beyond the Back
of Beyond

DOUGLAS
CHADWICK

Photographs by Joe Riis
and Douglas Chadwick

Bears and humans are among the few mammals that rely on plantigrade locomotion—using the full bottom surface of their feet, including the heels (and palms, in the bears' case). Photo: Joe Riis

Contents

Tracking Gobi Grizzlies

Surviving Beyond
the Back of Beyond

FIRST EDITION

Editors: Abraham Streep & John Dutton
Art Director: Scott Massey
Photo Editor: Jane Sievert
Project Manager: Jennifer Patrick
Production: Rafael Dunn
Additional Design & Photo Editing Support: Jennifer Ridgeway
Director of Patagonia Books: Karla Olson

Printed in Canada by Friesens
on 100% recycled paper

ISBN 978-1-938340-62-8
E-Book ISBN 978-1-938340-63-5
Library of Congress Control Number
2016912364

[Above] Base camp in the eastern mountain complex of Great Gobi Strictly Protected Area (GGSPA). Photo: Doug Chadwick Collection
[Next Spread] This female is one of the last three to four dozen Gobi grizzly bears, *Ursus arctos gobiensis*, left on Earth.
Known as *mazaalai* in Mongolian, all of them live in southwest Mongolia's GGSPA. Photo: Doug Chadwick

Preface

Two Quick Bear Stories

For more than a decade, my home was a log cabin in the Montana Rockies, off the grid and way off the clock. My to-do list on many days looked like this:

Chop firewood,
Pump water,
Go watch wildlife next door in Glacier National Park,
Especially bears.

Late one August, I camped for a while along the ridgeline of a mountain range overlooking a series of shallow subalpine lakes. It was huckleberry time, and the crop up there was beyond good that year. You could have told as much from the purple stains that tattooed my fingers and encircled my mouth. Or from the big clods of what looked like compressed pie filling all over the slopes. They were the dung left by tons—literally—of grizzlies drawn to huck heaven from home ranges near and far.

Before long, I had an adult bear in view at a lake. I dropped from the ridge to a lower band of ledges and set up a telescope. The animal was wading out from shore with only portions of its back and snout showing, furry alligator-style. This grizzly wasn't in the water to hunt for fish or for anything else, though. It wasn't there to drink its fill or to interact with another bear. It was just doing what any of us might while free-roaming the slopes on a hot afternoon—getting wet and keeping cool. Feeling fine. Every so often, the bear would stand to swipe at the surface or pound it with its paws to create a splash. At other times, Aqua-Grizz would submerge completely and then rise on its hind legs again to shake itself, whipping rings of water from its head and upper torso.

Returning to shore, the bear came upon a washed-up tree trunk. After rolling this around for a few moments, the grizzly lay on its back among the green sedges, wrestled the heavy length of wood atop its body, lifted it, and began to juggle the thing with all four feet. Why? Well, why will a grown-up grizzly repeatedly slide down a tilted patch of snow? Why does one foraging in a meadow sometimes break into a wriggly, loose-limbed frolic, swinging its head and zigzagging this way and that? I think the better question—and also the answer—is: Why not? Imagine you own hundreds of pounds of muscle packed atop muscle, claws that measure three to four inches along the outside curve, and the ability to accelerate from zero to thirty-five miles per hour in seconds. What you want to do, you can do, no worries. You're a heavy-duty organic power generator with a fresh tank of fruit sugar fuel, and this log is just lying there waiting to be tossed around.

While science can't quite bring itself to say that grizzlies like to goof, the experts acknowledge that, young or old, these bears do devote an intriguing amount of time to play behavior. Exuberance is part of what defines them. So is a strongly developed sense of curiosity. Grizzlies are given to thoroughly investigating objects of interest, manipulating them with their mouth as well as with those broad, flexible paws, trying in their own way to learn more about how the world works. It's one of the main reasons I've always found it natural to relate to grizz—to imagine myself in their place as they move through a landscape, poking around. I also try never to forget that the same animals can instantly turn volcanic when upset.

The grizzly eventually lost interest in the log and waded back into the lake. There, the bear resumed whapping the water with its paws, alternately dunking and rising to do the subalpine swimming hole shimmy-shake. For a few minutes, it spent more time than usual with its head underwater. I thought the bear might be investigating something below. That was before a closer look through the telescope revealed that it was blowing bubbles with its nose. The water's surface tension, layered with a fine summer film of pollen and dust, kept many of the bubbles bulging in place after they rose, glistening atop the lake like a flotilla of small jellyfish. The grizzly bit at some. It stood upright once more, chest-deep now, and appeared to look the bubbles over carefully. Then it started popping the largest by pricking them one by one with the tip of a claw.

———

MY WIFE, KAREN REEVES, SPENT SEVERAL SUMMERS MANAGING A HIKE-IN chalet high in the Glacier Park backcountry. One year, a spell of rain wrapped the heights in heavy clouds, hiding the spectacular topography from sight for days. One of the guests, a woman with an infant child, grew more and more restless as the storm kept its shroud over the land. At last, she decided that, rain or no rain, view or no view, she and her husband were going to get out on the trail to a pass south of the chalet. The high point was barely a mile distant, but the route was steep. By the time the couple negotiated the pass and started through the alpine meadows beyond, their baby had grown hungry. Picking out a level spot, the woman sat, opened her jacket, and began to suckle the child amid veils of mist.

As the baby nursed, the parents took more notice of their surroundings. They became aware of an occasional break in the fog. Then out of the swirls stepped a grizzly. Coming from the opposite side of the pass, the bear was no more than forty or fifty yards away, well inside the zone where a startled bear may reflexively attack. Not only was this a grizz, it was the kind said to be the one you least want to meet at close quarters: a mother with young. She had two little cubs at her heels.

The bear noticed the people at almost the same time. She stopped walking, swiveled to check on her offspring, and turned back to stare directly at the parents and child again. After what must have felt like an awfully long pause, this grizzly made its move. She plonked down on her hindquarters, gathered the cubs up onto her lap, and began nursing them. Maybe it was the smell of the other mammal's milk that inspired her; maybe something else. I don't remember Karen relating how long the mothers sat there on the pass, not far from one another, nursing their babies. I only remember hearing that after the young were fed and content, the two females rose and went their separate ways.

━━━━━━━

ONE WAY TO DEFINE GRIZZLIES WOULD BE AS BIG, HAIRY, EYE-POPPING opportunities to get your heart rate up and start thinking fast. But what are the animals truly like? All kinds of people seem to believe that they know. In reality, nobody does. And nobody will until we gain more insight into the species' complex suite of behaviors and learning abilities. That's not a criticism of our efforts. It's a tribute to a potent mammal that, like us, is able to operate on many different levels and in many different environments. It's also an open-ended invitation to discovery.

In a remote and pitiless desert on the other side of the world from North America lives a bear that science understands only poorly so far and the general public isn't aware of at all. One of the scarcest creatures on the planet, it is a type of grizzly so extraordinary that its existence is hard to imagine even

A wolf pack waits its turn at an elk carcass monopolized by grizzlies in Yellowstone National Park, United States of America. Photo: Dan Stahler

after you get to its homeland; in fact, *especially* after you get to its homeland. Traders, bandits, holy men, and warriors have passed through over the centuries, adding legends and layers of history. But they didn't stay, and this setting was never tamed. It still isn't. Not yet, although....

Oh, hell. Let's just go so I can show you.

01

Lost
Amid the
Dust
and Gold

Pre-dawn. The trap door at Shar Khuls was up, as usual. I left my vantage point on the high spine of a ridge and climbed back down to my tent. It was pitched near several others in a draw where the mountains give out onto an immense gravel plain. On one edge of the encampment was a *ger*, the Mongolian name for a yurt. Built of wood and concrete instead of fabric, this round hut stood buried in the side of a hill for extra shelter from the elements. There were ten of us living here, the only humans for thousands of square miles. The *ger* was the communal burrow where we gathered to dine.

Breakfast the day before had been noodle soup with dried camel meat that our cook pre-softened with a beating from a tire iron. This morning we were looking at a two-course affair: tinned sardines on fry bread, followed by a rice soup with chunks from the dwindling supply of overripe sheep parts that hung from the *ger*'s walls. It was April 29, 2014. The dust in the air outside had grown thicker overnight, and a cold wind was blowing gale force. Nevertheless, the crew—a group of wildlife scientists and protected area rangers—was determined to explore a water source far to the north that had been discovered only three weeks earlier. The plan was to head across the plain to a distant mountain range we failed to get over the day before. Since the southern slopes had proved too steep and unstable for our Russian-made, four-wheel-drive van, we were going to try circling the base of that range today to find a route up the north side.

First, one of the patrol rangers needed to inspect the Shar Khuls trap more closely and check three more traps we had set in the terrain farther east, each roughly fifteen to twenty-five miles from the next. Shar Khuls ("Yellow Reed") was named for its beds of tall *Phragmites* grass growing beside copses of poplar trees and tamarisk bushes where an underground spring flows to the surface. The other three traps were also set near live springs. All four oases lay amid a maze of parched mountains and canyons deep in the Great Gobi Desert, beyond the back of beyond.

Gobi, in Mongolian, means "waterless place." Half a million square miles in size, the Great Gobi is one of the Earth's five largest deserts (outside the frozen polar expanses receiving so little fresh precipitation that they, too, technically qualify as deserts). The drylands stretch for a thousand miles east to west and as many as six hundred miles north to south, taking in the southern third of Mongolia and much of northern China. This is right at the center of the Asian land mass, so far from any ocean that clouds bearing moisture drop nearly all of it over other landscapes before they ever get here. Rainfall in the Gobi averages just four to six inches annually. Some years, parts of the countryside never see a drop. Temperatures can reach

122 degrees Fahrenheit in summer and sink to minus 40 in winter. If you imagine the result to be a vast realm of shifting sands, well, you shouldn't. The Gobi Desert is mostly stone.

Each of the traps was a sheet metal box about three feet wide, four feet high, and eight feet long. The one at Shar Khuls stood with a heavy door raised above an open end. Inside were grain pellets, raisins, dabs of jam and honey, and a raw egg: bait. A wire ran from the door's release mechanism to a hinged plate slightly raised off the box's floor. Pushing down on that treadle would trigger the door to fall shut. The tension was carefully adjusted so that it would take a heavy footstep to do that.

A couple times in the past, I'd trotted back to camp from the ridge, which I climbed most every morning, with news that the Shar Khuls trapdoor was down. I'd rushed to gather up gear, piled into a van alongside as many crew members as could fit in, raced around the ridge to the box, and discovered nothing but the food inside. Violent wind gusts sometimes caused the door to drop by shaking it until the stays gave way. Although the trap weighed hundreds of pounds, one Gobi windstorm rolled the whole thing over onto its side. We wrestled it back into place and toted boulders from a nearby talus field to pile on top. Since then, the box was at least staying right side up. Still, with springtime temperatures cycling between sweaty hot and freezing in the course of twenty-four hours, metal parts were constantly stretching or shrinking a bit. Maybe balances shifted. Maybe weak spots developed. For all we could tell, *gazriin ezen*—local rock and tree spirits—came and messed with the system too. Something had to explain the windless times when we found the door fallen, crept toward the trap, and peered in only to find a bewildered hare or pint-size hedgehog peering back.

What we wanted to find in these live traps were bears. Big, unruly, long-eared, bed-hair-shaggy, chocolate-colored, bronze, or golden Gobi grizzly bears. *Ursus arctos*, found across much of the Northern Hemisphere, is commonly called either the brown bear or grizzly. Gobi bears are a unique variety or subspecies, *Ursus arctos gobiensis*. Mongolians call them *mazaalai*. Scientists weren't even able to confirm their existence until 1943, and not many details about their lives have been uncovered since. During the second half of the twentieth century, portions of the Gobi were hit by a combination of expanded livestock grazing and drought, both of which reduced the desert's already sparse vegetation. The bears lost half to two-thirds of their range, and their numbers fell sharply. Today, no more than three to four dozen individuals remain. Gobi grizzlies have become the rarest bears in the world. There are none in captivity. All the known survivors inhabit outlying ranges of the

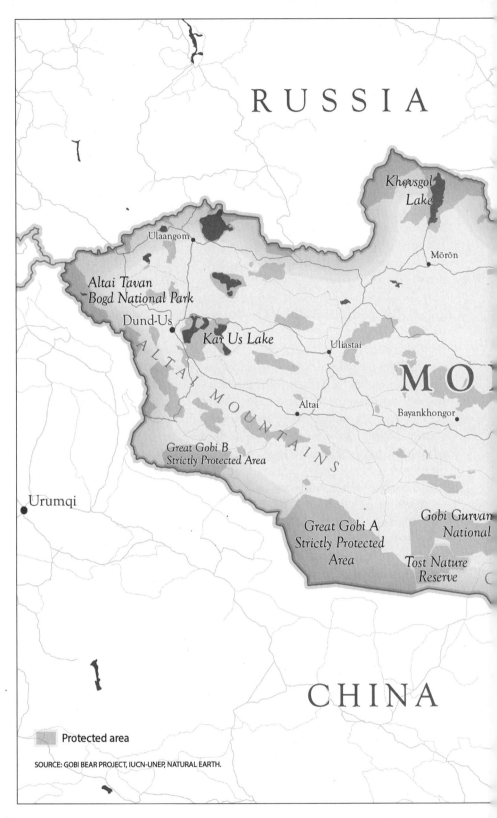

RUSSIA

Khovsgol Lake

Ulaangom

Mörön

Altai Tavan
Bogd National Park

Dund-Us

Kar Us Lake

Uliastai

MO

Altai

Bayankhongor

Great Gobi B
Strictly Protected Area

Urumqi

Great Gobi A
Strictly Protected
Area

Gobi Gurvan
National

Tost Nature
Reserve

CHINA

For decades, the Gobi bears' sole home and refuge has been Great Gobi A Strictly Protected Area (GGSPA),
situated in the desert mountains of southwestern Mongolia. The new Tost Nature Reserve now links the GGSPA

with Gobi Gurvan Saikhan National Park. This creates one of the world's largest continuous protected landscapes and opportunities for these bears to begin reclaiming portions of their former range.

Gobi-Altai Mountains in southwestern Mongolia, keeping almost entirely to three of the tallest, most rugged portions of a reserve established there in 1976. This is the Great Gobi Strictly Protected Area–A. Called the GGSPA for short, and it covers roughly 18,000 square miles, an area slightly larger than Israel and Kuwait combined.

Since 2005, the Gobi Bear Project team of Mongolian biologists, GGSPA personnel, and lead scientist Harry Reynolds, an American bear expert who started this study in his mid-sixties, has been working together to catch and radio-collar *mazaalai*. They continue to do this for a month every spring between the time most bears emerge from hibernation and the start of searing temperatures that bring with them a risk of fatal heat stress for a captured animal.

Nearly all Mongolians have a nickname. Purevdorj Narangerel, aka Puji (or Puugee), is the ranger assigned to patrol the central third of the reserve. When trapping operations are based in his sector, he joins the team and is typically the one who makes the daily rounds to check the baited boxes. He does it the same way he keeps an eye on thousands of square miles of the reserve the rest of the year—alone astride a motorcycle. It is the fastest means of travel in this roadless desert terrain. Equally important, a dirt bike like his sips lightly from the limited fuel supply the Project is able to haul in to a remote base camp.

Of medium height with close-cropped hair, Puji often wore a stern expression; not severe, just set in place. I could never tell how much of this reflected a personality trait and how much was a carryover from endless hours of riding through great empty landscapes, cutting the wind and sharp cold or baking heat with his face, concentrating hard on the path he was choosing, where any one of a million rocks could send him and his machine cartwheeling. Puji, who looked to be in his mid-thirties, readily shared information when it was needed. Otherwise, he tended to keep his thoughts to himself, a serious man with the serious skills needed to crisscross a hard place month after month and return intact. This morning, he once again pulled a balaclava over his head, wrapped his greatcoat more tightly around himself and bound it in place with the sash at its waist, fit his motorcycle goggles over his eyes, fired up the bike, and raced off to run the trapline without a backward glance.

On average, the team caught just two bears in a season. So far in 2014, we had been trying for two weeks without any luck. All eyes were on the moto-ranger as he returned in midmorning, cut the bike's engine, and rolled to a stop beside his tent. Looking up, Puji shook his head. Zero for four again; no bear in the traps. The rest of the crew soon set off in the van, leaving Puji

Following rough dirt tracks and wildlife trails, GGSPA patrol ranger Purevdorj (Puji or Puugee) Narangerel covers the middle third of the enormous reserve by motorbike. Photo: Joe Riis

at camp along with Boldbayar (Boyoko) Mijiddorj, who grew up in a village close to the reserve and was now a Mongolian university student in biology. Geerlee Namkhai, the tireless older woman from the GGSPA headquarters who kept the *ger* in order and cooked for the team, would sometimes drop everything to join in a day's exploration if it sounded promising. Not this morning, though. With this much dust and wind streaming by, she chose to stay behind too.

The plain to the north was shaped like a colossal dish. At its center, we rolled along over a series of flat alkali pans (*takyr* in Mongolian) where water from rare heavy rains had pooled and then evaporated. The sun baked the briny deposits of clay-rich silt into hard white speedways. But it seemed as though the Russian van manufacturers must not have intended their products to be driven south of Siberia, for we never raced far before we had to turn the machine's nose into the hard wind and shut off the engine to keep it from burning up.

Harry and I had the same habit of using van cool-down breaks to go on short walkabouts, searching for animal signs and unusual stones. Both of us kept rock collections beside our tents at camp. Our favorites were pieces cut and polished by airborne grains of dust and sand. The term for such stones, I learned later, is ventifacted—literally, wind-wrought. Outcroppings of crumbling bedrock amid the *takyrs* offered a striking variety of examples, because the passing air picked up velocity traveling across these smooth pans. Intense solar radiation interacts with minerals both within the stone and in the fine clay particles that winds plaster onto its surface. This adds a shiny patina to the sculptures—a desert glaze. With their odd lumps and curvatures and almost liquid smoothness, many of the results seemed less like rock than like some as-yet uncategorized Gobi life-form.

When I knelt on the ground for a closer inspection, I could feel my face being ventifacted—getting a free dermabrasion treatment at the Gobi spa. The stronger gusts really hurt, though, and left nicks in my sunglasses. These stones didn't speak of the eons at work. They told of a geologic rush job. The specimens under my nose would be a few microns smaller and altered in shape by the time the van engine was ready to haul us on the next leg of the journey.

"*Yawi-awi*." My Mongolian language abilities are worse than rudimentary. I'm only repeating a phrase we all called out on journeys, and I'm probably spelling it wrong. I knew what it meant, though: "Let's go!"

Eventually, our traverse of the plain was complete. Next we rounded the target mountain range, beginning a long, butt-banging, kidney-rearranging drive upslope. As the angle of the incline gradually increased, we found ourselves halting every twenty minutes for an engine cool-down of fifteen minutes. This was my fourth consecutive spring expedition with the Gobi Bear Project. Between bad weather, impassable ground, and vehicle break-downs, I'd taken part in many an all-day odyssey that never reached our destination. Having undergone one just the day before, I didn't like feeling condemned to another, but the only thing I could do about it was shut my eyes and retreat into other thoughts.

I began to nod off. You know how strange dreams can be. If I had drifted into a truly bizarre one like, say, being packed into a Russki van with a small horde of Mongols careening around after grizzly bears nobody knows exist way the hell and gone in the middle of Thirstland watching people's heads bounce off the ceiling ... nothing would have changed after I woke up. But I knew why I was here.

Ten thousand years ago, the planet's human population was around 5 million. As of 1930, there were 400,000 times that many folks—about 2 billion. The total hit 3.5 billion by 1970. Between then and 2012, it doubled to 7 billion. During that forty-two-year interval, Earth's total population of vertebrate wildlife—fish, amphibians, reptiles, birds, and mammals—fell by more than half, according to the World Wildlife Fund. The International Union for the Conservation of Nature predicts that one of every four species of mammals will vanish in the near future. A third of all species presently known, and possibly more, may be gone by the end of the century.

This was the context in which our attempts to learn more about Gobi bears played out. For me, it kept our daily dramas with malfunctioning equipment, accidents, dwindling supplies, or big-jawed camel spiders that can race thirty feet in two seconds in perspective. When a series of minor setbacks began to feed a real sense of frustration anyway, I'd focus instead on how heartening it would be to actually carry off a rescue of these most critically endangered bears. The existence of grizzlies in the Gobi Desert defies long odds to begin with. If the Project proved able to help them rebound, that wouldn't change the world. But it would keep Gobi bears in it—and perhaps raise hopes for other implausible-seeming efforts to provide fellow Earthlings with a future. I pictured the team climbing a nearby peak to stand on the summit with middle fingers raised, flipping off the forces denaturing the only living planet we know.

Any thought is worth trying if it helps pass the miles, right? This really was a long ride.

By late afternoon we had chugged far enough up the base of the range that a canyon opened up below us to one side. The van made better time along its rim, where the gravel was firmer. Unhappily, the drop down to the canyon bottom soon became so long and steep that I wished we weren't hugging the edge quite so closely. Enkhbold (Boldoo) Erdenekhuu had the wheel today. Tall and turned out in full camouflage fatigues most days, he was a senior ranger with an air of authority but an easy laugh. Rather than use his strong voice to order anyone around, which would have been a pretty un-Mongolian way to operate in a group, he preferred to lead the sessions of traditional songs that the Mongolian crew carried on for miles at a time during our travels, chorusing away about lost love and found love, a tireless horse, and the greatness of the land and immanent blue sky. Boldoo was an excellent driver and a fearless one—a little too fearless for my liking. All at once, he turned the wheel, shouted a Mongolian version of "Are you ready?" and drove right over the canyon rim. *Yawi-awi*! Yeehaw! And holy shit! We schussed downward while he fought to keep the van from slewing sideways and rolling, reached the bottom, and from there continued gradually upslope again by following the lower canyon's curves.

Project travel depends on Russian-made four-wheel-drive vans. Loaded with people and supplies, they required periodic stops to let the engines cool. Photo: Doug Chadwick

Three-quarters of an hour after that, we were nearing the upper reaches of the mountain range when another canyon abruptly appeared, falling away from the heights we had now reached. The serpentine bottom of this new cleft lay a long way below, wrapped in deep shade, beckoning like the pathway into a lost world. Boldoo drove right up to the gorge's rim as though he intended to drive straight down this one too. It would have been suicidal. I grabbed a door handle, preparing to leap. But he braked and killed the engine and started laughing; he'd just been messing with us. Still chuckling, Boldoo pointed at the ground just outside the window and said, "*Baavgai.*" The word sounds like "bawa," and it's the generic Mongolian term for bear. As soon as I stepped out, I saw the fresh tracks next to the van. They continued over the edge of the chasm and down a dune stacked against the canyonside.

We put on daypacks and followed the bear's steep route to the bottom, sliding an extra yard for every step we took in the soft sand. While descending, I looked across this new canyon to the crest of the mountain range looming above. I could make out the notch in it that we had tried to reach with the van from the south side the previous day. Had we made it that far, we would have found ourselves looking straight down past the front wheels at a thousand vertical feet of cliff.

On the floor of the gorge, the bear's trail merged with the scat and tracks of wolves, black-tailed gazelles, wild camels, wild asses, and the region's wild cliff-dwelling goats with horns like great knobby scimitars—Siberian ibex. It was a reminder that the reserve was established to protect not just *mazaalai* but an entire community of desert fauna whose rich variety of big mammals had been a revelation ever since my first trip into the Gobi. The convergence of their paths foretold of a spring waiting somewhere along the dry wash. A second clue came from the thickets of tamarisk. They spoke of water already present underfoot within reach of these plants' specialized deep-root systems. Before we had gone another half-mile, a small amount of that liquid seeped to the surface and formed shallow pools. The remains of a black-tailed gazelle lay among the tamarisk stems at one side. More bones and scraps of hide were scattered in the powdery white alkali dust that forms around the evaporating edges of the Gobi's rare springs. On the scree slope just above, an ibex skull and horns rested facing the water hole as if placed there to keep watch.

At least two of the sets of bear tracks looked relatively fresh. A compact pile of scat among them consisted almost entirely of darkling beetle remains—further evidence, perhaps, of how Gobi bears adapt when a rainless spell, such as the desert had experienced for months now, suppresses early springtime plant growth. Although we encountered more tamarisk thickets and several big poplars along the next mile of the canyon floor, no additional surface springs appeared. There may have been some lower in the gorge, but the hour was growing late. We called a halt to our trek after coming upon the body of an ibex surrounded by torn-off tufts of its fur and bear droppings packed with more of the hairs.

This was the narrowest part of the canyon so far—a bottleneck ideal for ambush by a predator. In the movie running through my brain, it was wolves that had made the kill; their scat lay close by. After them came gimlet-eyed ravens and vultures. Next, the bear, arriving at the gorge to slake its thirst, followed its nose to the carcass and chased off the birds to take its turn scavenging. In reality, the carcass was too dismembered to reveal how the animal died. The marrow in its leg bones, normally white and fatty, was red and runny, a sign of malnutrition. The ibex might have been easy prey, and the killer wasn't necessarily either wolves or a bear. It could have been microscopic disease organisms. Or it could have been one of the snow leopards living among the Gobi's mountains, which include summits close to 9,000 feet high. These nocturnal hunters with a whisper-soft tread descend to many of the same oases used by the rest of the area's wildlife. Nor could we rule out the possibility that the ibex was brought down by a similar predator within the reserve: the Eurasian lynx. Weighing as much as sixty-five pounds, this larger cousin of the Canada lynx is a successful ungulate predator as well as a hunter of smaller mammals and birds. I would have liked to search the gorge more widely for feline footprints or territorial scrape marks. By the time we finished investigating the area around the carcass, though, dusk was already overtaking us.

━━━━━

WE RETRACED OUR ROUTE TO THE HEAD OF THE GORGE, CLIMBED BACK UP the dune to the van, and started driving away into the night. I thought we were headed straight for camp, which was hours distant. Instead, Boldoo detoured to a higher slope and pulled up at the base of a promontory. We got out and climbed until our headlamps illuminated a pit where illegal miners had been hacking their way into the solid rock under the spell of gold. Mongolian authorities have nicknamed them ninjas, since they generally slip into the reserve under cover of darkness and wear face masks or scarves to counter the cold and the wind. Most come riding motorbikes, but a few use cars or trucks. Usually driving without lights, they count on being able to elude the handful of rangers who patrol the vast area.

The ninja miners who get caught are subject to fines, and many have their equipment confiscated. That doesn't deter some from returning or newcomers from trying their luck. Hundreds have been arrested throughout the protected area over the past few years. More keep coming, ignoring the hardships, pushing ever farther into the reserve, gripped by visions of becoming freed from a lifetime of want in a sudden blaze of light reflecting off precious metal. Gold, copper, and coal have been found in many parts of the Great Gobi Desert. One of the largest deposits of gold and copper yet discovered on the globe—Oyu Tolgoi (Turquoise Hill)—lies a couple hundred miles directly east of the GGSPA.

Some of the ninjas who invade the reserve search in old runoff channels with metal detectors. A few set up dry placer operations using screens that sift the gravel for flakes and nuggets one shovelful at a time. Others prospect routes across mountain walls and bore their way inside with pickaxes and chisel-tipped bars, following strata with glimmers of the precious ore. That's what the ninjas had done here, high above the gorge. They carved a shaft straight down through solid rock for a dozen feet and then hewed a horizontal tunnel—what miners call an adit—deeper into the bedrock. The ninjas must have been tracing a good vein. When I first arrived this year at the protected area headquarters, located in Bayantooroi (Rich in Poplars), a hamlet just beyond the reserve, eight men were being held in custody next door at the police station. They were fresh ninja recruits—the third group nabbed at

These villagers toting a metal detector look suspiciously like illegal miners—"ninjas" as the GGSPA rangers call them—who sneak into the reserve illegally at night to dig for gold. Photo: Joe Riis

this illegal mine within two weeks. A few days after we continued on to our base camp from the headquarters, we learned via a radio call that four more ninjas, who had fled the most recent raid, just got collared. They were trying to make their escape through the reserve on foot when rangers and police caught up with them. That may have saved their lives. Out of water and on the verge of collapse, the men had been drinking their own urine to survive.

Ninjas originally discovered the springs in the gorge we explored. Rangers following suspicious tire tracks came upon the illegal mine and then learned of the water source the outlaws relied upon. As a rule, the mostly hand-powered digging activities of gold-seekers don't directly disturb all that much acreage. Nor has evidence been found of *mazaalai* being poached for their gall bladders, claws, and other body parts, an all-too-common fate for bears in Asia. But some of the trespassers do kill other wildlife for food. Wherever ninjas go to dig for precious metal within the reserve, they gravitate to the nearest water, as they had here. Their frequent presence at and near springs discourages desperately thirsty animals from coming in to drink, thereby taking away the Gobi resource most valuable to the animal community as a whole.

Of the bear dung we noted in the gorge today, the most telling sample was collected by Dr. Amgalan (Amgaa) Luvsanjamba. A slightly built, gray-haired man with a rapid stride and an eye for details of the natural world, he was a long-time member of the Gobi Bear Project and former department leader at the Institute of Biology, part of the Mongolian Academy of Sciences. Near the ibex carcass, he found a scat containing a white plastic label from a food wrapper. As Amgaa said when he held the label out for inspection, it came from "ninja food." Here, then, was an animal rewarded for sniffing around a site frequented by people, most likely a dining spot or garbage pile close to the mine. The learning abilities of *Ursus arctos* are considerable. However, using them to form a positive connection between human activities and something to eat would be one of the surest ways for this Gobi grizzly to end up shot for "raiding" an illegal camp.

Whatever else the outlaws might have left near the mine opening was obscured by the night and the dust streaming past. The wind felt close to freezing now, and it had grown so bullying that we could scarcely stand against it. We descended and began a long return drive through the main canyon along the dry wash covering its floor. I had been wondering how we were possibly going to get up the hundred-foot wall Boldoo had previously dived down in the van. What he did was let us out at the bottom, circle the vehicle across the wash to build up speed, hit the steepest part of the slope—the cutbank of the wash—with the accelerator floored, and take to the sky. The van flew five or six feet clear of the ground, headlights arcing upward like searchlights as the engine screamed and the wheels spun in the air. When the tires came down onto the surface, they bounced off it several times before the treads dug in to add to the upslope momentum. With the engine faltering toward the top, Boldoo squeezed just enough power from it to inch over the rim. He never heard our cheers from below over the blast of the gale. If you're going to get very far driving in the Gobi, being a little too fearless is a real help.

The canyon's steep sides had partly sheltered us from the main surge of the growing dust storm. It hit full force during our descent of the mountains' open lower slopes. A constant pinging and drumming of airborne grit against the van's body joined the wails of the wind. When we reached the plain, the storm's roaring grew louder. The van's tracks from earlier in the day, marking our way home, were being erased by the second. To follow what was left of them, Boldoo had to slow the rig to a crawl, for the dust was so thick that it cut visibility nearly to zero at times.

Then we reached the alkali flats—the series of *takyrs*. Conditions went from bad to stupid-bad to raging, blinding, Captain-we've-landed-on-the-wrong-planet! movie bad. With the air coming at us like a reddish-brown landslide, swirling in the headlamps, crashing relentlessly against the front of the van, I remembered the expression "It'll be a cold day in hell when...." Now I knew what a cold day in hell must be like. Our inbound tracks were lost altogether. We tried to navigate instead by keeping a constant angle relative to the direction of the oncoming waves of dust. It reminded me of night voyages on boats trying to maintain a fixed bearing in a maelstrom at sea.

It's always easier to keep your spirits up in the daytime. We knew that we had traveled a relatively straightforward route through the *takyrs* earlier, but we couldn't find it at night with this desert going airborne. The paths Boldoo chose ended at ridges of deep sand or sudden drop-offs into gullies. I wasn't worried until I realized that the Mongolians had gone completely quiet for a while. That never happened unless most everyone was sleeping. Nobody was sleeping. The crew's silence wasn't a symptom of fear. Everybody was used to dust storms. What I was hearing was the soundless admission that we were exposed to the teeth of an exceptionally strong blow on an enormous plain with no place to hide from the furious blackness and no solid idea of where we were or how we were going to get un-lost.

I couldn't follow what little conversation there was. After someone pointed out a faint set of tire tracks, Odko translated some of the comments:

"Ours from today?"

"Maybe another day."

"Yes, they look older, and I think they go a different direction."

"Ninja?"

"Or ours when we were looking for the ninjas?"

Then a huge wave of dust obliterated the last of those tracks, and everybody was back to pointing hopefully in different directions.

I expected that we might spend the night out here, and it would be long. The temperature continued to drop. Even with the windows tightly shut, the wind was forcing enough fine dust through the tiniest seams of the van that I could taste it in my mouth and feel it caking the inside of my nose. Mineral air. I kept enough surgical masks in my pack to pass around if it came to that. And if the van broke down and the storm continued? Finding our way through the chaos to our base camp on foot was a near-impossibility. I'd brought six quarts of water. I wished the other team members had done the same. Collectively, we barely had enough for another day, maybe two.

Boldoo kept the van moving, though, picking paths around obstructions, aiming in what he thought was the general direction of a rough track that ran between the nearest village north of the reserve and the central mountain range where our camp stood. Many changes of trajectory and opinions about them and storm-skewed readings on GPS devices later, we seemed no closer. Somehow, though, we did reach the track after angling away from a mess of sandy ridges.

We turned onto the route. It looped and meandered, and we'd gone a fair distance before Nyambayar (Nyamaa, pronounced Nima) Yanjin, a ranger-biologist, began making a sound as if he were repeatedly clearing his throat. That, in everyday Mongolian, was saying, "No, no, no, no," while he curved his hand to describe a 180-degree turn. A genuine giant of a man in his twenties, very tall and muscular and also very stout and fond of food, Nyamaa rarely wore much besides a T-shirt, shorts, and open sandals. He seemed generally oblivious to cold. The one item of extra clothing he had brought, a thin coat, was still lying on the seat beside him. Nyamaa was in a happier mood than he had been before we found this track. He was just letting us know that he thought we had turned the wrong way and were now headed in exactly the opposite direction from where we wanted to go. He was right.

Reversing course, we crossed two or three different mountain ranges that I didn't remember, even though I'd traveled this track before. After the last of the high passes, a brief lull in the storm allowed us to glimpse a light way off in the distance. An hour after that, midnight had come and gone, but we were racing up the final rise from the gravel plain toward camp. At the

Only a little lost, the Project crew discusses the best route to a newly
discovered spring where ninjas had a nearby illegal gold-mining operation.
GGSPA director Dovchindorj (Dovchoo) Ganbold stands to survey the terrain.
Photo: Doug Chadwick

entrance, we found Puji waiting, looking like a ninja with his face wrapped
in a dark scarf and his motorcycle goggles on to protect his eyes from the grit.
The gleam we had glimpsed from afar was his flashlight. He was still shining
it as a homing beacon for our long-overdue scouting party.

I'd expected that the storm would have forced the team members who
stayed behind in camp to disassemble our tents and weigh them down with
rocks. Over the years, I'd seen winds from different directions turn tarps,
rain flies, and several standing tents into colorful kites sailing away over the
desert. Other tents, staked down more firmly, got torn open at the seams.
Yet our tents were all still upright, flapping and bending but un-shredded
and exactly where we had left them. This was because the encampment was

nestled in a draw carefully chosen so that the prevailing winds from the west, the most powerful ones like this storm, mostly passed overhead. Crawling inside my tent, I pushed my backpack and bags of gear up against the sides and corners to keep the fabric taut, depriving the wind of creases to strum. I had no trouble falling instantly asleep.

———

DAWN BROKE CHILLY AND CLOUD-COVERED. TO MY RELIEF, THE UGLIEST conditions seemed to have moved on to the east. I climbed to the ridge for a look. The trapdoor at Shar Khuls was still up. After descending to camp, I sat down to eat with Dovchindorj (Dovchoo) Ganbold, the protected area's director. Having previously worked in the reserve as a biologist, he had an abiding interest in fieldwork with wildlife and jumped at the chance to be part of the trapping expedition this season. A single man in his thirties, Dovchoo also looked forward to occasional trips from the reserve's remote headquarters to a city—any city—in hopes of meeting a prospective wife. I asked him how often the reserve saw heavy dust storms. "Last year," Dovchoo said, "we recorded high winds on 130 days—more than one out of every three." Not all of those would rank as real tempests, he added, but they included winds you could lean into hard without falling over. "And," he reminded me, "the winds come strongest in the springtime."

My next question was, had the rangers decided on a name for the springs we visited in the gorge near the mine? "Yes—*Khashiin Us*," Dovchoo replied. "It means New Springs."[1] They were new not only because the place had only been found on April 5 of this year, when the rangers first arrested ninjas there, but also because that date fell within the season of renewal following winter. Another translation for Kashiin Us, therefore, would be Springtime Springs, or Spring Springs. That's fun to say in English. But for me, the name will forever conjure images of ibex remains, fur-stuffed predator scat, an inky hole hacked into a promontory by gold-fevered outlaws, and a bone-chilling blizzard of dust.

Between the first glimmers of dawn and the time Puji returned from his morning trap circuit, I could usually fit in a two- or three-hour hike plus breakfast. Afterward, if he reported that we were zero-for-four again, there were camp chores to be attended to and promising habitats in the vicinity to be explored. If we felt up to a long drive followed by a long hike, we could try to retrieve one of the radio collars that had dropped off a bear in previous years. The search would entail probing outward from the unit's last GPS

1   Years earlier, a ranger patrolling by camel came upon a previously unknown spring while traversing *Edrengiin Nuruu*, a major ridge that also rises north of Shar Khuls. Before his death, he described the location to other rangers. They have searched for the site many times since, but the ridge is huge and rugged, and no one has yet managed to rediscover water there.

radio location recorded before the batteries died. As often as not, the result was an exercise in peak-and-canyon maze solving with no collar at the end. Still, it was always good to see a new batch of topography.

But today, following the dust storm, I was content just to lie in my tent and read. Harry had passed along a paperback collection of short stories he recently finished. The tales revolved around the lives of urbanites in relationships rife with infidelities and guilt, psychological punishments by spouses, knotty expectations imposed by lovers and friends, shopping crises, and unsatisfying emotional compromises.

What the hey, Harry? He usually favored American frontier history and Scandinavian detective novels. Now he'd stuck me in the company of these people overwhelmed by culture, comfort, and convenience busy engineering crises for themselves as a kind of antidote to ennui or approaching middle age. I occasionally found myself silently yelling at these characters: JUST GO OUTSIDE!

I waded into the next short story and was reading about the disintegration of a stale marriage when Harry walked up to the tent's entrance and shouted at me in his best attempt at a Southern work gang boss's drawl, "Git yer lazy ass up outta bed, boy! We got bears to collar!"

Puji had followed *mazaalai* tracks leading all the way from Shar Khuls to the second trap site, *Tsagaan Tokhoi* (White Rock or White Cliff), more than fifteen miles distant, and found the bear inside the metal box. Everyone in camp squished together into one van and followed Puji back toward Tsagaan Tokhoi. When you accidentally jostle someone in Mongolia, the polite thing to do is immediately grasp the other person's hand and shake it. There was a lot of hand-shaking and joking going on inside the vehicle for the better part of an hour while one of the rangers, Ankhbayar (Ankhaa) Buyankishig, gunned the rig over the rough track and the rest of us bounced and swayed and banged into one another and sometimes toppled onto two different laps at once.

The trap rested near the edge of a broad wash coming out of a canyon where water appeared at intervals. While the rest of us stayed at a distance, Harry walked slowly and quietly up to the big box to peek through slits cut in the sheet metal on the sides and top. He needed to estimate the animal's weight in order to know how much of the drug containing a mixture of a sedative and a muscle-immobilizing compound he would need to anesthetize this bear. When he returned to the van, he filled a syringe with a measured dose and fitted it on the tip of a long jab-pole. He crept quietly back to the trap, again hoping to keep the bear's level of stress to a minimum and avoid a burst of violence. Patiently, he stood with his science spear poised over a small opening in the top of the box. He was waiting for the bear to turn in just the right position so that he could thrust the needle into a meaty shoulder or, better yet, a flank, thereby minimizing the possibility of hitting tendon or bone.

He struck suddenly. We could hear the bear roar and whirl and slam its paws against the sides of the trap, but all we could see from our vantage point was Harry walking away from a shaking metal box. We all hunkered by the van until the grizzly storm subsided, and when it did, we stayed in place, speaking only in whispers to avoid rousing this *mazaalai* in the slightest before the drug took full effect. Finally, Harry went to look into the trap again. He used the blunt end of the jab stick to gently prod the animal. It was unresponsive. After watching a little longer, Harry signaled the crew. Ankhaa climbed on top of the box and lifted the door. Harry reached in and poked the grizzly a few times with an outstretched hand, then tugged on one of its legs. He gave an "all clear" nod, and five crew members joined in carrying the inert animal's body from the trap to the lee of the van, where they could work out of the wind.

Knowing that the drug had rendered the bear unable to react but by no means unconscious, everyone made an effort to avoid making loud noises. Nevertheless, the crew's adrenaline level generated a steady rush of whispered conversations that proved impossible to damp down. Amgaa and Nyamaa got busy with a measuring tape and calipers, and Boyoko began jotting down the animal's overall length and girth, muzzle size, neck circumference, and so forth on a data sheet. I was intrigued by the animal's ears. Like those of the other Gobi bears I'd seen, they struck me as larger and longer than those of typical grizzlies. Tufts of hair sticking straight up from the top made them appear longer still, as if a dab of desert jackrabbit had somehow made its way into the gene pool.

Odbayar (Odko) Tumendemberel, a young geneticist who had been with the project for years, was perfectly comfortable among centrifuges, spectrometers, and formidable statistical equations back at her lab in the Mongolian Academy of Sciences. Yet she had grown up in a herding family far from a city and was, if anything, more at home out here wearing a traditional ankle-length greatcoat to deflect the wind and squatting in the dust to collect a small vial of blood and samples of hair for later DNA analysis. Dovchoo pitched in to help move the bear onto one side or the other for more measurements. He also took its temperature with a rectal thermometer every so often to be sure the animal's system wasn't reacting abnormally to the

[Top] Gobi Bear Project leader Harry Reynolds tries to jab a captured bear using a pole tipped with a sedative-filled syringe. [Bottom] Harry looks on while biologists Bayasgalan (Bayasa) Amgalan (center) and his father, Dr. Amgalan (Amgaa) Luvsanjamba (right), measure the skull length of a sedated animal before fitting it with a radio collar. Photos: Joe Riis

drugs. Camera in hand, Boldoo circled the group and recorded as much of the process as he could. As for Puji, he had roared off to check the two traps he never got to earlier.

The bear was a female. Though missing a patch of fur along one shoulder and part of her neck, she showed no obvious signs of recent injury or infection. This Gobi bear, like others I'd seen up close after capture, showed an astonishing amount of wear on her teeth. If she were a North American grizzly, I'd have guessed her age at more than twenty years. By Harry's estimate, she was about six years old. As I ran my fingers over the blunt fangs and ground-down molars, she growled as she exhaled. The sound wasn't ·fierce; more of a bearish sigh. Who could say what this grizzly's mind was processing as she lay there helpless, unable to connect any messages from her nerves to the muscles that had always overpowered whatever stood in her way? She couldn't even blink, so we had squeezed lubricant drops into her eyes to prevent them from drying out and covered them to keep out the dust. When her blindfold slipped off, I bent down to readjust it and felt her breath moisten my skin. Her body gave off all kinds of fragrances—some musty, some sharp, others rich and gamey. The sum of them smelled sweet.

Once the crowd hovering over the bear had the measurements and samples it needed, I took a turn at her side and put my hands on her fur—that strange, shaggy, distinctive *mazaalai* coat that doesn't drape over the body so much as stick out in all directions, wildly mussed-looking. From the layer of light brown outer guard hairs, I worked my fingers down into the bear's second coat, consisting of fine, densely interwoven hairs. Unlike that of the North American grizzly, the *mazaalai* inner layer of fur is brilliant white, as if borrowed from a polar bear. It is also remarkably thick. I could feel the warmth trapped within. How a desert-dwelling bruin coped with summer's heat wearing this woolen underwear was hard to imagine, but then I couldn't imagine dealing with the unobstructed icy winds and bitter cold that grip this part of the world from fall through spring without extra insulation. Odko spied a camel tick crawling through the fur and nabbed it—not for science but simply because this bear's life might be a little more comfortable with one less tick on its hide. It was the least we could do to make up for all our pulling and probing.

The claws told the same story of life in this environment as the teeth did. On a typical *Ursus arctos*, those nails would be three inches or longer and tapered to a sharp point. But this bear's were cracked, chipped, and stubby, and less than half the usual length. They can keep growing back of course, but I wasn't expecting *mazaalai* claws to be long and sharp anymore, not on animals that spend a lifetime walking over stone and digging through gravel to get at plant roots and burrowing rodents. An adult's teeth look as they do because they don't grow back even though the bear goes through the rest of its life unavoidably chewing on chunks of sand and mineral grit along with much of its food from the desert's floor. The foot pads that had carried this female across so many miles of sharply eroded stones and burning hot gravels were cracked and worn smooth in places, yet surprisingly soft and supple. The more I examined them, the closer I felt to her, because of the resemblance of the bottoms of her front feet to human palms and the way the elongated soles of her rear feet reminded me of my own.

Looking around, I saw that my window for close-up observation was about to close. The crew was preparing to hoist the female off the ground with a rope tied to a scale. We didn't have a lot of time to squander. It can take an hour and a half for an immobilized bear to get up. Then again, it can take as little as thirty minutes, depending on the individual animal's metabolism and the precision of the dosage it received. Whenever a grizzly starts coming out of its stupor, you don't want to be playing with its toes.

The scale gave a reading of 207 pounds, a heavy April weight for a young but sexually mature female *mazaalai* that had spent a long winter in a den living off her fat reserves. Enlarged nipples indicated that she had been nursing cubs. We saw no sign of the offspring. If two-year-olds, they might have become independent of her early in the spring. If they were new cubs or yearlings, they had more likely perished. Then again, it was possible that the female had somehow hidden them away while she alone visited the trap. We'd been wondering how the drought that began the previous year might be affecting the bears. Although it may have reduced this one's ability to provide enough milk to nourish her young, she seemed in good overall condition—solid with muscle, rather than bony.

As the team finished fastening the satellite radio collar around the bear's neck, the dark sky released a few raindrops. Not many reached the ground, and those that did disappeared quickly, leaving the desert's surface dry. Even so, we took this sprinkle as a promising sign that moisture-bearing clouds hadn't given up on visiting the Gobi this year. Because the day stayed quite cool and the immobilizing drug tends to lower body temperature somewhat, Harry covered the bear with a red space blanket before we departed. We weighted down the corners with rocks to keep the wind from tearing her brightly colored cover away. Seen through the van's rear window as we left, she looked like a tired hiker who had decided to bivouac near the canyon entrance.

The normal collaring protocol calls for keeping a continuous watch over a bear coming out of the drug's effects until the animal regains enough strength and coordination to amble off. The reason we tucked the stirring but still-groggy female into her makeshift blanket and left her to wake up alone is that Puji had come hurrying back on his motorcycle from checking trap site number three—Tsagaan Burgas (White Willow). We had a bear in the box there, too.

As he gave the crew this news, I could see that everyone was waiting for Puji to crack a smile and let on that he was making a joke. The Mongolians have a talent for straight-faced kidding. Not this time; he was being serious. Every one of us was soon slinging an arm over a companion or exchanging high-fives. When Harry had told me to get my lazy ass out of bed because we had bears to collar, he only knew about the one at Tsagaan Tokhoi. No one imagined that we really did have bears—plural—to deal with, or that we would, within the space of a few hours, match our yearly average of two successful captures.

With Odko translating, Puji said, "I didn't get a good look into the trap because I didn't want to bother the bear, but I think that it is a small one." He was wrong. It was a male, maybe eight years old, taller and a good foot longer than the female. By the time we arrived, he had torn away part of the metal ventilation grate welded onto one side of the box. He carried 231 pounds on a rangy frame, and that was his low, post-hibernation weight. His general condition, like the female's, appeared good. The double-layered coat he wore was luxuriantly thick. We found a number of ticks burrowed into it and a recent scar running down one side of his head. Nobody, it seems, gets

The sedative used on captured bears tends to lower body temperature. On this particularly cold day, researchers kept this female warm while waiting for the drug to wear off. Photo: Doug Chadwick

by completely unscathed in the Gobi. And yet this pitiless environment had produced two large, beautiful mammals contoured with belts of powerful muscles and wrapped in plush fur. Two lives that, if granted the usual span for their kind, would continue for fifteen to twenty years. Or longer.

On the way home from fitting a collar on the second bear, we stopped at Tsagaan Tokhoi to retrieve the space blanket. The female was nowhere in sight. We sent good wishes her way, wherever that might be. It wouldn't stay a mystery for long. GPS locations from her collar were already being picked up by a satellite orbiting overhead. They would soon be downloaded onto a computer at Harry's home in Alaska.

At Shar Khuls, we stopped again and filled one large barrel and some smaller containers with water before driving the last mile to camp. The air temperature was dropping fast again, but the wind had faded to a stiff breeze, and the sky was clearing of dust. As the sun sank, it tinted the remaining clouds with crisp streaks of vermillion. We were halfway through the spring field season. I had two more weeks' worth of tomorrows to see what surprises Gobi bear country would bring.

———

DURING A DIFFERENT LONG RIDE THROUGH THE GOBI SOMEWHERE, I ONCE asked Harry what kept him doing this kind of research. He said, "Working with bears in Yellowstone and Alaska gave me a good life. This is my chance to give back. Where you save bears, you save the land and a lot of other kinds of wildlife. Look, Gobi bears might not make it. But you can't think like that. To see a problem and not want to fix it, not try while these bears still have a chance, well ... it's a sin. This is the most extreme environment a bear could be in. But Gobi bears have found ways to survive. They've adapted. They've done it partly through learning how to use the desert's scarce resources, and each generation keeps passing that knowledge along to the young. They're still here after who knows how many tens of thousands of years. You can't just turn your back on them." When I asked how long he intended to keep coming to the Gobi, he replied without hesitation: "I'll quit the project when I get too old to move around or I fall over and die. Whichever comes first."

Ursus arctos, the brown, or grizzly, bear,[2] first arose in Central Asia between half a million and a million years ago. Some genetic evidence

---

2 By tradition, most scientists stick with the common name of brown bear, which is how the species was originally described in Europe. They reserve the term grizzly for *Ursus arctos horribilis*, the North American subspecies with silver-tipped—grizzled-looking—fur. But a growing number of biologists and naturalists have begun to use brown bear and grizzly interchangeably, as I do, for several reasons. In the first place, not all brown bears are brown; individuals can be gray, reddish, straw-colored, deep gold, pale blond, or practically jet black. Adding to the confusion, other bear species, including the common American black bear, *Ursus americanus*, come in brown or brownish color phases, while varieties of the brown bear in Eurasia have grizzled fur. For instance, the big bear buddy of an American mountain man in the U.S. television series *Grizzly Adams*, popular during the 1970s, was played by a Syrian brown bear, *Ursus arctos syriacus*. To my ear, the name grizzly sounds a little wilder and more growly than brown bear and thus captures more of the species' indomitable quality.

suggests that *mazaalai* are closely related to those ancestral *Ursus arctos* and may in fact be the oldest continuous line of grizzlies among the subspecies present today.

Some taxonomists have classified Gobi bears together with the Tibetan bear, also known as the blue bear, *Ursus arctos pruinosus*. The widespread range of the Himalayan brown bear, *Ursus arctos isabellinus*, includes northwestern China's Tian Shan Mountains, which top out at 24,406 feet. Since eastern extensions of the Tian Shan Range approach Mongolia's Gobi-Altai Mountains where the last Gobi bears are found, this has led other experts to suspect that *mazaalai* might be a relict enclave of *isabellinus*.

When geneticists analyzed samples of hair said to have come from Yetis, the famed Abominable Snowmen of the Himalayas, the fur turned out to belong to *isabellinus*. One reason early Gobi scientist-explorers were never able to vouch for the existence of bears in this desert is that the information they gathered from herders included confusing reports of another big, hairy, somewhat human-like creature roaming the place. This was the Mongolians' version of the Yeti, or Bigfoot. They called it *Alma*.

No one knows how long *mazaalai* have lived isolated from other types of grizzlies in Asia. It might not have taken very long for inbreeding within a relatively small population confined to an extreme environment to transform the bears of the Gobi into *Ursus arctos something else*. It's also possible that Gobi bears became different by remaining largely unchanged through time while grizzly bears elsewhere, able to wander and exchange genes more freely, evolved along different lines.

Taxonomy is the professional chore of assigning Latin names to lifeforms and trying to fit them into fixed categories, the better to organize our understanding of nature, even though the essence of life is change. No wonder the correct classification of creatures is a source of continuous debate. Whatever label Gobi bears eventually end up with won't alter their essence as a unique population of bruins with a unique way of life at the outermost edge of the outer edge of possibility for their kind. They are not huge, they are not white, and they don't inhabit the snowbound heights of the greatest mountains on Earth. But they are big and tousle-furred and call for a serious stretch of the imagination on our part.

The Himalayan brown bear qualifies as a Yeti you can prove you saw. *Mazaalai* may or may not have originally been connected to that subspecies. Call Gobi bears *gobiensis*, *isabellinus*, *pruinosus*, or *improbabilis*. It doesn't matter to me. They are my Yetis. They're my Bigfoot, my Mongolian *Alma*, my lost tribe of powerful hairy beings, rearing up to walk on two legs at times,

An artist's rendering of a "Yeti Bear." Much as samples of Yeti hair have turned out to be Himalayan brown bear fur, legends of big, hairy sasquatch-like *Alma* walking upright in the Gobi may have been sparked by sightings of this desert's grizzlies. Illustration: Julian Watson

roaming a landscape as remote and mysterious, demanding, and beautiful in its own way as the Himalayas. And although no one tracking down rumors of them managed to prove their existence to the world at large until almost the middle of the twentieth century, they are as real as warm breath and a beating heart. At the same time, they are in danger of not being real for much longer.

02

Indiana Jones and the Gobi Death Worm

During the 1920s, Roy Chapman Andrews of the American Museum of Natural History organized four long expeditions through the Gobi Desert of China and Mongolia. Wearing a trademark campaign-style hat cocked on his head and a pistol on his hip, he led mixed caravans of early-model automobiles and gas-laden Bactrian camels across the great waterless tracts between herders' huts and the ruins of ancient Silk Road palaces, occasionally trading shots with bandits. Prickly warlords, devious traders, indifferent Manchu potentates, dust storms, desertions, and dwindling rations—he handled them all with panache.

Andrews was also a prolific writer. His many popular books, together with photographs and films taken by team members, gave Americans and many other Westerners breathtaking glimpses into what, for most, had been a blank spot on the map of the world. The tales Andrews told personified exotic adventure and made him a rock star among the scientist-explorers of that time. The creators of the *Indiana Jones* movies apparently didn't draw upon any one historical figure to fashion their hero. Nevertheless, Andrews is widely assumed to have served as a model, if only indirectly because his image was so pervasive in American culture during his heyday.

And like Indiana Jones, Andrews always found really cool, priceless stuff out there in *terra incognita*. On the initial trip, in 1920, the Museum team unearthed the first fossil skull of *Baluchitherium* (since renamed *Paraceratherium*), the largest land mammal known at that time. This tree-top-browsing member of the Indricothere family, related to early rhinos, stood sixteen feet high at the shoulder, was twenty-four feet long, and weighed fifteen to twenty tons. That's larger than *Tyrannosaurus rex*. Yet extinct big-ass mammals have never quite been able to compete with extinct bad-ass reptiles in people's imaginations. It was the second Gobi expedition's finding of fossil dinosaurs that truly caused a sensation, for among the mineralized treasures were dinosaur eggs—a first.

"Some ... have been crushed but the pebbled surface of the shells was as perfect as though they had been laid yesterday instead of eighty or ninety million years ago," Andrews wrote in his eleventh book, *Under a Lucky Star*. The eggs were thought to belong to a smallish plant-eater whose remains were abundant in a section of bright red sandstone hills that expedition members dubbed the Flaming Cliffs. Previously unknown to science, the dinosaur was later named *Protoceratops andrewsi*.

A second new dinosaur found in the same area was labeled *Oviraptor*— egg-plunderer—because its lithe, predatory form suggested that it was there making omelets out of the plant-eaters' progeny. A couple decades afterward,

Led by Roy Chapman Andrews, the American Museum of Natural History expeditions into the Gobi during the 1920s unearthed the skull of an Indricothere, an extinct relative of the rhino and one of the largest land mammals ever. Photo: Stéphane Compoint

paleontologists realized that the eggs had actually been laid by *Oviraptor* itself. Modern studies revealed not only that *Oviraptor* probably sat on a nest to incubate the eggs but also that its skin was covered with feathers. The Andrews expedition unearthed the first fossil *Velociraptor* as well. Resurrected in digitized form, this hunter won fame as an unholy terror in the *Jurassic Park* movies. As the name implies, *Velociraptor* could run very swiftly. It was smaller in reality than in the films, though, and experts now say that it, too, wore feathers. For that matter, some believe even mighty *T. rex* sprouted feathers, at least in its early years of life.

The list of fossils from that second expedition included larger dinosaurs. In addition, while prying into rocks from the latter part of the so-called Age of Great Reptiles, team members came up with the remains of a shrew-like mammal. Only one other mammal from that stage of Earth history had ever been found, and some doubted that the specimen had been aged correctly. The Andrews expedition confirmed that small mammals were scurrying around underfoot toward the end of dinosaurs' reign. From the Natural History Museum, director Henry Fairfield Osborne cabled the returning party: "Congratulations. You have written a new chapter in the history of life upon the earth."

With its frosts and winds continually exposing more long-buried bones, the Gobi remains a hotspot for paleontological discoveries, yielding bonanzas of bygone species and insights into their biology and evolution. Discovery is an exciting word—and a slippery one. Although they received worldwide acclaim for collecting dinosaur eggs, Andrews and his museum colleagues were certainly not the first humans to come upon them. The last of their four expeditions uncovered evidence of a Stone Age culture present in the Gobi 10,000 to 20,000 years ago at a site where lakes filled the lowlands between towering drifts of sand. Among the artifacts were fragments of fossilized dinosaur eggs with holes drilled in them. The Dune-Dwellers, as the team named these ancient people, probably wore the eggshell pieces strung together into necklaces.

[A] The griffin, half-lion, half-eagle. Its legend may have started when Iron Age gold-miners in the Gobi noted fossils of [B] the small, beaked dinosaur *Protoceratops*. The Andrews expeditions rediscovered these fossils together with the first reported dinosaur eggs. [C] The Gobi death worm. Do not disturb if ever found. Illustrations: N/A, Nobumichi Tamura, Gwenlyn Norton

A powerful mythic beast called the griffin, or gryphon, combining the body of a lion with the head and wings of an eagle, appeared in Middle Eastern art at least 3,000 years ago. Griffins were said to live among red mountains in the wilderness where they guarded great treasure, particularly gold. Adrienne Mayor, a research scholar in the Department of Classics at Stanford University, has offered an intriguing theory that the legend began with the Scythians, a loose confederation of nomadic hunting and herding tribes in the steppes and drylands between the Middle East and Central Asia. The Scythians dug gold from the Gobi Altai and neighboring Tian Shan Mountains. They may well have noticed the fossils of *Protoceratops* in sandstone formations like the Flaming Cliffs. Although these dinosaurs walked on four legs and were no larger than lions, they had massive heads with large, sharply pointed mouths closely resembling a beak. If you were a Scythian gold-miner who stumbled across those preserved skeletons near preserved eggshells, you wouldn't have found it hard to picture a spectacular mammal-bird hybrid guarding nearby veins of precious ore. Mayor suggests that depictions of the griffin made their way from Scythia into the Middle East via the Silk Road, then to Minoan and Greek artisans, and eventually from there onto the banners and shields of medieval Europe's aristocracy.

In 1926, Andrews described another Gobi creature in his book *On the Trail of Ancient Man*—the death worm. Mongolians, Andrews wrote, called the creature *olgoi-khorkhoi*—large intestine worm—presumably as a way of describing the thickness of its body. Reaching lengths of several feet, the bright red desert-crawler, also known as a Gobi bloodworm, spit an acid that instantly corroded the toughest metal and dissolved any flesh it touched. The bloodworm, he wrote, could also kill a nearby victim with a high-voltage electric discharge from its mouth even faster.

Andrews was reporting tales he'd heard. He never saw one of the monsters—no reliable source has—and plainly stated that he didn't think they were real. But the man was a good storyteller, and good stories have a way of sticking around. Not long after Andrews introduced the notion of Gobi death worms to the world at large, they began to appear in artwork, pulp fiction, and movies. Much as the Scythians' griffins spread far from the Gobi in artists' renderings, the sights Andrews and his colleagues beheld in the bone-dry and desolate core of Asia fired the dreams of people halfway around the globe—including aspiring field naturalists like myself. Reading about Andrews's Gobi adventures when I was young left an indelible impression of that great desert as a repository of mysteries and marvels still waiting to be brought to light.[1]

---

1   If you open an Andrews book, you'll soon find him routinely shooting many of the new animals he meets on his journeys simply for "a bit of sport." He was given to running down, and over, Gobi wolves with his car, picking off eagles and hawks from their perches because they made such alluring targets up there, and on and on. Had he come across a Gobi bear, he would almost certainly have put a bullet in it. Our self-described man of action belonged to the tail end of the era of the so-called great white hunters. It was also the era of great white collectors, whose affiliation with museums only made them more systematic about killing specimens. The rarer the animal, the more avid those "naturalists" were to shoot at least one before its kind disappeared. This was spoken of as conserving the creature for future generations to see—stuffed and mounted in a diorama. The movement toward actively managed protection of wildlife was still in its infancy in the United States during the 1920s and wholly absent in much of the rest of the world. As for Andrews's habit of flavoring the chronicle of an expedition with sometimes disparaging opinions about whole ethnic groups and cultural traditions encountered en route, this also requires from the modern reader the one thing the famed adventurer did not explore: the virtue of tolerance.

The author reflects on his situation from a van seat, removed so the driver can work on the engine. Photo: Joe Riis

GROWING UP IN THE AMERICAN WEST, I WAS FASCINATED BY NATURE AND never-tamed places. That didn't change as I got older. I majored in biology during college and did my graduate field research on the social behavior and ecology of mountain goats. Under heavy pressure from sport hunting combined with the expansion of road networks ever farther into the backcountry, the goats were in widespread decline. Grizzlies, whose numbers had fallen to perhaps fewer than 700 south of Canada by the 1970s, needed protection even more urgently. I carried out some small-scale surveys and follow-up lobbying that played a minor role in getting the bears listed as threatened under the Endangered Species Act.

Next, I went to work as a seasonal biologist for the National Park Service, studying the mountain goats along the continental divide in Glacier Park. In my spare time, I hiked to my favorite settings for watching grizzlies, because ... I'm not sure why. I feared these great, humbling, electrifying master mammals; I admired them more for their blend of power and playfulness directed by an obvious intelligence. I think I sought out their presence in part just because it made me so fully alive, from the oldest compartments of my glands and senses and brain to the newest. Grizzlies can absolutely rip and tear stuff apart, but for me they made the world feel more whole.

Over time, I stepped up my involvement with grassroots conservation efforts in northwestern Montana, where I lived, and started writing for various magazines. One of those publications was *National Geographic*, which, in 2007, had an article in the works about snow leopards. Photographer Steve Winter was capturing spectacular images for the story, but a writer had not yet been chosen. The assignment called for traveling through fabled mountain realms in Asia to learn firsthand about big, rare, enigmatic cats with fur like mottled moonlight. Would I be interested? the editors asked.

Dear National Geographic Editors: Is this a trick question?

By June of that year, I was driving tent stakes into the ground 15,000 feet above sea level in Ladakh, India. A large district within the country's northernmost state, known as Jammu and Kashmir, Ladakh borders Tibet and shares much of its traditional culture as well as the lofty landscapes that earned Tibet the title Roof of the World. My camp was in the Zanskar Range, which parallels the Ladakh and Karakoram Ranges to the north and the mighty Himalaya to the south. No matter which direction I turned, peaks above 20,000 feet, gleaming with the snows of untold centuries, defined the horizon.

Jammu and Kashmir also borders Pakistan. As for exactly where the boundary ought to be drawn through the ragged Karakoram topography, the governments of India and Pakistan have differing ideas. From time to time, the two nations have tried to resolve the issue by sending troops up among the glaciers to shoot at each other. Reaching the Zanskar Valley requires a long drive on a highway fringed with military bases and guarded at checkpoints. The last supply stop my companions made was in a town previously shelled by Pakistani artillery. But all that was miles behind us now. The nearest outpost was a peaceful Buddhist monastery far below, where we had shouldered our packs and set off on foot.

Once the snows retreated farther and the uncovered slopes greened, shepherds would drive goats, sheep, yaks, and yak-cattle hybrids from the valleys to graze these high pastures. That raised the potential for conflict with snow leopards because the cats snatch livestock now and then. The herders have always retaliated by executing snow leopards in the vicinity, which is one of the main reasons this leopard's numbers across Asia have fallen to a few thousand and the species is considered endangered.

For the moment, though, it was just us up here: Me. Two camp assistants. Several pack ponies. The mountains' untamed creatures. And a guardian of that wildlife, Dr. Raghunandan (Raghu) Chundawat, regional director of science and conservation for the Snow Leopard Trust. The nonprofit Trust helps herding families counter livestock losses by predator-proofing night-time corrals, improving veterinary practices, and setting up village livestock insurance pools, among other projects, in return for a pledge by the locals to cease killing snow leopards and the wild hoofed animals they prefer to hunt.

Under Raghu's tutelage, I got better at following the cats' pawprints over hard ground, examining the bones and horns of old kills, and learning to recognize the type of conspicuous boulders or overhanging ledges that snow leopards choose to spray with urine as territorial markers. I even worked at gauging the freshness of that pungent scent to estimate when a leopard had last padded by. Who wouldn't want to get better at sniff-testing mountain panther piss? Actually, the stuff smells better than it sounds.

I wanted to learn more about the kind of routes snow leopards choose for moving through the terrain so that I could perhaps think a little more like one—feel as if I were taking in the world through its golden eyes, if only for a few moments now and then. I'm not invoking anything mystical here. It's more like a game combining the human powers of observation and imagination to make useful guesses. Humans have played at projecting themselves in animal form since time immemorial, the better to hunt and gather food, avoid danger, and survive. The more you can tap into the intuitive and even subconscious parts of your brain, the better tracker you'll be.

━━━━━━━━

THE MORNING OF OUR RETURN HIKE TO THE VALLEY, I LEFT CAMP BEFORE the others to scout for tracks in the film of frost that had coated the ground overnight. Pawprints appeared just a couple hundred yards down the trail. Very fresh pawprints. Yet they were neither from a leopard nor one of the wolves whose dung we had seen here and there. Both of those carnivores leave roundish, four-toed tracks. These were considerably bigger and elongated, somewhat like a broad human foot complete with a rounded heel and five toes. Had the impressions been made in deep, soft snow, blurring the details, I might have started thinking harder about Yetis.

Describing the tracks this way might make it seem as though I spent a while running through a mental checklist to identify them. No. I knew at once what kind of animal had walked here—felt the answer prickle my skin like a blast of wind off the ice. Although Asian black bears inhabit the Himalayas, they keep mainly to the foothills and forests. And even if a large adult wandered this high above the treeline, its claws wouldn't be long enough for the tips to leave marks so far in front of the toes.

Heads up, man. You may be halfway around the world from Montana's Rockies, but you're in grizzly country.

The range of *Ursus arctos isabellinus*, the Himalayan brown bear, stretches from Bhutan westward into Pakistan and northward into the Hindu Kush, Pamirs, and other imposing mountain systems of Central Asia. This grizzly had likely been drawn near our campsite by cooking aromas and perhaps the smell of horses. It must have shied away from investigating too closely. Great. But where was it now?

Raghu was descending in my direction when I first noticed shaggy fur above a boulder off to one side of the trail section between us. I whistled to get Raghu's attention and motioned frantically for him to look to his right. The bear stepped out from behind the rock into full view. As soon as Raghu saw it, he pulled out his camera. Then he began trotting downhill directly toward the animal. Where I come from, we don't charge at grizzly bears. Apparently, things were different here.

As for the grizzly, it did what its kind most often does in the presence of humans. It ran away—across the slope through stunted willow brush, over the edge of a deep canyon, down the long walls of loose debris, scrambling and sliding in a barely controlled fall, and across the heavy rapids of a river flowing fast and milky gray with pulverized rock ground off the peaks by glaciers.

Once on the far shore, the bear finally paused to look back over its shoulder and shake the ice water from its fur. Himalayan brown bears are usually described as wearing a coat with a uniform color. This particular Zanskar bear dressed differently. Its sides were golden brown, its legs a deep chocolate hue, and the hairs on its back shimmered with silver ends. I'd seen almost identical-looking bears in central Alaska. People call them Toklat grizzlies, after the Toklat River watershed in Denali National Park, where the light body/chocolate leg pattern is common.

Forty minutes after we encountered this bear, it was lying on a ledge partway up the other side of the canyon, relaxing in the sun. Raghu, on the other hand, was still fired up and taking photos with a long lens. At last, he turned and asked, "Do you know how many brown bears are left in Ladakh?"

No idea.

"Maybe twenty or twenty-five," he said.

Raghu had been able to watch the wraith-like snow leopards as often and closely as anyone I've heard of. In all the high-country trail miles he covered, he had never experienced a good view of a Himalayan brown bear. Which explained why he had gone running toward this one. My guess was that it weighed no more than 300 pounds. That still didn't make charging it a very good plan.

On the other hand, I knew next to nothing about *Ursus arctos isabellinus*. Reading reports on the animals later, I learned that, like snow leopards and most of the other great cats—indeed, like most large carnivores in the world today—they have undergone a dramatic decline and vanished from most of their historic range. *Isabellinus* may still number between five hundred and a thousand, but the animals are scattered in small, increasingly vulnerable populations. As of 2007, for example, all of Pakistan, with its towering Karakoram, Hindu Kush, and Himalaya Ranges, held fewer than two hundred of these bears, and they were separated from one another in seven subpopulations. Six of those consisted of twenty or fewer animals. The International Union for the Conservation of Nature lists the Himalayan brown bear as "critically endangered"—the category for wildlife with the very highest risk of extinction.

When I read about the recent DNA study of two alleged Yeti hair samples—one from Ladakh, the other from Bhutan—and the conclusion that they came from *isabellinus*, I thought about North American grizzlies I'd seen that looked platinum blond. It's possible that a few Himalayan grizz may have exceptionally light-colored or silvered fur too; maybe not pure white, but close enough to conjure an Abominable Snowman in someone's eyes. Or maybe the bears were just coated with snow at the time and standing up on their hind legs as grizzlies often do, the better to see and to catch scents wafting on the winds. Various Himalayan cultures have their own names for Yetis. One, it turns out, specifically refers to a type of bear. Should someone ask if I have ever seen Yeti tracks during my travels in the mountains of Nepal and Ladakh, I can pretty honestly reply, "Yes, I saw some one morning. Then I watched the Yeti a while."

———

BEFORE I FLEW TO NORTHERN INDIA, I'D BEEN DOING FIELDWORK FOR THE snow leopard story in the Altai Mountains of northwestern Mongolia. My wife, Karen Reeves, and I traveled there with Bayarjargal (Bayara) Agvaantseren and her assistant, Tserennadmid (Nadia) Mijiddorj, both with the Snow Leopard Trust. Through an arm of the Trust called Snow Leopard Enterprises (SLE), Bayara oversaw more than two dozen community-based programs built around the production and sale of handcrafted wool goods.

In traditional Mongolian culture, fur shorn from a household's goats, yaks, camels, and other livestock is wetted and tightly compressed to form sheets of felt. Wrapped over a light wooden framework, felt made the roof and rounded walls of the house itself—the *ger*—before sturdy but lighter modern fabrics became available. Felt is also turned into blankets, sleeping mats, and articles of clothing for the families living inside. A soft-spoken former schoolteacher, Bayara trained the women to make smaller felt items— children's booties and caps, placemats, trivets, and so on—incorporating more decorative designs than the practical nomadic herders ordinarily bothered with. The Trust then sold these handicrafts as well as skeins of yarn from camel hair or fine goat wool (cashmere) online and through select outlets in the West. Bayara would pay well for the specially made goods. In return, the families that benefited were expected to lead the way in convincing the rest of their community to cease killing snow leopards.

While Bayara continued on her rounds, Karen and I would take off into the high country for several days at a time, bringing Nadia with us as a trans-lator. Not long out of high school, Nadia had been entering inventory data on a computer in an office when we met in the capital city, Ulaanbaatar. Soon, we were tracking snow leopards and their prey—ibex and wild boars—on the slopes of Altai Tavan Bogd National Park with Khazakstan on the west, Russia on the north, and massifs like 14,201-foot Kuiten Uul looming overhead. We followed more leopard and ibex signs farther east in the Siachen Mountains. I remember how easily Nadia slipped into the role of a field naturalist and practical campmate as we bivouacked in the snow, and I can recall the highlights of each trek we shared. Yet I have completely forgotten where it was that she told me something that would open a new phase in my life.

I had asked Nadia for more information about Eurasian brown bears, *Ursus arctos arctos*. They were supposed to be present in the Altai region and other portions of far northern Mongolia. We hadn't found evidence of them even within protected areas. Although hunting of bears was no longer legal anywhere in the country, it looked as though they were being shot by poachers and herders anyway. That was when Nadia mentioned that there was another kind of bear in Mongolia—one even more scarce. Where? Not in the north, she said, but in the Gobi-Altai, where the southern end of the Altai Range curves eastward and becomes a succession of smaller mountain chains rippling deep into the Great Gobi Desert.

"These bears are in the true Gobi—the really dry lands?" I asked.

"Yes."

"Brown bears like the brown bears here?"

"Yes. But different brown bears. They are called *mazaalai*. Gobi bears."

I remember that part well enough, because it was the first I had ever heard of the animals. Nadia's English was good but uncertain at times, and I had maybe ten words of Mongolian in my entire vocabulary. I assumed there was a mistake in the translation or else this brown bear actually lived somewhere else but had become associated with the desert in folklore.

Ursus arctos is an adaptable omnivore able to live in a variety of habitats by exploiting a wide range of high-energy foods. That makes it a direct competitor of humans. Over the centuries, we eradicated this species from so many favorable environments in temperate regions that we've come to envision grizzlies as naturally most at home in cold northern forests, rugged mountains, and tundra—places we haven't yet overrun. Who thinks of these bears swiping at salmon in streams of the British Isles as late as King Arthur's time? They did. Who remembers that in the nineteenth century, grizz populations flourished alongside the bison of North America's Great Plains? Others lingered in the US desert Southwest into the early decades of the twentieth century. I once went to check out rumors of holdouts in northern Mexico's Sierra del Nido Range with its slopes of oak, manzanita, and agave, where grizzlies were reported as recently as the late 1960s. But the Gobi? From the photos and videos I'd viewed, it was all I could do to imagine

A subadult male makes his way up a dry wash. Photo: Doug Chadwick

lizards squeezing a living from that landscape. Yet Nadia was insistent about *mazaalai* being at home there.

I must have looked exactly like most of the people I've since told about Gobi grizzlies: baffled. And politely trying not to give the impression that I didn't believe what I was being told. I was making a mental note to look into the fauna of the Gobi at a future date, hoping to clear up our obvious mis-communication, when Nadia went on to say that her father had personally studied these bears for years. He was a wildlife scientist and the head of a special nature reserve within the Gobi.

The gears in my brain unfroze and began to spin. Some of the com-munities Bayara and Nadia worked with through the handicrafts program were in the Gobi-Altai. If snow leopards could make a living in those remote desert mountains, why not a population of some type of *Ursus arctos*? Gobi bears! What were they like? How did they differ from others? And then the all-important question:

"How many are there?"

"My father thinks maybe about thirty," Nadia said. "They are the only ones left."

"In all of Mongolia?"

"In the world."

And I instantly yearned to see them. Visiting their haunts in the Gobi outback would surely open up my view of what a grizzly bear is and what it is capable of. Perhaps I'd find a way to help the survivors. I thought about this fairly often after returning to the United States. But when I took off again on natural history reporting assignments, they landed me in other corners of the globe. In between, I was busy with volunteer conservation activities in the Rockies. Many were aimed at recovering the United States's own grizzly population, still listed as threatened south of Canada. Bit by bit, my intention to explore the Great Gobi Desert in search of improbable-sounding grizzlies, more mysterious than snow leopards and far more rare, was becoming like a New Year's resolution—readily made but not quite as readily as the excuses for putting it off.

———

ALTHOUGH I WASN'T GETTING ANY CLOSER TO GOBI BEARS PHYSICALLY, I DID begin gathering some background information on the subject. Explorers from Russia and other European nations had been probing the Gobi since the late 1800s. One Russian, V. Ladygin, reported what he was sure were brown bear tracks and diggings in the area in 1900. During the 1920s, while Andrews was rummaging through layers of stone from the Dinosaur Age, an expedition sponsored by the State Geographical Society of the Soviet Union made a concerted search for the rumored bears. The party returned with a tantalizing collection of accounts from local people but nothing more solid than anyone else had come up with to prove that *mazaalai* weren't yet another Gobi mirage. By the time a Russian-Mongolian team of scientist-explorers traveling on camelback finally saw one of the desert's bears, it was 1943.

Arising in Asia during the Ice Ages, the brown bear spread westward to Europe and eastward across the Bering Land Bridge to North America. The species took on an assortment of forms as it radiated into the new environments. In the days when taxonomists prided themselves on detecting enough minor variations in a specimen's physical appearance to announce the discovery of a new type, they divided *Ursus arctos* into as many as ninety different subspecies. With modern genetic tools at hand, most scientists now recognize fewer than a dozen. Their homelands across the Northern Hemisphere vary from Alaska's Kodiak Island (*Ursus arctos middendorfi*) to the northern Japanese island of Hokkaido (*Ursus arctos lasiotus*).

While the ice sheets covered a good share of the northern latitudes, the Gobi's uplands were growing forests and grasses, and herbs carpeted the

Two caves create the appearance of a sculpted animal head atop a knoll. Photo: Doug Chadwick

now largely mineral plains. Brown bears living in the region might have been part of a broadly distributed population before a major advance of the glaciers covering Central Asia's highest mountain chains cut the Gobi group off from neighboring bears. That's one possibility. Yet the dominant trend over time was a gradual drying of Asia's interior as the still-rising Himalaya and other mountains blocked the flow of moist air from the Indian Ocean. The rain-shadow effect increased toward the end of the Pleistocene. So another possibility is that the bears of the Gobi became a separate enclave as increasingly arid conditions caused their homeland to shrink toward portions of the Gobi-Altai Mountains where water still issued from springs.

On the subject of exactly how to classify *mazaalai*, the only bears of any kind wholly tied to a severe desert environment, the reference material I read offered different opinions, but most authorities recognized Gobi bears as the distinct subspecies *Ursus arctos gobiensis*. The Zoological Society of London, Mongolian Redbook of Endangered Species, and Convention on International Trade in Endangered Species did the same and further identified *gobiensis* as critically endangered. By any definition, this unique group of grizzlies was on the brink—a short slide, a stumble, or a jostle away from nothingness. Ever since Nadia made me aware that there was such a thing as a Gobi bear in the first place, the days had been marching relentlessly onward. And if her father's count of around thirty animals was anything other than a serious underestimate, it seemed unlikely that time was on their side.

In the winter of 2010, I answered the phone and heard the voice of Dr. Michael Proctor, an ecologist based in southern British Columbia. He was inviting me to take part in the Gobi Bear Project, primarily as a natural history journalist. He and Project leader Harry Reynolds were hoping I might be willing to write an article about the bears in order to focus more attention on their plight, both from the public at large and from the Mongolian government. This came straight out of the blue. I knew both men for their work with North American grizzlies but was not aware of their connection with Gobi bears. I told Proctor that I didn't need much persuading to join them in the desert.

Joe Riis, a young outdoorsman from South Dakota, graduated from college with degrees in wildlife biology and environmental studies. He went on to become a natural history photographer and worked for *National Geographic Magazine*, first in Thailand on a tiger story and then on a Ugandan wildlife story. When we got in touch about Gobi bears, Joe was twenty-six and had just completed shooting a series of exceptional images about a round-trip migration of more than three hundred miles made each year by pronghorn

Photographer Joe Riis with the remains of two camera bodies set on the ground to record a *mazaalai* departing a capture site. Both were severely punished by the bear for loudly clicking as it passed. Photo: Joe Riis Collection

antelope in Wyoming. His work was part of a campaign to protect the animals' natural travel corridors, known as the Path of the Pronghorn. Joe and I convinced *National Geographic Magazine* to send us together to accompany the Gobi Bear Project on the month-long spring expedition in 2011.

When we first set out with the research team in late April that year, I had no intention of staying personally involved with the fieldwork after the journey ended. That plan was not successful. I returned to the Gobi as an unpaid volunteer to take part in the 2012 spring expedition—and in every subsequent spring expedition through 2015. I knew the chances for recovering a small, isolated population of desert-dwelling grizzly bears were not good. And a warming global climate was almost sure to make the odds worse. But the mix of exploration, adventure, science, and, above all, sheer, stubborn optimism embodied in the Project got a grip on me that wouldn't let go. One of my field geologist father's favorite expressions kept coming to mind. Watching someone struggle with an overwhelming task, he would sometimes turn to me and sigh, "Vigorous ... but futile."

Then he would jump in to help.

A

E

F

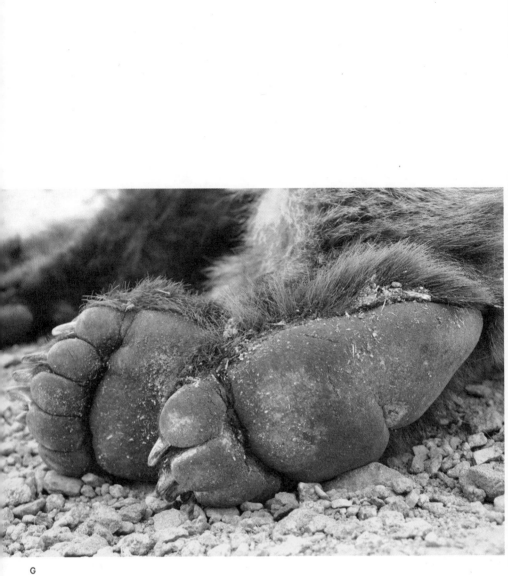

G

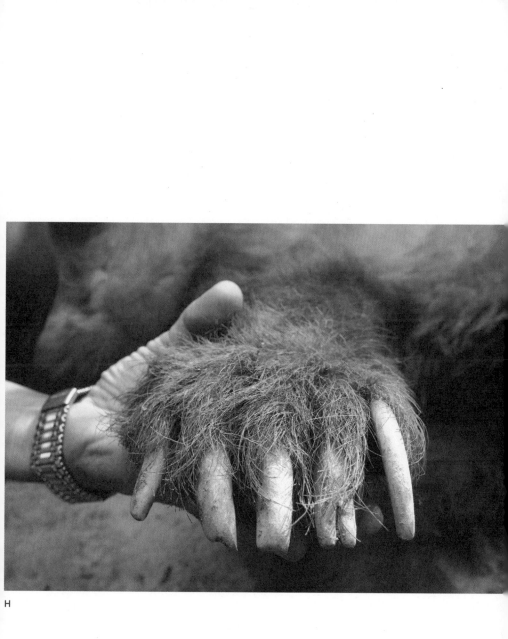

H

J

K

M

P

A   On average, strong winds blow across the Gobi more than one day in three. The most powerful gales come in springtime, our project season. Mostly, they just pummel you, but every so often they'll almost let you believe you can fly. Photo: Joe Riis

B   Evening and a temporary camp somewhere in the mountain maze. Photo: Joe Riis

C   An adult female angles up a canyonside above an oasis in the last evening light. Photo: Joe Riis

D   Gobi Bear Project cook (and amateur athlete) Khosbayar (Khosoo) Munkhjargal sorts through sheep parts stored in the shade of a field hut. Photo: Doug Chadwick

E   Washing off the dust before dinner. Photo: Doug Chadwick

F   Removing hair from what will be the centerpiece of our evening banquet. Photo: Joe Riis

G   These are the hind paws that carry a Gobi bear across a realm of jagged stone, burning hot in the summer, freezing in the late fall and again in early spring. Photo: Doug Chadwick

H   And these are the front claws that move across that same rock terrain month after month and dig deep into the gravel for roots. Photo: Joe Riis

I   Harry (left) and Michael check the mouth of a captured male immobilized by drugs. Tooth pattern and sharpness are good indicators of a grizzly's age, but in the Gobi, estimates have to be adjusted to account for wear and tear from gravel and sand when foraging for roots, insects, and burrowing rodents. Photo: Joe Riis

J   (From left) Michael, bat expert Cori Lausen, the author, and Harry make plans inside a *ger*, or yurt, built into a hillside for extra protection from the elements. Photo: Joe Riis

K   While the Gobi wind plays with Cori's locks, she tries to trim her husband, Michael's, hair. Photo: Joe Riis

L   GGSPA rangers Purevdorj (Puji) Narangerel (in camouflage) and Ankhbayar (Ankhaa) Buyankhishig (in a traditional greatcoat) display confiscated metal detectors after returning from a midnight arrest of ninja miners. Photo: Joe Riis

M   Genetic specialist Odbayar (Odko) Tumendem- berel passes blood samples to Harry while other members of the Project team collect and record measurements. Photo: Doug Chadwick

N   Harry checks the weight of a sedated young male. Gobi bears are notably smaller and lighter than their grizzly counterparts elsewhere. Photo: Doug Chadwick

O   Throughout Central Asia, rock cairns serving as markers in the landscape are often adorned with animal skulls and horns. Here, ranger Nasanjargal (Nasaa) Battushig poses with the head of a Gobi argali, a subspecies of wild mountain sheep. Photo: Joe Riis

P   Moving on as another day dawns in Thirstland. Photo: Joe Riis

03

Altan

Four years after first hearing about Gobi bears, I returned to Mongolia, landing in the capital, Ulaanbaatar. It is the country's only real metropolis. Many simply call it UB. When you ask directions here, you are likely to hear something like: "Keep going down Genghis Avenue until you hit Genghis Square. Turn right onto Genghis Street. Go past the big Genghis Bank building, you'll see Genghis Auto Parts on the next block...." There's also a fair chance that whoever is giving you directions is a descendant of Genghis, whom the Mongolians know as Ghingiis or Chinggis.

Under the greatest of khans and his offspring, Mongol rule extended from Vienna in Eastern Europe to the coast of China and from Siberia south into India and Vietnam. This was nothing less than the largest empire in history. At least 10 percent of all Mongolians and roughly 8 percent of the folks in surrounding portions of Asia carry Genghis DNA. Genghis had a senior wife, the Empress Borte, multiple auxiliary wives, and lots of offspring by them. Only Tenger, the steppe nomads' god of the overarching Blue Sky, knows how many other women the great khan bedded during his continent-ranging campaigns. Not unexpectedly, the sons and grandsons who governed various parts of the domain Dad conquered did exceedingly well on the dating scene, too.

Born around 1160, Genghis lived until 1227. According to Jack Weatherford, author of *Genghis Khan and the Making of the Modern World*, courtiers kept telling Temujin—his given name—that as the ruler of damn near everything, he was expected to ensconce himself in a humongous palace overflowing with bling. Genghis wasn't interested. He preferred modest quarters and liked to get away even from those to relax in a *ger* and ride among the rolling hills where he grew up. His successors were another matter. Grandson Kublai Khan, who reigned over the Orient from the captured Chinese capital, Dadu (later re-named Beijing), raised jewel-encrusted opulence to such heights that Europeans at first dismissed Marco Polo's descriptions of them as nothing but sheer fantasy. As in many a dynasty before and since, the line of heirs eventually succumbed to the distractions of pomp and overindulgence, lousy advice, and internal rivalries culminating in fratricide, uncle-cide, in-law-cide, and so forth. The descendants lost chunk after chunk of the empire until only Mongolia remained, divided among minor khans and warlords.

Following centuries of territorial conflicts with its neighbor to the south, Mongolia was absorbed into the Qing Dynasty of China's Manchus. This helps explain today's confusing custom of referring to portions of northern China as Inner Mongolia and the area occupied by the modern-day nation of Mongolia as Outer Mongolia. In 1911, Mongolia declared its independence from the Chinese. Just thirteen years later, the country became a Russian satellite territory. Seven decades of collectivization and other communist efforts to re-shape the Mongols' nomadic culture followed. In 1990, amid the dissolution of the Soviet Union, Mongolia revolted. By 1992, it had established itself as a constitutional democracy with a parliamentary system of government and a market economy.

Encompassing 604,200 square miles, an area more than three times the size of Spain, all of Mongolia held perhaps half a million people back when Roy Chapman Andrews was introducing the American public to the Gobi Desert. Today, Mongolia has three million people, yet still ranks as Asia's least densely populated country. In rural areas it remains a nation of herders whose basic patterns of life haven't changed much over time. Families continue to dwell in easily transported *gers* on the open steppe, moving between seasonal pastures with their livestock. Most families keep goats and sheep, but many also have cattle, yaks, cattle-yak hybrids, horses, or camels; the mix varies from region to region.

At the same time, an increasing proportion of the populace, especially in the younger generations, is drawn to the economic opportunities and faster-paced lifestyles available in towns and cities. One of every two Mongolians can now be found in UB, a former religious center once known as Urga. It lies within a handsome river valley where outlying strands of the Great Silk Road once converged. Under communist influence, the city was re-named Ulaanbaatar (meaning Red Hero and often written as "Ulan Bator"; there is seldom only one way to spell a Mongolian word in English) and reshaped with blocks of office buildings and factories. Before long, the surfaces of this testament to Soviet-style planning were peeling and coated with a combination of soot spewed from giant coal-fired power plants placed in the valley's center, exhaust from ever more congested traffic, and the dust raised from thousands of unpaved side streets and alleyways. The outskirts meanwhile became a sprawl of hastily built high-rise housing mixed with clusters of dingy canvas *gers*.

It will be a while before anyone describes UB as charming. But the downtown shops and restaurants were bustling when I visited during the last week of April 2011. The sidewalks filled each morning with a mix of older citizens in the long woolen herders' coats called *dels*, young men in stylish jackets with lots of zippers, and young women in designer jeans picking their way through the patches of rubble and dirt in high heels. Overhead, construction cranes were beginning to transform the old squared-off concrete skyline with soaring modern towers of glass and steel.

I'd flown from the States with Joe Riis, the wildlife photographer, and Harry Reynolds, the longtime grizzly bear researcher. Michael Proctor, the Canadian expert in grizzly bear genetics and population ecology, arrived about the same time. Even jet-lagged, he was already spouting plans while rocking up and down on his toes with ready-to-launch energy. Dr. Cori Lausen, a quiet-spoken scientist who had carried out fieldwork in remote areas around the globe, was on the same flight as Proctor. A noted authority on bats, she arranged to join the expedition because, first, the GGSPA region of the Gobi had never been well sampled for these nighttime flyers and, second—well, she was married to Proctor and had been hearing stories about his desert travels for years. This was Proctor's fourth trip to help with a population survey based on the collection of hair samples for identifying individual DNA. It was Harry's fifteenth visit. He'd come for a month of fieldwork focused on trapping every spring and a month of follow-up field research every fall since 2005.

We were soon met by Odko, the genetics graduate student with the world's readiest and greatest smile, and Amgaa, the silver-haired wildlife ecologist, both working at the Academy of Sciences in the city. Amgaa's son, Bayasgalan (Bayasa) Amgalan, who was involved with a United Nations Development Program project called Conservation of the Great Gobi Ecosystem and its Umbrella Species, joined our team as well. Amgaa and Bayasa had participated in the Gobi Bear Project from the start. So had Ankhaa, the GGSPA ranger. He showed up in UB after driving 600 miles from the reserve's headquarters to provide one of its vans for transport. We would rent two more to haul all the people, gear, food, and fuel for the Gobi Bear Project's operations this spring.

Arranging vehicles and drivers, purchasing supplies, and meeting with Ministry of Environment officials to discuss *mazaalai* protection and obtain special permits for travel within the GGSPA kept us hustling back and forth through the capital for three days. During that time, Ariunbold Jargalsaikhan, a National University of Mongolia mammalogist in his thirties who shared Cori's interest in bats, made plans to be part of the Gobi venture. Hunter Causey, a lanky young PhD candidate in hydrology visiting Mongolia on a Fulbright Scholarship, got wind of our expedition and volunteered to come along too, curious to see what he could determine about the sources and condition of the springs the bears relied upon.

Finally, on April 29, after stuffing gear and groceries ceiling high in the three vans, we made our escape from the city—almost. One last stop at a market on the fringe: Another crate of bottled water for the road? Better grab two. More cookie snacks? Duh. Spare sun hat? Throw it in the cart. We drove away shortly before noon. Prepared for weeks of unrelenting bright sunshine and heat, I was still tucking a just-purchased tube of extra sunblock into a daypack when the sky darkened and snowflakes began collecting on the windshield.

———

THE SNOWSTORM CONTINUED FOR MILE AFTER MILE ACCOMPANIED BY WINDS of up to thirty miles per hour. Waves of fresh crystals streaming sideways over the ground began to blur the highway's outline. As our four-wheel-drive vans climbed steadily over a range of uplands, we hit snow already eight inches deep and stacking up higher in drifts. The vans cut through the piles, but other traffic was not doing as well. At one point, the way forward was blocked by a mess of tanker trucks, freight haulers, and passenger cars strewn across the road, thoroughly tangled in what was by then a full-on blizzard. Some sat abandoned while the owners struggled on foot toward the only roadside inn for miles. A few people stayed by their vehicles, digging to free the tires from the drifting snow. Vigorous, but futile. The wind instantly filled in every shovel hole with additional flakes and then packed on some more.

Our vans were old and hard-used. With the weather-stripping around the doors and windows in tatters, fine snow crystals fell inside, sprinkling

The author retreating to find cover from a sudden April blizzard. Photo: Joe Riis

Joe, Odko, Amgaa, and myself, huddled in the center. I fought to extract my duffel from beneath the packs and equipment cases heaped around us and yoga-ed into more layers of clothing. With daylight fading, the drivers wove through the vehicle pileup in low gear until we were free to keep rolling on toward the Gobi—or get stuck in a drift farther along the route.

A lonely roadside inn en route from Mongolia's capital, Ulaanbaatar, to where the steppe begins to give way to the Gobi. Photo: Joe Riis

After a cold night at a lonesome, wind-rattled roadside hotel, we drove out of the fading storm and continued southwest on dry roads. The asphalt grew spotty, then ended. We left the last hilltop pine forests behind as well. Now the only trees were a scattering of poplars lining streams in some of the bottomlands. The rest of the countryside was a seemingly endless succession of hills and low mountains separated by broad plains, all sheeted with winter-brown grasses just starting to go green, dotted with clusters of grazing livestock, and never, ever, broken by a fence. Proctor, whom I was traveling with that day, commented, "Cowboy country." This is the steppe that characterizes so much of Mongolia. It has been a horseman's paradise since long before Western cowboys were invented. The sight of mounted herders racing across the unbroken prairies reminded me that the first pony express was instituted by Genghis. Stationing hell-for-leather riders with strings of fast horses at intervals throughout his empire, he was able to relay messages from one far end to the other at the maximum speed for communications in his day—a gallop.

Larks took to the air everywhere around us. Amgaa pointed out demoiselle cranes wading in the low spots flooded with meltwater. Eagles and hawks swept by overhead. Hours passed between the occasional roadside cluster of *gers* offering meals or vehicle parts. Gradually the grasses thinned. More stony soil showed between the clumps, and whole windswept hillsides turned bare in places. The dirt road itself dissolved into tire tracks braiding through the increasingly stark terrain. We forded two rivers in the vans, wading out ahead each time to determine the shallowest passage. Though we were barely halfway along the 600-mile route between UB and the Gobi reserve, I could already sense that, before long, wading a river and pausing to splash my face with its water would seem like something from a dream.

Yaks, cattle, and sheep became less common. In their place appeared goats and domestic Bactrian camels, both of which get by on rougher forage than other livestock and need to drink less frequently. The transition from steppe to arid steppe lay behind us now. Then the arid steppe, sometimes called desert steppe, started to be replaced by true desert. The scale of this stark open landscape grew so enormous that I could no longer judge distances. Sometimes the view would dissolve into a shimmering mirage that lifted the horizon up to float in the air. At other times, the horizon stayed sharp but bulged a little through the center and bent slightly downward toward the sides. I realized I was looking at the curvature of the earth.

When the vans pulled to a stop for a minor repair or simply because everybody needed a break, Odko sometimes had trouble finding a bush anywhere to hide behind for a pee. I'd take a brisk walk in a different direction to stretch my legs. I only intended to have a good look around, but as soon as the dirt track and vehicles vanished from sight behind a slight rise, I would get this odd image in my head of Antoine de Saint-Exupéry's Little Prince standing alone on the asteroid that was his new home.[1] The planetary panorama that deserts offer can be liberating, stretching your awareness way beyond the usual boundaries. It can also leave you feeling smaller and more vulnerable than you're prepared for at first—in my case, less a prince than a batch of transitory organic molecules out on a coil of the Milky Way. Yet the same boundless mineral panorama can make you much more sincere when you pause to give thanks for being alive.

Late in the afternoon, the ridges we crossed became higher and steeper. I wondered aloud where we were.

"We are on the north side of the Gobi-Altai Mountains," Odko said.

"Will we be working here?" I asked. Odko translated for Amgaa. He smiled and drew an arc in the air to indicate that we would be going over this range. Then he drew a series of air arcs.

---

1 A crash-landing in the Sahara Desert by the author, an adventurous early aviator, is thought to have served as inspiration for his book *The Little Prince*.

"So, more mountains to cross after this," I said.

He nodded.

"How many?"

Soon, Amgaa, Odko, and I were all drawing arc after arc in the air and laughing.

"Oh a lot of mountains," Odko said.

In the Gobi-Altai Range, even the heights most often touched by rain clouds held scant vegetation. Down on the intervening plains, the only things standing above the gravel and dusty clay in some stretches were a few of the shrubs called saxaul. This woody bush has tiny leaves to help limit evaporation, green bark that carries on photosynthesis in the place of larger leaves, deep, wide-spreading roots to gather whatever water is available, and spongy layers of bark to help store the life-giving liquid until the next rain falls. Besides being drought-tolerant, saxaul is also highly salt-tolerant, cold-tolerant, heat-tolerant, and resistant to both wind and intense solar radiation. It has to be all those things at once to reign as the Gobi's dominant plant, and it still looks more dead than alive much of the year.

Most of the Gobi is a plateau between 2,500 and 5,000 feet above sea level. The Altai Mountains sweep into the Mongolian portion from the west to add ranges of peaks thousands of feet taller. Positioned roughly halfway between the Equator and the North Pole, a desert this high is bound to be a chilly one outside the summer months. It didn't look that way from inside the car on the last day of April. The sky was spotless, the sunlight strong. More mirages shimmered in the distance, and dust devils twisted through the basins. But the wind blowing steadily from the northwest stung the flesh. When we stopped to eat, the crew quickly spread out gathering fallen saxaul branches to fuel a fire, and the warmth from the flames was welcome no matter what the hour was.

I forget whether the night of that journey to the reserve's headquarters was one that saw us camped beneath the stars on some windy undulation of the Gobi-Altai Range or driving on through the dark. I only remember an unending succession of desert plains and desert mountains until we arrived. A small forest rose around the springs at the village of Bayantooroi. Ten yards beyond the fringes of the trees, the desert took over again. The Gobi no longer felt like a faraway exotic place. The rest of the world did.

Dr. Batmunkh (Miji) Mijiddorj, whose daughter Nadia had first told me about Gobi bears, was still the reserve's director in 2011. He housed us in a low concrete building at the center of a courtyard with a well, a wooden outhouse, and metal storage sheds. His office was in the next room. The following

Moto-ranger Puji scouts the way for the Project crew following in a van. Photo: Doug Chadwick

morning, he met with us there to talk over the Project's plans for the season. A handsome man in his fifties, Miji showed up freshly scrubbed and wearing a suit jacket. He sat in sharp contrast to our gang of rumpled travelers, but I knew from Harry that this man speaking to us in a soft voice with a direct gaze was as capable in the field and as passionate about Gobi bears as anybody in the room.

In between his other responsibilities at this remote outpost, Miji had been making forays to gather information about *mazaalai* for three decades. More often than not, he was the only biologist in the world paying any real attention to Gobi bears. He also made a special effort to survey wild Bactrian camels. Only about 800 of these double-humped giants (*Camelus ferus*) were left on Earth. Some roamed China's portion of the Gobi. "But the majority of the species now relies mainly on habitats within this reserve," he said, with Odko translating. "This is a stronghold for *khulan* (wild ass) too—maybe 800 to 1,000. About 600 argali, 500 ibex. And maybe a 1,000 black-tailed gazelles."

The weather was delivering a gift to the reserve's wild herbivores as Miji spoke. When we stepped out of his office, we instantly got wet. My first day deep in the Gobi, the storied "waterless place," and I had to go paw through my gear to find a rain jacket. I was never happier to put one on. The rain fell in fine drops. It lasted for hours while a soft, warm mist enveloped the countryside. Later, after the skies began to clear, Miji announced, "Eight millimeters! (*Just under a third of an inch.*) We had a snowfall of fifteen millimeters (*over half an inch*) this winter." Harry had told me of waking up one memorable spring morning in 2007 to more than nine inches of fresh snow across this desert. The half-inch of white flakes Miji described wasn't much by comparison, but every fraction was still a big deal in the Gobi. And now nearly a third of an inch of rain had arrived right at the start of the growing season. It was as hopeful a welcome as a newcomer like myself could wish for.

GOBI BEARS WERE VERY RARELY REPORTED OUTSIDE THE SOUTHERN mountains of the GGSPA after 1970. Over the years, estimates for the number of survivors within the reserve ranged from twenty to thirty-five, based on tracks, other signs, and occasional sightings. In the early nineties, the renowned wildlife biologist George Schaller, who had conducted the earliest in-depth studies of mountain gorillas, lion social behavior, jaguars, pandas, and Tibetan antelope (chiru), among other species, extended his groundbreaking research on snow leopards into Great Gobi Strictly Protected Area-A. In the course of following these cats, he became intrigued by evidence of the reserve's shaggy bears. Schaller and his Mongolian colleagues collared several with VHF radios. The result was the first scientific paper providing details of Gobi bear movements and other aspects of their natural history.

In 1993, Tom McCarthy, a US graduate student, arrived in the GGSPA to build upon Schaller's work with both Gobi bears and snow leopards. Schaller and McCarthy felt that the bears' numbers were similar to earlier estimates. Miji's continuing research led him to the same conclusion. Despite a fourteen-year drought that halved the average annual precipitation in this region of the Gobi from 1993 until 2007, he thought that there might still be something like twenty-five to thirty *mazaalai* in the GGSPA. Like all the earlier figures, his was a best guess. No one had yet been able to carry out an actual census over such an enormous batch of remote, convoluted terrain. How would that even be possible?

I'll confess that as I swung my gaze back toward the landscape we had passed through, and then south and west toward the equally naked and crumpled landscape we were going into next, I toyed with the notion that everything they'd been telling me about Gobi grizzlies was one hell of an elaborate joke. Hey, Montana, you really believed that story about bears being here? Ha! Take another good, long look around, sucker. This ain't Montana.

On the morning of May 3, we managed to stuff more supplies and another fifty-five-gallon drum of gasoline into the vans. Then we added two people from Bayantooroi—the cook Gerlee, whose husband worked at the headquarters office, and Nasanjargal (Nasaa) Battushig, a ranger in his early twenties with a budding interest in wildlife ecology. They and their gear somehow squeezed in too, and we departed for Shar Khuls. Moto-ranger Puji sped ahead on his dirt bike. He was already out of sight by the time the vehicle became so enveloped in its own dust that it was hard to keep track of the others in the caravan. By evening, we were carting boxes of supplies into an underground *ger* a mile from the oasis. With help from Ankhaa and Amgaa, who planned to sleep in the *ger*, Harry and I won the battle against the wind and each managed to get a tent set up in the canyon wash. For his part, Puji was smoking a cigarette and repairing a low tire. It would become a familiar scene in the days ahead. The inner tube was completely Gobi-fied; the thing had so many patches everywhere that Puji's only option was to layer another on top. It held when he pumped in air.

We spent the next two days preparing and adjusting the trap at Shar Khuls and those at the three other capture sites near water sources within the central mountain complex. Close to each trap stood rectangular metal bins about eight feet high with a slot opening near the bottom on opposite sides and a feeding trough welded to each opening. The bins had been filled earlier in the spring with livestock pellets made of compacted grains, primarily wheat. Surprisingly, the native hoofed animals didn't touch the stuff. This was fortunate—the pellets were intended as supplemental food for *maazalai*. It can be especially valuable for these predominantly vegetarian bears between the time they emerge from dens and the time spring temperatures turn warm enough for the native plants to start growing.

Begun decades earlier to help the bears contend with a lengthy drought, the artificial feeding program was also a way of compensating the population for the loss of much of its original range earlier in the twentieth century. Soviet planners wanted to increase wool production in the Gobi by drilling wells farther into the core of the desert, making it possible for livestock to use that range. Herders moved in, and their flocks quickly stripped off the thin cover of native desert plants, moonscaping the place. It's likely that some *mazaalai* were shot as perceived threats, despite the fact that these generally shy bears were not known to take livestock or harm people. Others presumably left in search of range with more food and less human disturbance, but no one was keeping track. All anyone knows for sure is that the only part of the original population able to hang on through the years was the one that kept to the three remote mountain complexes in the southernmost part of the GGSPA.

The following morning, I walked to the trapping site at Shar Khuls with most of the team. There, a single strand of barbed wire had been strung between posts to form a knee-high fence around the feeder and trap. The

[Top] Michael and Odko collect fur snagged on barbed wire strung around a
feeder—DNA from the hair helps identify individual bears. Photo: Joe Riis
[Bottom] Bins filled with grain pellets—supplemental food for the bears—are now
in place at most of the reserve's scattered oases. Photo: Doug Chadwick

first thing all of us did upon arriving was help Proctor and Odko check for bear fur snagged on the prongs. Odko tucked each frizzy sample into a little envelope and labeled it. We had *mazaalai* fur, and we were standing amid all kinds of *mazaalai* pawprints in the dust around us. For me, it was evidence, at last, that these desert grizz were no mirage. For further proof, I had *mazaalai* dung stuck to the bottom of my shoes. Big glorious piles lay everywhere by the feeders. Most consisted of digested grain pellets, but some held the remains of natural food. I broke pieces apart for a closer inspection and a sniff. Trust me: semi-fresh grizzly shit full of partially fermented wild onion sprouts is definitely not a hoax.

Step two was fence repair, since incoming bears going over or under the strand often did more than just brush against it. They stepped on the wire, pushed against it until the posts loosened and it sagged, sometimes broke the strand, or knocked the posts over by rubbing against them to scratch an itchy back. While Nasaa and Amgaa re-set a couple of the posts in the rocky ground and tightened wires, I took my turn using a tire iron to dig the next post hole a bit deeper. Puji and Ankhaa began transferring some of the grain pellets from the feeder to the trap for bait. They then wired boards in place to close off the bin's openings so the bears couldn't get at the remaining chow.

Bayasa removed the digital card from the automatic camera fixed to one of the posts, inserted it in his camera, and begin clicking through the photos. Seeing his expression change, people dropped what they were doing to look over his shoulder. We had *mazaalai* pictures! "You should look at this. Seven days ago," Bayasa said, showing me the most recent photo from the camera card at Tsagaan Tokhoi. "I think it is a male." The photos just before that revealed the bear in different positions, causing Bayasa to exclaim, "He looks good—pretty fat for this time of year. Uh-oh." We laughed together at the next images, which showed the bear investigating the camera. Run forward like a slide show, the sequence culminated with an extreme close-up of a grizzly nose followed by a photo of the inside of its mouth. Bayasa scrolled back through a month's worth of pictures. Foxes, chukars, and ravens had all triggered selfies. Every so often in between, a different Gobi grizzly had as well. "The earliest bear here is from April 5th," he told me.

We set up traps at two of the other oases that day. The day after that, we got to the fourth and farthest trap site, the oasis called Khotul Us, located some forty or fifty miles from camp. There, Bayasa waved me over to see photos with two adult bears in the same frame. They were wrestling. "Fighting? Maybe playing?" he asked. "Maybe a boy bear and a girl bear getting to know each other?"

It was hard to tell from the images. The date stamp was from mid-April. If the pair was still in the neighborhood, Kohtul Us, where four small puddles of water glimmered in the otherwise dry wash near the mouth of a canyon, might prove to be a lucky spot for us. When the sweet treats and an egg were added to the pellet piles in the metal box there, that was the final touch. We were open for bear business in the central mountain complex. The rest was up to the *mazaalai*.

BACK AT SHAR KHULS, EVENING DID NOT BRING MUCH OF A SLOWDOWN IN activity. After Ankhaa finished wiping the day's coating of dust off the van's windows, he walked over to a knot of team members, chatted with them a while, then went into a slight crouch and slapped the inside of his thighs. This was an invitation to begin a round of the national sport: *Bokh*. Wrestling, Mongolian-style. The sport is more similar to sumo than to Greco-Roman grappling on the ground. Adversaries grasp each other by the shoulders or waistband and try to lift and throw their opponent down. As soon as either contestant's body hits the earth, the match is instantly over. If the grapplers fall together, whoever's shoulder or back touches first is the loser.

Ankhaa had competed in village and regional championships. An agile natural athlete, he is broad-shouldered and muscle-packed from his toes to the top of his crew-cut head—a length of around six feet two inches. Fortunately

During a lull in bear research, Mongolia's national sport,
bokh—wrestling— enlivened life around camp. Photo: Joe Riis

for challengers, he is extremely good-natured. Unfortunately for challengers, graciously allowing someone else to win once in a while is not in Ankhaa's repertoire. That didn't stop crew members from trying. One after the other, they ended up in the gravel and dust. Ankhaa invited Ariunbold, a well-built man and the only one in camp equal to the champ in size, to have a go, but Ariunbold declined with a smile. He had work to do.

As I walked toward my tent after dinner, Ariunbold and Cori were assembling poles and nets pulled from their gear bags, getting ready for a night out with the bats. These nocturnal mammals, particularly the nursing mothers among them, consume a lot of water. They drink on the fly, scooping up a sip at a time while skimming the water's surface. Moreover, the insects that most of them hunt tend to be thickest over wet places. Therefore, the plan was to set up a mist net where a rivulet trickling out of the Shar Khuls reed thickets ran for a short distance over open ground before vanishing into the gravel.

Imagine a volleyball net with threads too thin to be picked up by the bats' sonar. Flyers that became entangled in this webbing were then carefully taken out and held in sacks. After a sufficient number had been collected, each was unsacked and positively identified before having a long string attached to one leg. Holding onto the string's other end, Ariunbold or Cori released the captive to wing its way outward and begin flying in circles. The researchers had an electronic device set out to record the tethered bat's ultrasonic calls as it wheeled through the night. By playing the calls back at a frequency audible to humans, the scientists learned the distinctive vocalizations that came from each type of bat they captured. Once this association was established for the different species in an area, the bat people would simply put out this call detector night after night and let the playback tell them which bat species were out and about at specific times and in what numbers.

A cloud cover moved in and helped keep the nighttime temperatures warmer than they would have been under a clear desert sky. Even so, it grew cool enough that Cori started to worry about leaving the bats waiting in bags for their turn to be flown at the end of a string. The types she was finding at this spot were a whiskered bat (*Myotis*, with golden fur the color of some Gobi bears), a parti-colored bat (*Vespertilio*), and a pipistrelle (*Hypsugo*). She also caught a serotine bat (*Eptesicus serotinus*), which prefers to crawl on the ground, snapping up beetles, rather than catch meals on the wing. These are all small-bodied species that can lose heat quickly when inactive and exposed to low temperatures. Eventually, Cori stopped putting whichever bat she had just removed from the mist net into a bag. Instead, she resorted to her technique of tucking the animal into her bra to stay warm against her skin.

To answer the questions that naturally arise about bosom bat-snuggling, she explained, "Yes, I do get bitten. Yes *there*, but mostly on my fingers. You get used to it. Rabies? It's not the big scary issue everyone thinks it must be. I take vaccine shots to keep my titers (levels of antibodies stimulated by the injection) up. Michael does too." Cori Lausen is a bona fide Batwoman.[2] Maybe *the* Batwoman. She certainly ranks as a leading authority on the animals, having studied bats on almost every continent and produced stacks of scientific papers. As the clock ticked toward 2 a.m., she and Ariunbold, assisted by a sleepy Proctor, were still on the job.

While these night-workers were busy flying their bats, the rangers, looking out from the slightly elevated position of our camp, saw lights in the far distance. Ankhaa and Puji wrapped themselves in *dels* to fend off the cold and roared off into the darkness—Puji on his motorbike and Ankhaa following in a van, racing toward where the lights last showed. As expected, the intruders turned out to be ninja miners. The rangers seized the men's metal detectors and wrote out tickets, fining them a hefty amount.

While all this nocturnal commotion was happening, I snored peacefully away in a sleeping bag, oblivious to everything but my dreams. The sound of the rangers returning woke me up. I trudged from my tent toward the *ger* and found a small crowd assembled, passing confiscated metal detectors around and pretending to discover buried treasure. I asked Ankhaa what would happen if the ninjas failed to report to the reserve's headquarters and pay the fine. Translated, what he said was, "The police will go to the men's home and take the keys to their motorcycles. They can confiscate the motorcycles if they want. Then the ninjas will pay a bigger fine if they want to get the motorcycles back." Hinting at larger operators behind the scenes, he shrugged and added, "Or someone pays the fine for them."

"When I came here six years ago, there were no ninjas," Puji told me. "Last year, I arrested nearly 100. Some come to the springs for water, especially Shar Khuls, and some kill wild camel and gazelle for food. If there are many ninjas together, it can be dangerous. If I think they might have guns, I just talk to them, tell them about the law. I don't try to arrest. More are coming all the time now." There had been shots exchanged between rangers and ninjas. But the rangers were plainly uncomfortable talking about that subject. Their reluctance wasn't some sort of attempt to hide excessive use of force on their part. Only a few were allowed to carry guns, and then only after extensive training and certification. Lacking sufficient manpower and vehicles to stop the influx of ninjas, the rangers were the ones most at risk from violence.

---

2 One of every five species of mammals in the world is a bat. Phenomenally diverse, they are found in nearly every sort of habitat except in polar regions. The only mammals truly able to fly, they play vital roles keeping insect numbers in check, pollinating flowers (fruit bats are responsible for much of this in tropical and subtropical regions), and dispersing seeds (ditto). Their overall influence within ecosystems is at least as substantial as that of the better known and bigger creatures. Bats are also just as imperiled. Yet they receive far less attention from the public, which by and large fears them and tends to be repulsed by their appearance. I admired Cori's passion for her research subject—and her restraint in keeping her thoughts private while the rest of us talked nonstop about conserving Gobi bears, camels, snow leopards, and other beguiling megafauna.

In the midst of an unprecedented mining boom, Mongolia was enjoying enviable economic growth. It was also facing issues arising from inadequate planning, accusations of corruption, and pollution from the authorized extraction operations that were underway. The widespread illegal mining activities were an additional challenge. However, officials in the higher echelons of power were inclined to downplay the seriousness of the problem. My impression was that the rangers didn't want to appear to be contradicting or complaining about current government policies. I had more or less parachuted into the Gobi Bear Project without very much preparation. The rangers, friendly from the start, were opening my eyes hourly to a desert environment I knew little about. Understanding even less about the country's political realities, I decided not to badger GGSPA personnel for details about ninja encounters—at least until we got to know each other better.

———

ON MAY 6, THE MORNING OF OUR FIRST DAY WITH ALL THE TRAPS READIED, Puji sped back from his check of them into the middle of camp and sat still for a moment on his bike. It deserved to be the center of attention, for it was pimped out with big metal conchos aglitter on the oversize saddlebags and a brightly colored blanket covering the seat. Mitts made of sheep hide turned inside out had been sewn over the handlebars. The thick wool kept his hands warm enough to work the throttle and brake in the coldest wind. Wearing a heavy camouflage jacket and pants, eyes hidden behind wraparound sunglasses, Puji projects purpose and authority. Just don't look closely at the seat blanket, designed for children and featuring a happy teddy bear in the center.

Now Puji's normally stoic face cracked a broad smile, and he pulled his hands loose from the mitts to give a thumbs-up sign. There was a real bear inside a trap this morning. Which trap? Distant Khotul Us.

While the rest of us scrambled to gather up loose gear, Harry played it cool. Since the capture part of the Project began in 2005, he'd had to get ready to deal with a Gobi bear in a trap seventeen times.[3] But he wasn't *that* cool. He was adrenalized enough that he forgot to make a final check of his equipment as we loaded up a van. After an hour and a half of travel, with Ankhaa accelerating more than usual—imagine an extended car-chase movie scene played on fast-forward, only with more dust—we arrived at the trap. That's when Harry realized he had everything he needed to radio collar a *mazaalai* except a radio collar. Ankhaa took off again at warp speed

3 Harry had thus far put collars on eleven different Gobi bears. Some of the additional captures were of individuals trapped during previous years. He gave each of those a new collar unless the individual looked to be in poor condition, in which case he simply turned it loose.

to bring one. He returned not much more than two hours later—I was really glad that I hadn't gone along on that ride. Harry proceeded to drug the bear with his syringe-tipped jab-stick, and we waited for the chemicals to kick in.

Overhead, the midday sun grew steadily stronger. When the crew hauled the immobilized animal out of the trap, they carefully set it down in the narrow shadow of the box. Working with other biologists, I'd been in on dozens of grizzly bear captures in North America. Now, though, part of me wished I was a rookie, so I could experience a first contact high all over again. I hoped grizzlies would never begin to seem ordinary to me. At the moment, I didn't see how that could happen. Even doped into a stupor, this bear seemed to radiate force from its dense musculature and big, broad head. Looking at grizzlies is like seeing creatures underwater through a face mask. They tend to appear larger than they really are. The logical part of my brain was resisting that effect, trying to tell me that this grizz wasn't large at all, especially for a male. In reality, it was closer in size to a black bear than to a North American *Ursus arctos*.

One of the male's most striking characteristics was his golden brown fur with a blaze of white on the shoulders and neck. The fact that this hair was sticking out all over the place made a strong impression, as did the other *mazaalai* characteristics that I would later come to understand as typical—the long ears, the thick snow-white underfur, the beat-down-to-stubs claws, and,

Grizzlies in the Gobi Desert, where winter temperatures may fall to minus 40 degrees Fahrenheit, need more insulation than you might expect for a desert dweller. Photo: Joe Riis

especially, the blunted ends of the teeth. The degree of wear on them was startling to me, for this animal had the relatively short muzzle of a youngish bear. Harry affirmed that it actually was a very young adult, most likely six years old.

Dark hairs along with blackish skin around the eyes gave this male the look of someone who needed to think about cutting back on the late-night partying. I didn't know if the dark circles were a common Gobi bear trait or an appearance temporarily emphasized by early shedding of fur around the eyes. I'd seen a couple of grizzlies in the Rockies with a similar look during the early summer shedding period. There were two ticks embedded in the male's eye rings. While we removed them, Harry commented that he had handled individuals with ticks crowded all around the eyes. Our male also had several scars on his head, some of which seemed to be old bite marks. He weighed exactly 100 kilograms (220 pounds), an impressive size for a male Gobi bear his age, in Harry's opinion. For comparison, a six-year-old male grizzly in Montana might weigh 300 pounds or more.

Inspecting the bear, directing the crew's measurements and drawing blood samples, constantly checking the animal's breathing, pulse, and temperature, Harry was in his zone, genuinely cool now. He'd morphed into a stone-cold grizz pro, the man who had captured and collared more than 1,700 *Ursus arctos* in North America. Harry once had a drugged grizzly revive enough to turn its head and sink its teeth into his leg; he then stood in place, stifling the urge to howl, which risked further reviving the bear, and waited several minutes until the animal finally relaxed its jaws. Proctor, normally one of the more exuberant humans ever invented, was ice too, having handled hundreds of North American grizzlies himself. Watching the Reynolds-Proctor duo move through the process was tremendously reassuring. If we were going to subject the world's rarest bears to the impositions of science, it had to be done with all the calm and care and experience I was seeing.

The Mongolians decided the bear's name would be *Altan*, or "Golden."[4] We waited into the evening to be sure the drug was wearing off normally. The male regained his footing and woozed around the trap site wearing his new collar. Harry had explained to everyone that grizzlies tend to rush at the first thing they hear or see when coming out of their drug-induced state, which was why we were huddled by the van at a distance, talking in whispers. Moving farther from the trap, Altan heard the click of Joe's automatic camera, set on a stake low to the ground to grab a portrait of him departing. Harry was right; Altan instantly ran over and bit the lens, busting a couple thousand dollars' worth of top-of-the-line optics. With night about to close in, we watched

4 The fact that a line known as the Altan Khans (Golden Khans), descended from Kublai Khan, ruled the western Mongol tribes during the sixteenth and seventeenth century also figured into the choice of this name for the golden young male. An attack on the outskirts of Beijing by the original Altan Khan (1507-1582) stimulated the Chinese to replace the rammed earth ramparts of the Great Wall with brick and stone.

[Top] Photographer Joe Riis tests the remote camera he has positioned along an oasis trail used by the bears. Photo: Joe Riis Collection [Bottom] Another of Joe Riis's remote cameras falls victim to a bear released from a trap after being radio-collared. Photo: Joe Riis

him power away down to the wash and into the Khotul Us canyon, a sturdy, young, golden bear from a rare line in an ancient, wild setting. And there he went, wearing a digital necklace in touch with orbiting satellites to tell us of his future travels and perhaps his fate in the modern world.

On the ride home, I asked more about Altan's bed-hair look. Why would a desert-dwelling grizzly end up having fur at least as thick as that of a grizzly roaming the Arctic? "Winters are long here," Proctor answered, "and temperatures sink far below zero. Without deep soil to tunnel into for a den, these bears have little choice but to find a shallow cave and sleep partly exposed." In other words, *mazaalai* can't dig a bear-size burrow because every mountainside in the GGSPA is pretty much all stone. They can't find a hollow tree to crawl into either, there being no forests other than the rare oasis poplar grove.

If you watch coastal salmon-feasting grizzlies in late fall, you'll see their butts jiggling like jelly as they walk. Those animals go into their winter dens with a body fat ratio of close to 50 percent. Rocky Mountain grizzlies that have been gobbling berries through the late summer and early fall might be 17 to 25 percent fat before denning. Nobody has measured this quality for Gobi bears, but it would be at the low end of the scale. Smaller and leaner than grizzlies in more generous settings, Gobi bears have less body mass to retain heat. An extra thick double layer of air-trapping fur has to do the job of providing insulation in lieu of layers of flesh and fat. A *mazaalai* can add to the cushion between itself and the floor of a cave den by carrying in vegetation. Most grizzlies gather some plant material in for their winter beds: conifer boughs, beargrass, heather, and the like. The few reports of possible Gobi bear winter beds described collections of dry branches and twigs; not the most comfortable sleeping mat, perhaps, but it sounded better than freezing rock.

The night concluded with shots of vodka inside our bunkerlike *ger*. By tradition, the owner of the bottle pours a short glass and hands it to the oldest person in the seated circle, who takes it with a bent head and a hand ceremonially bracing the elbow of the outstretched arm. Before you gulp, you're to dip the finger next to your pinky into the liquid, then flick that finger over your head, sending the vodka drops up as an offering to the powers in the immanent blue sky. Do it again if it feels right. Then guzzle away. The glass returns to the owner, who pours again and hands the glass to the next person in the circle, etc. And so the vodka makes the rounds, fueling comments and jokes and the occasional speech—tonight in celebration of the season's first bear. The crew had experienced seasons without a single capture until the last week of the expedition. One year, the sole bear caught entered a trap on the very last day. Our first catch of the season happened almost instantly.

Cheers.

MONGOLIA

AREA OF
FOCUS

G O B I -

Bayantooroi •

Great Gobi A
Strictly Protected A

CHINA

Atas Bogd ▲
A T A S   R A N G E   I N G E S
Bogt Tsagaan Ders •

Khukh Khuls •

G O B I

• Oasis
▲ Summit
■ Ger/Basecamp

0 _____ 25 MILES

SOURCE: GOBI BEAR PROJECT, NASA,
IUCN-UNEP, NATURAL EARTH. ASTER
GDEM IS A PRODUCT OF METI AND NASA.

Although GGSPA is more than five times the size of Yellowstone National Park in the United States, all its
wild inhabitants rely almost entirely on water from a small number of scattered oases.

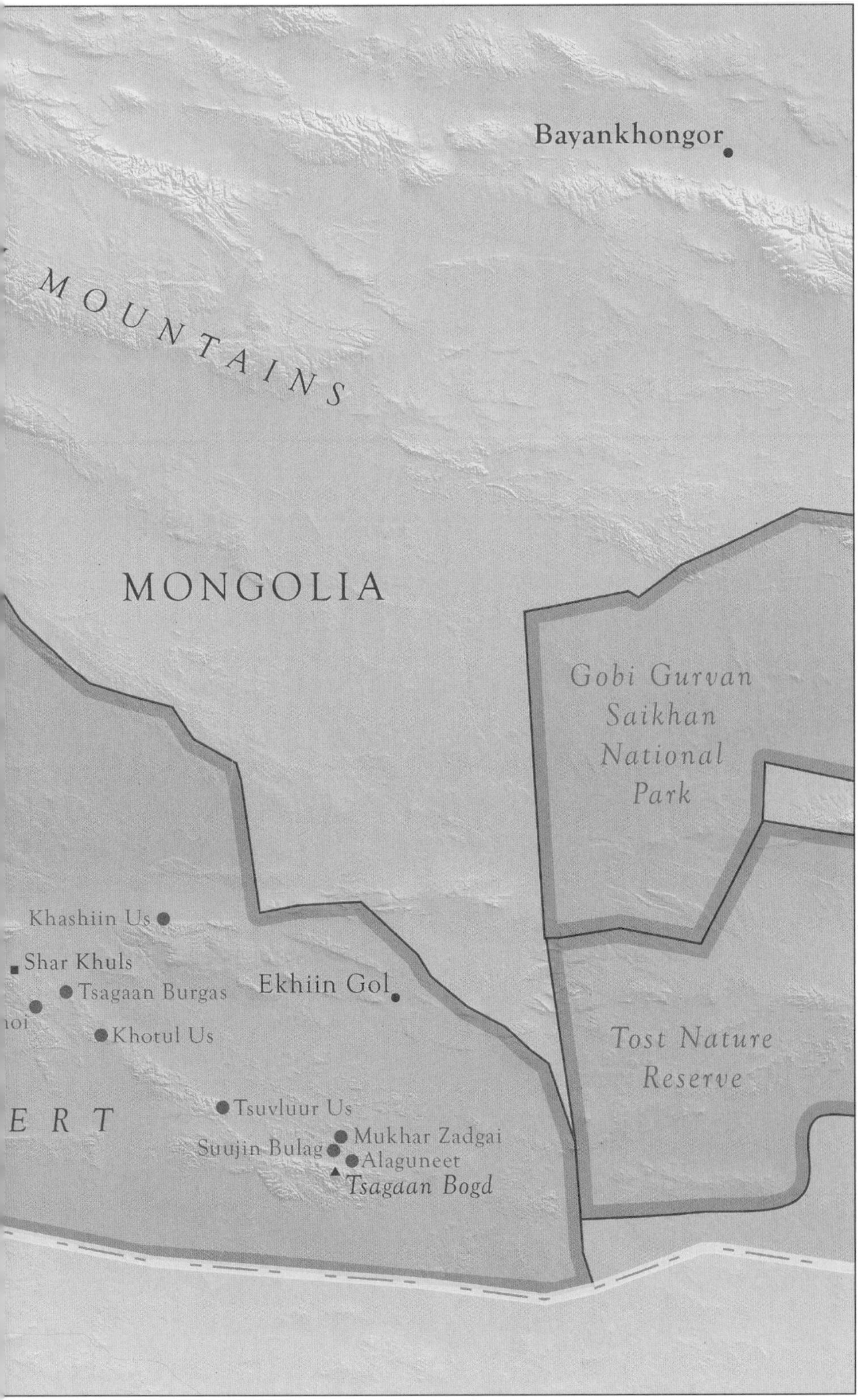

Bayankhongor

MOUNTAINS

MONGOLIA

Gobi Gurvan
Saikhan
National
Park

Khashiin Us

Shar Khuls

Tsagaan Burgas   Ekhiin Gol

ol   Khotul Us

E R T   Tsuvluur Us

Suujin Bulag   Mukhar Zadgai
Alaguneet
Tsagaan Bogd

Tost Nature
Reserve

The Botgos (Baby Camel) Mountains between the Atas (Male Wild Camel) and Inges (Female Wild Camel) ranges in the western mountain complex. Photo: Doug Chadwick

04

The Learning Curve in Thirstland

I was out in the mountains of British Columbia with a Canadian biologist one summer day long ago when we heard a noise and turned to see a figure emerge from the woods. It was a man wearing torn clothing so spattered with grime and blood that he was being followed by a swarm of flies. He looked like the sole survivor of a backwoods drama whose details you would rather not hear. My companion knew this guy, though, and introduced me. It was Mike Proctor, wearing his standard work garb for a day of packing overheated, gore-dripping chunks of road-killed ungulates around. They were to serve as bait in traps set to capture grizzlies so he could place radio collars on them. The researcher I was with had been doing the same thing. I was helping, and, to be honest, we too had clothing issues and a devoted fan club of flies.

Radio-tracking is still the most efficient way to gather data about movements, the use of specific habitats, and many other dimensions of bear behavior. Proctor has relied on this technique, which field biologists call "collar and foller" throughout a long career. However, at an early stage, he began thinking about how to tap the additional data stored in the DNA of every mammal's hair filaments and follicles. Working in the Rockies of southern Canada, he was the first person anywhere to conduct a major field test of the effectiveness of deploying scent lures together with strands of barbed wire to snag grizzly fur. Coupled with genetic analysis to identify individuals and their parentage, "hair-trapping" proved an efficient, low-cost way to census populations over a broad geographic area and define the relationships between subgroups. That's one reason this methodology has

The author and Michael model lightweight
GPS radio collars intended for the bears. Photo: Joe Riis

[Previous Spread] Michael displays a pair of Siberian ibex horns. These ibex
inhabit the reserve's steepest terrain. Photo: Joe Riis

since been adopted by bear researchers worldwide. Another reason is that trapping hair is nonintrusive; it's an alternative to capturing and drugging the animals, a stressful operation that comes with risks to the bears and the researchers alike.

Not that Proctor is risk-averse. In Borneo, he once climbed a tree to look for hairs in the nest bed of an orangutan when one of the apes swung in from the forest to sit beside him. Proctor, the scientist, couldn't help himself; he reached out and tried to gently pluck some fur from his new companion. No luck. It wouldn't pull loose. So he took a breath and yanked hard. The orangutan barely moved. It just looked at him with an expression that slowly changed from surprise to something else. "Not anger," Proctor told me. "It was more like sheer disgust. Then the orangutan left." So much for the possibility of a transcendent moment of bonding between long-separated primate cousins. "I sat there thinking I must be the rudest ape in the world," Proctor admitted. "But I got some hair!"

Over the years, I'd met Proctor in various settings, from mountainsides to wildlife convention rooms and restaurants. His own hair looked worth collecting, as it was forever sticking out at stray angles. No matter what he'd done to try taming his head-fur beforehand, he always appeared to have just wrapped up some business in a tangle of branches somewhere, an impression strengthened by the fact that he rarely wore anything but field clothes. The one time I saw him fancied up was in an office where we were to meet with high-ranking Mongolian officials. Proctor arrived sporting a sharp-looking camel hair suit coat just purchased in downtown UB. To go with it, he had on a well-used pair of dungarees and hiking boots—stuff you'd need to wear to wrangle a grizz.

In 2008 and 2009, Proctor and Odko systematically surveyed the *mazaalai* population by collecting bears' fur at springs. Counting sites that amount to little more than small puddles of water, there are more than twenty oases scattered across the three GGSPA mountain complexes inhabited by the bears. Nearly all the springs had feeding bins set up near them, and the Project crew made sure a strand of barbed wire got strung around each of those. More barbed wire was wrapped around the trunks of poplars that *mazaalai* liked to rub against[1], mostly near the springs but also in spots where a few of the trees grew from a canyon floor with subterranean water but none that reached the surface. This simple system snagged 950 samples of grizzly fur over the two-year period. Odko analyzed them back in her UB genetics lab. She discovered that all the hairs came from eight females and fourteen males, making for a total of just twenty-two different animals.

---

1   Rub trees do more than serve to scratch itches for brown bears. They also appear to function as signposts where the bears leave scent from their bodies. The smooth rubbed areas often appear together with claw marks higher up on the tree's trunk and emphatic pawprints pressed into the ground underneath, which may be a way of depositing scent from glands on the soles of the feet.

Twenty-two was *not* the definitive number of Gobi bears left in the world. It was the absolute minimum. Did some individuals ease past the wire strand without touching a barb? Did barbs that came into contact with visiting bears fail to grab onto any hairs at times? Were a few bears keeping away from feeders to avoid meeting a dominant individual at the site? (Big males represent a potential danger for subadults and for mothers with young cubs in particular.) Were there *mazaalai* that kept to areas with water sources the team couldn't reach or didn't know about? The answer in every case was: maybe. Applying statistical formulas to their sample—science's approach to quantifying probabilities—Proctor and Odko calculated that the population most probably stood between twenty-two and thirty-one, in line with the estimates made by Schaller, McCarthy, and Miji.

The number of females within this population was alarmingly small, so few that they could all go for a ride together in one of our vans with room to spare. Of those, fewer still would be of breeding age and fertile. They were the bottleneck in the population, the key to its future, and a constant focus of concern for members of the Project. The loss of just a couple within a short period could mark the start of an irreversible decline to zero for Gobi bears. At the same time, the fact that a very small cadre of sexually mature females had somehow kept this population's count fairly steady decade after decade was encouraging. In my mind, every bear still out there, and particularly each female, deserved honor and acclaim as a symbol of that ineffable force, the cell-deep fire we call the will to live. Biospirit.

It helps a great deal that the natural lifespan of a grizzly can exceed thirty years. Researchers in Montana radio-tracked a wild female who produced new cubs at the age of thirty-five. It also helps that *Ursus arctos* are smart, possessing the largest brain-to-body weight ratio of any mammals in the big and varied Carnivore order.[2] Fast learners, bears absorb and store a good deal of information about their surroundings over a lengthy lifespan and pass at least some of that knowledge on to offspring, giving them a leg up in the game of life. Burly knowledge. To contend with the Gobi requires a lot of plain, old-fashioned toughness and strength as well, but being grizzlies, *mazaalai* come with those qualities built in. Meanwhile, the creation of the strictly protected area, combined with the supplemental food placed near

---

2 Experiments with captive black bears showed them able to "count," insofar as they proved able to distinguish circles of identical size from one another when they contained different numbers of dots. Captives also displayed the conceptual ability to categorize objects or patterns with common characteristics, selecting them from among an array of alternatives in tests. A grizzly in coastal Alaska was documented picking up barnacle-encrusted rocks and rubbing them against its fur to give itself a more thorough scratching. This isn't genius-level behavior, but it does qualify as tool use. And that places *Ursus arctos* in a (so far) rarefied group of animals that includes members of the canny crow family, dolphins, and some of our fellow primates. Six of eight individual captive grizzlies given stumps or plastic boxes in the yard of an enclosure proceeded to push or drag the materials into a heap. The animals then climbed this mound they had built to reach a sweet food reward dangling high overhead. When captive chimpanzees (which share more than 96 percent of the human DNA sequence) first did something like this in the second decade of the twentieth century, the news electrified the scientific community. Which reveals something significant about chimps and bears but tells us even more about how tightly humans have clung to the dogma that we, and we alone, are capable of reasoning, or insight.

Puji tries to locate one of the GPS collars, which emit a standard straight-line (VHF)
signal along with one that can be picked up by satellites. The collars are programmed to drop
off the bears after eleven months. Photo: Joe Riis

water sources, played a crucial supporting role through the years by offering
the survivors sanctuary plus extra nutrition.

Since the same animal might leave fur at several different springs, the
hair-capture study gave the Project a way to track individual movements by
untagged bears. The three main mountain complexes with springs are separated by forty to sixty miles of bleak, waterless, and largely foodless expanses.
A key question was whether or not the small *mazaalai* population might be
separating into subgroups isolated from one another. If the bears within the
different mountain complexes weren't exchanging genes, the population
would become more subject to the harmful effects of inbreeding with each
generation. Before Proctor started taking fur samples, GPS locations from
collared animals had shown some males traveling between the mountain
complexes. Yet with only one to three bears giving off signals in a given year,
the sample size was too small to tell the team very much about the level of
interchange. The researchers hadn't even known for sure that each mountain
complex still contained at least one breeding-age female. The fur samples
made it clear that one was present in each group. The samples also showed
that a female moved between two of the mountain complexes during the
hair-snagging study. Five males did the same. One roamed across all three
complexes, covering a minimum of 120 miles en route.

Counting backward from the ages of the bears he had collared, Harry
calculated that at least nine had been born between 1999 and 2009. Our recent

capture of big, healthy, six-year-old Altan brought the number to ten. Thus, the Project had put two major sources of anxiety to rest for the moment: The *mazaalai* continued to meet and mingle genes. And they were still making babies that survived to become young adults, replacing members of the population lost to old age or other causes of death.

Ursus arctos gobiensis showed no obvious sign of giving in. Its numbers appeared to have stayed more or less constant for the past four decades. Thus, the main question for the biologists, for the Mongolian government, and for anybody and everybody who cared about these creatures had become this: What will it take to help the world's rarest bears increase enough to spread outward, reoccupy former range, and gain a firm grip on the future instead of just tenaciously hanging on in their shrunken home?

——————

BEFORE I COULD UNDERSTAND WHAT MIGHT BE DONE TO HELP GOBI BEARS recover, I needed to understand what allowed them to live in this desert to begin with. When I'd buried my hands in Altan's fur while it moved up and down with each breath, it was almost as if I subconsciously craved the added layer of proof that *mazaalai* truly exist. Receiving it through my fingertips was a privilege, and Altan was as real as could be, but I still had no feel for the realities of these animals' daily lives. What kind of routes were they following through the mountain labyrinths and over the sprawling gravel plains? Where were they able to scrounge enough calories and protein from this stonescape to stay nourished? My intuition was insisting that this species and this environment simply weren't a fit. The only way I knew to change that was to hike the place—to take one step at a time with my eyes wide open and keep walking and looking until I began to glimpse how the Great Gobi might grow a grizzly bear.

Wherever I wandered alone on foot, I found myself under the spell of two sensations aroused and amplified by the desert. The first was one of absolute exposure—to the sun and eternal blue sky; to vast, uncluttered vistas of Earth's bare skin and bones impinging from all sides; to sharp stones underfoot, pushes and probes of the wind; to more stars than I had ever seen. Outside my tent or the *ger*, there was no place to hide from any of it—no overhanging branches, no organic tangles, no corner or cubby to nestle into except maybe somewhere against a bare rock face.

The second sensation was of the desert's profound stillness. Nothing moved out there save the occasional dust devil or wisp of a cloud. There was never even a jet contrail marking the sky, for no commercial airlines flew routes over the empty spaces of Central Asia. The absence of motion was matched with an absence of sound. If you make a point of listening to the Gobi wind, you can nearly always hear it whispering something. But its surges and susurrations become the kind of white noise you cease to pay attention to. And when the wind that has been blowing you around suddenly idles, the depth of the silence will practically knock you to your knees.

And then, fast as a shooting star, the silhouette of a saker falcon cuts a line through the sky and disappears behind a peak. Perhaps twenty minutes later, a single raven call comes echoing down one of the side-canyons. The rest is stillness again, the Gobi's all-encompassing, unchanging views and the sound of no sound. It was a while before I fully grasped why this stasis wasn't broken by big wildlife more often. Wherever I turned, my gaze took in such a broad span and I could see so far into it, I anticipated finding a band of wild asses, perhaps a line of wild camels, or at least a lone gazelle if I scanned the panorama carefully through binoculars. Nope. The only animals I could count on seeing were the pied wagtails that hopped around base camp picking up insects and scraps. Only once in a while did I manage to view large mammals. It was usually at a distance, and most often because I was tipped off by long streamers of dust rising from the ground where they were on the move. Many and many a square mile was required to sustain a single animal through the changing seasons and years and cycles of drought in this desiccated domain. If the numbers that I had heard listed for hoofed wildlife in the GGSPA sounded high, it was because the reserve is colossal. To hike so far and come upon so few to watch wasn't disappointing; it was the Gobi. I took it as inspiration for walking farther and looking harder.

The thing that had thrown me at first, raising my expectations for frequent sightings of big critters, was that signs of their presence abounded, and not only near springs and in the narrow passageways where dry washes led through canyons. The plains and mountain slopes everywhere were etched with the braided trails of hoofed wildlife and stippled with their droppings. What was going on? The answer is that I wasn't factoring in how natural processes operate in a desert.

Around my home in the northern Rockies of Montana, the weekly weather forecast for early May likely included rain. Daylong, soaking rain. The drops would fall atop tons of melting snow in the high country. I envisioned the rivulets that would be cascading all over the place, carrying loads of sediment downhill. If I were there, I'd hear avalanches and landslides being loosed on the steeper terrain and see where sections of saturated hillsides had slumped at lower elevations. Boulders were working free from frost-heaved slopes and tumbling down into the woods, smashing vegetation. In the valleys, the fields were speckled with meltwater ponds in some areas, completely flooded in others. In between, the topsoils, rich in organic material, were sodden as a wet sponge. Nighttime temperatures turned the water in them to ice. As the crystals expanded, they lifted the dirt up, broke it apart, and re-mixed the contents.

While almost the entire surface of the countryside stayed in a state of physical flux, it was in motion biologically too. Bacteria, fungi, and single-celled algae thriving in the moist conditions were busy recycling organic material and adding to it as they multiplied. Earthworms by the bajillion were doing the same, eating, excreting, and enriching the soil, constantly turning over the upper layers alongside countless mites, nematodes, and other invertebrates at home in the humus. In short, potent forces of erosion, decay, and reconstruction were at work 24/7 from the peaks to the lowland meadows. That's what I was used to.

But what was happening in the Gobi landscape? Not too much. Maybe a band of wild asses cut a new track across the rubbled slopes with their sharp hoofs months ago. Weeks later, another group chose the same route, carving it a bit deeper. Scant rain fell on the path. Hardly any melting snow trickled across it. The ground froze during the cold months—nighttime temperatures still sunk below freezing some nights during our mid-spring visit—but there

If enough spring rain falls, fields of the wildflowers called golden buttons arise to gild the desert. Photo: Joe Riis

was precious little moisture in the stony surface debris and little or no humus to absorb any precipitation that did arrive, so frost-heaving was minimal.

Even if only a handful of animals journey along that particular route once in a great while, it will linger for decades, and maybe centuries, as another strand in the webwork of paths. Such trail systems pattern the land so conspicuously you can't help suspecting—if you're a newcomer from Montana—that great throngs of ungulates must be somewhere just over the next hill or two. Scat in the desert seems to last forever too. Microbes don't get very far with degrading the stuff before it dries out. For the same reason, dung beetles and flies can't make much use of it either. Most droppings just turn into brittle turd mummies that lie around year after year like the occasional dead branch fallen from a saxaul bush.

Another lesson the desert had in store was how many seeds and root systems lie dormant inside the mineral soil underfoot. Stimulated by the recent light rain and the onset of warm May weather, vegetation suddenly started erupting from sterile-looking ground. We awoke to more wildflowers every May morning. The most conspicuous was a member of the sunflower family that shot up four to six inches to produce a marble-size ball of yellow petals. *Altan tovch*, the Mongolians called it: golden button. Before long, thick clusters of them were nodding in the winds. In the low-angled light of sunrise and sunset, they peach-fuzzed and gilded whole spans of our world. Even better for our purposes, these glowing golden blossoms fed *mazaalai*. I found the plant's remains in bear scat at trap sites and springs.

Soon a larger type of herb began to emerge among the golden buttons. Each plant produced two or three round, dark green leaves big as dinner plates close to the ground. From that base, a stout reddish stalk arose to put forth a many-branched display of red flowers. The result looked very familiar. This was rhubarb, a wild desert version with the scientific name *Rheum nanum*. How could a perennial plant this large and showy grow from fields of gravels too hot to keep your hand on at midday?

After puzzling over the question for about ten seconds, I grabbed a flat rock and used it to dig next to a flowering rhubarb. The gravel on the surface was replaced by fine sand and compacted dust underneath. Yet at a depth of no more than eight inches, the granules felt damp. The dust's clay content was holding onto the moisture the sky had delivered. I dug twice as deep, and the soil felt twice as damp. The thick taproots of the rhubarb went deeper still. I'd been told that they would, but I had to see for myself because members of the Project had said that the plant was a staple in the diet of Gobi bears. Now I could understand why.

This key food was most abundant in slight creases of the terrain and along minor gullies, where just a bit more sediment and water runoff converged after a rain than on smoother contours. In years like this, the plant flourished and added to the stores of starch and protein in those long, chubby roots.

"We call the rhubarb *bijun*," Bayasa told me. "People in the Gobi make bread and donuts from the roots." (It is also spelled *bajuuna*.)

After summer shriveled the flowers and leaves, the bears could still sniff out the underground bulk of the plant and dig it up. They could do the same in drought conditions, when the rhubarb might show little or no growth aboveground.

In my wanderings, I got better at recognizing old pits where a *mazaalai* had clawed its way down to a rhubarb's roots. Pieces of dried-out leaves and stalks sometimes lay mixed with the excavated soil, but I no longer took this as proof that the digging was fairly recent. I'd readjusted my timescale to the slow pace of decay in this desert. Here and there, clusters of mounded burrow entrances also patterned the terrain. They were gerbil colonies, and it looked as though bears had been digging into some of them. Although the gerbils don't hibernate, they turn sluggish in their subterranean tunnels when bitter cold weather holds sway over the desert. The weeks before and after the bears go into dens of their own are probably when they have the best luck digging for rodents.[3]

Several gerbil species inhabit the Gobi. In our rocky area, the most common were great gerbil and the Mongolian gerbil, or *jird*. The latter was taken to France as a curiosity during the nineteenth century. From there the captives went on to other Western countries. Their descendants are the gerbils looking back at you from a cage in a pet store, if not a cage in your kids' room.

Here's the deal with most of us grown-up naturalists: While we can toss around Latin names and biological principles, there's a huge part of us that's still just an eleven-year-old on a treasure hunt. We'll keep going all day on the chance of turning over a stone or peering around a bend to find something that makes us say, "Ooooh!" and then, if we're lucky, "What the heck *is* that? I've never seen anything like it before." This impulse defines all kinds of adventurers. The difference is that the naturalist is captivated by the mystery of organisms, their majesty/intricacy/oddity/fantasticality. And their behaviors: "What's it *doing*?"

With time, you store up enough facts that you find yourself saying, "I can identify the species, but how does it fit in here?" This means you've reached the stage of being engaged with animals' life histories, their habitats, their

3 Though their remains show up in *mazaalai* scat, gerbils aren't a key food source. In fact, nobody knows whether the bears that plow into colonies enjoy more success catching the gerbils or scavenging the seeds and roots stored in their tunnels. A bit of related history: Mongol hordes who plundered some European kingdoms and so frightened the rest in medieval times inflicted only negligible damage compared to the bubonic plagues that later swept through in the fourteenth century. The epidemics claimed a third of Europe's population. As it turns out, the first outbreak during that era may have originated in Mongolia. The disease spread from Central Asia to both China and Europe, and the original carriers were likely not rats but gerbils.

relationships with neighbors, and the ecosystem that supports the community as a whole.

Almost inevitably, in the twenty-first century, this leads to the crunch question: "What do we have to do to keep all this from disappearing?" Human curiosity is boundless. The wonder of the natural realm ought to be unending too. Eleven years old or all grown up, you don't want the best treasure hunt ever to end.

What I'm trying to get at is why observations of all these obscure details about footprints, plant parts, and pawings in the dirt seemed so important during my first days in the field in between bear captures. Proctor summed up the GGSPA setting when he described *mazaalai* as living in "the most extreme, dry, hot, cold, sparsely vegetated bear habitat on Earth."

But how?

Whenever the crew did a maintenance check on a capture site, it gave me time to go off backtracking the pawprints left by recent bear visitors. Their trails were not the usual linear set of tracks that animals make. Ambling along in the rolling, slightly pigeon-toed gait grizzly bears use, the *mazaalai* created distinct double sets of tracks—parallel paths, one for the feet on each side the body. From a distance, it almost looked as though someone had driven a vehicle with two close-set tires up and down the wash.

A grizzly will often step precisely in the pawprints left by an earlier bear. Proctor told me that this was particularly characteristic of male *Ursus arctos*, and Gobi bears were no exception. Elsewhere, small prints—not from a cub but from a yearling or two-year-old, a recently added member of the population—filled in between the adult-size tracks. The most heavily used double trails in the dust and gravel of a wash sometimes hugged the cliff walls on one side, perhaps for shade from the sun's heat or concealment in the shadows. Wherever individual prints strayed from one of the main routes, I, too, strayed, hoping to identify the object of interest that had caused the diversion. Where a bear appeared to have stopped and turned sideways I, too, stopped to sniff the wind and look around, making guesses about what might have grabbed the animal's attention. I couldn't be sure that I would ever get to see a Gobi bear apart from a trapping operation, but walking in their tracks, pausing where they paused, digging where they dug, and picking apart the odd scat left en route let me assemble a sort of virtual *mazaalai* as I wandered along.

While searching for more grizzly signs one morning, I did finally get a fairly close look at a band of camels from behind a rock outcropping. Considering how hard I was struggling to make sense of the presence of grizzlies in this setting, it was fascinating to suddenly come upon larger and even shaggier mammals perfectly designed to be here. Each was equipped with a double row of long eyelashes to guard against the intense sun, sand, and dust. And a special transparent third eyelid to wipe away grit that gets past the lashes onto an eye's lens. And a long, narrow nose that conserves the moisture in exhaled breaths and can close tightly to seal out hurtling sand and dust during storms. Plus those long, long legs to keep the torso high off the hot ground. And the ability to allow the body's temperature to rise as high as 104 degrees F without harming the brain.

As far as anyone yet knows, *mazaalai* don't own unique physical adaptations for desert environments. They are basically built like other grizzlies. Starving camels will turn to chewing on the flesh, skin, and bones of carcasses. *Mazaalai* can do that. But they can't subsist on the toughest, saltiest, prickliest vegetation around, and they can't drink fifteen to thirty gallons of water in a quarter of an hour, walk away, and keep going without another sip for weeks. Camels, of course, are expert at both. They digest the rough forage by fermenting it in vat-like, multichambered stomachs with the help of microbes. Troops of bacteria, protozoans, and fungi combine to transform raw plant cellulose and lignin (woody fibers) into usable starches and sugars, proteins, fatty acids, vitamins, and other essential nutrients.[4]

The gazelles, argali, and ibex possess the same kind of ruminant guts loaded with helpful microbes. Like desert bighorns in North America, the argali sheep are able to tolerate significant dehydration of their body tissues. Gerbils and most of the other Gobi Desert rodents hardly need to drink at all. They generate water from the way they metabolize seeds, buds, and other food, and they excrete very little liquid in their concentrated urine.

Bears, though omnivorous, operate with a carnivore's anatomy, which includes a relatively small stomach and short, straight intestinal tract. This is a digestive system designed for animals whose diet consists chiefly of meat and other animal tissues—concentrated energy food that doesn't require a lot of processing. To obtain a similar level of nutrition from a largely vegetarian diet, Gobi bears can't just compensate by eating more plant bulk. They have to high-grade what's available, seeking out the richest parts of the most palatable species.

Such a stark, pared-down realm, and yet there was so much to take in. Rambling through its contours looking for signs was always exciting—and often a little frustrating because I'd begin to feel as if I was hiking through a landscape stippled with question marks. I needed to learn how to read this

---

4 Ruminants are far from alone in their partnership with microbes. The usual estimate is that the human body consists of something like a hundred trillion cells. Impressive. Yet there are at least an equal number of single-celled organisms inside a human. Most of them inhabit our digestive tract, where they play crucial roles in the breakdown of foods, the manufacture of key nutrients, and, though many people still think of these microscopic creatures as "germs," the prevention of disease. We live within ecosystems, and ecosystems that amount to largely unexplored frontiers live within each of us.

Ranger-biologist Nasaa displays a rhubarb's long, thickened roots. Gobi bears crater
some slopes digging up this trove of starch and protein. Photo: Joe Riis

desert—learn the language of the ground, the plants that pushed up through it, the calligraphy of tracks in the washes.

What I needed was a guide. For me, that was often Amgaa. Now in his late fifties, he had traveled all over the country during his wildlife research career. Through Bayasa, who interpreted one night while we dined, Amgaa said, "My special interest was the black-tailed gazelle. I studied the ecology and distribution of that species to know what is the best way to conserve it. Also," he added between bites, "because gazelles are very delicious."

During his many trips to the Gobi, he had seen bears near feeders on a number of occasions, but "only three times in the wild," meaning elsewhere in the GGSPA terrain. "Two were bears by themselves," he recalled. "The third time, it was a mother with two subadults." *Lucky man*, I remember thinking. That family group alone might have represented a tenth of the entire *mazaalai* population. Amgaa didn't have to watch them to know what they liked to eat, though. He was an ace at detecting animal sign, and he knew the Gobi vegetation.

When I asked him one day to help me find more examples of the plants *mazaalai* favored, Amgaa promptly led me to a stout bush that had just put forth a profusion of yellow blooms quivering slightly in the cool morning breeze. I wanted to know which part of the shrub the bears ate. Since his English was as limited as my Mongolian, I inquired by bending a whole leafy branch my way and shoving my face into it. Amgaa shook his head and instead mimicked nipping off the flowers one by one. The plant was a cara-gana, sometimes called peashrub, and related to varieties planted in gardens and hedgerows around the world. In the legume family, it has specialized nodules on its roots that host bacteria capable of converting atmospheric nitrogen into organic molecules the plant can use for growth. When the bears munched caragana flowers, they were gaining a share of the nitrogen compounds, which are essential building blocks for muscles and cartilage.

Later on, I waved Amgaa over to a white-barked bush erupting with flowers. He informed me that it was called *tsagaan mod* white tree or white bush. I never was able to pin down what species it was, but Amgaa indicat-ed—again mostly with gestures—that the bears did indeed eat the blooms. A different shrub with whitish bark, also fairly widespread in draws and other drainage channels, was *Zygophyllum xanthoxylon*, another legume. The prominent developing seedpods looked edible, and Amgaa let me know that they, too, served as bear food.

Odko, meanwhile, was gathering *Zygophyllum potaninii*, a nonwoody relative of the bush. "Mongolians call this one *khulangiin undaa*," she said when we crossed paths with her near camp. "That means wild ass—the *khulan*—drinks of it." The plant is what botanists call a succulent, having thick, fleshy, water-storing leaves with a waxy surface to prevent evaporation. It could have been named "*mazaalai* eats and drinks of it," for bears munch the soft tissues of this low-growing species and surely get a good sip of liquid at the same time. In addition, *Z. potaninii* may give them some protection from toxins. The species contains selenium-based antioxidants able to neu-tralize the kind of harmful free radicals that can cause liver damage—which is why Mongolians value it as a traditional folk cure for liver ailments. Odko planned to dry the leaves and take them to friends and family in UB.

On another foray, Amgaa pointed out shrubs called nitre bush, *Nitraria*, and described the dark blue or purple berries that would form in midsummer. Like the blueberries and huckleberries I knew back home, nitre bush fruits have a high sugar content to offer a grizzly. Gobi bears also lip the berries off box-thorn bushes—*Lycium*, the genus that includes species popularly called Goji berry or wolfberry. In the uplands, Amgaa helped me distinguish between two different types of *Ephedra*, a widespread genus of shrubs found in the temperate drylands of many countries. Known in North America as Brigham tea, Mormon tea, or desert tea, *Ephedra* is not actually a flowering plant, or angiosperm. Instead, it belongs to the more ancient group called gymnosperms, which includes conifers and gingko trees.

As I knelt down and mimed a bear munching the foot-high *Ephedra* species closest to us, Amgaa enthusiastically nodded encouragement, possibly just because he found my antics entertaining, but more likely because this shrub puts forth small berries as early as late May or the first part of June in a good year. In looking through Schaller's early paper on Gobi bear natural history again, I noticed a description of *mazaalai* eating the tips of both tamarisk and *Ephedra* bushes. That seemed like a good strategy for any browser, since the growing ends of the branches and their new leaves would be the most tender parts of the plants and offer the highest nutrient value before the berries ripened. *Ephedra* was common enough here that it represented a huge potential food source. Yet dining on it might have more consequences than simply filling the stomach.

The nitrogen-rich yellow blossoms of the caragana bush are food for desert-dwellers from bears to hares. Photo: Doug Chadwick

One of the compounds produced by this conifer, ephedrine, is a stimulant that increases blood pressure and acts as a bronchodilator in humans. Various cultures, especially in China, have used *Ephedra* concoctions as a tonic and treatment for asthma, coughs, and an array of other ailments for centuries. As a close chemical analogue of amphetamine and methamphetamine, ephedrine could be making Gobi bears the world's most buzzed bruins. Or the chemical might have no effect on them whatsoever—maybe they've developed ways to neutralize it. Who knows what practical applications advanced studies of these desert bears could yield for human medicine, not to mention for meeting the challenges of adapting to a warmer, drier world? But for the moment, the thrust of the Project was to hurry up and gather enough basic facts about the animals to keep them from vanishing.

Most of the annual precipitation that arrives in the Gobi and the Mongolian steppe in general does so in the form of summer storms. In an average or better year, this yields two growing seasons. The first is springtime, when whatever moisture is stored in the soil combines with occasional showers. Next come bursts of heavier summer rains that can spark a resurgence of plant growth. "We had rains last fall, some snow in the winter, and we had the rain this spring," Amgaa told me back at camp. "This should be a good year." Unlacing my boots, I noticed that their toes were tinted yellow from pollen brushed off the golden buttons.

I had seen a fair amount of sprouting wild onion as well as new clumps of low-growing *Stipa gobicum* grass during my walks. The bears grazed both these species, and all of us chopped up the wild onion greens to sprinkle on our dinner noodles. When newly sprouted, both types of plants are at their richest in carbohydrates and protein and hold the most liquid. According to Schaller, the moisture content of the onion shoots during spring is 86 percent; in the blades of the *Stipa*, 67 percent. The more the bears can find, the less often they have to trek to an oasis for water. If the summer rains prove generous, some onion and *Stipa* will continue sprouting and growing all season and into the fall. Another source of high-energy green food the bears grazed were the sprouts and lower stalks of the tall *Phragmites* reeds (technically, a species of grass) that flourish in beds at a number of the springs. Grasslike sedges grew from moist soil close to the water's edge, and I saw evidence of recent feeding on them. Brown bears around the Northern Hemisphere eat young sedges. So do most resident ungulates. The GGSPA oases held so many kinds of fresh tracks that I couldn't be sure which animals had been grazing down the sedges, but the *mazaalai* surely took part.

As the days warmed, I found the desert's ordinarily quiet surface becoming more and more animated by the scuttlings of toad-headed agama lizards three to six inches long, ground beetles, and other insects. I often noticed as many as half a dozen wingless grasshoppers within a few yards once I honed my search image for them a bit during strolls. Resembling pudgy flightless crickets, they walked slowly and were easy to catch. From a passing bear's point of view, it would be as though somebody had randomly scattered nougats with a protein content on a par with red meat across the desert floor. To the bears' plant diet, I could now add some amount of the following animals: carabid and tenebrionid beetles, ants, and wingless grasshoppers.

Schaller and Miji had identified lizards, gerbils, hamsters, jerboas, and other, unidentified rodents in *mazaalai* scat along with an assortment of remains scavenged from ungulate carcasses.

Bit by bit, pawprint by digging crater by turd speckled with beetle shells or grasshopper legs, I was beginning to form a mental picture of real grizzly bears moving through Thirstland from one source of concentrated food to another. Were there enough such sources to be found from early spring through late fall? Amgaa summed up the answer simply and, I think, best. He wasn't speaking in terms of a year or even a few years. He was talking about the long run when he said, "If the weather is good, the bears will survive. If the climate is changing so the weather is not as good...."

―――――――

AFTER SEVERAL SLOW DAYS WITH NO BEAR ACTIVITY REPORTED NEAR THE trap sites, Hunter Causey, the volunteer hydrologist, went out to set a PVC pipe with calibrated markings among the reeds of Shar Khuls to serve as a gauge of the water level in the oasis. In trying to drive the pipe into the ground, he was met by a solid field of underlying ice. His discovery pointed to the possibility that this Gobi permafrost layer, insulated by the reeds' roots and a thick mat of decomposing stalks, might reliably deliver meltwater even through a severe spell of drought.

The next cause of a stir around camp was a motorcycle wreck. It happened when Nasaa, who had a high-energy approach to most undertakings, substituted for Puji to make the round of trap checks. He tried a shortcut over the shoulder of a ridge. This cost him enough sections of skin off his face and arms that he looked a little like he'd got in the way of Altan's exit from the trap.

Then came May 11, an unusually warm night that happened to be Cori's fortieth birthday. Batwoman's original plan was to have a glass of wine and move on to the oasis edge to catch more bats, hoping to pick up a species or two not yet recorded for this region of the Gobi. Then a vodka bottle appeared in her honor.

Since turning the Big Four-Oh was an important occasion, the drinking protocol now was different. Whoever's turn it was to accept the drink offered by the bottle's owner was expected to respond with a dignified toast or a song before taking a sip. Lovely, plaintive solos poured from the mouths of some of the least talkative Mongolians in the crew. Some would begin a traditional song, and it never took long before the others all joined in. Several of the tunes were long enough that another vodka bottle appeared in-between stanzas.

The night was still young when Cori decided to forego bat-netting in favor of birthday partying. Someone drove one of the vans with a cassette player closer to the standing circle of toastmasters. Mongolian rock music blasted through the speakers. It isn't right to report on what your friends do out in the middle of nowhere once the bottles and glasses are being passed around freely and the dancing starts. I'll relate only that the next morning of traveling as a group by van to carry out a maintenance check of the trap sites was slow business. There were occasional stops for crew members to leap out, lean way over, and try to avoid splashing their shoes with their breakfast.

When a small crew went with Hunter to install a PVC pipe gauge in the Tsagaan Tokhoi canyon where water collected, I hiked on far up the course of the wash. After bouldering through one narrow section, I reached a fork where the rock had eroded into hoodoos—odd spires and towering walls honeycombed with shallow caves. Gale-force gusts surging up this deeply cut reach of the canyon turned the hoodoos into giant wind instruments. The place shrieked and wailed and uttered prolonged, anguished moans, as if I'd stumbled into the Gorge of Lost Souls. And not necessarily on my home planet. A moon two-thirds full stood in the ribbon of daytime sky above the slot like a second, unearthly sun. In my imagination, the cave-pocked cliffsides were mutating into the high-rise apartments of an alien culture.

While the open desert wasn't familiar to me yet, it was a hundred times more familiar than this abode of eerie stone voices. I was now countless twists and turns and drops of the canyon away from the van. All at once I felt beyond alone, isolated from every trace of normalcy. I tried to laugh off the strange emotions welling up inside—until the sound of a cry behind me swelled so clearly and so close that I instinctively reached for my knife. It was only a sudden barrage of wind currents strumming a set of peculiar undercut curves in the wall. *That had to be what it was.* But I was becoming less and less sure of anything. I made a hasty U-turn and hiked back down the canyon.

The night was another warm one. Cori caught about thirty bats. We breakfasted on marrow soup in the morning, and the day grew baking hot by noon. Once again, we were hanging out waiting for a report from Puji. The moto-ranger was overdue. Midafternoon had arrived by the time he rolled in to tell us that the Khotul Us trap had another bear in it. We arrived there around 5 p.m. The *mazaalai* was a female. She already had a name: Borte, Genghis Khan's first and principal wife—the empress. The Queen of queens.

Harry and the crew first caught Borte in 2006, when she was seven years old and weighed 163 pounds. Now, five years later, she weighed only 128 pounds. This was the smallest adult female grizzly I had ever seen. Yet she

Measuring rhubarb abundance and growth along a transect line to determine yearly
differences in relation to weather conditions. Photo: Joe Riis

had been nursing young within the last month or so. Though her teats were
not full, they remained slightly enlarged, and Harry was able to express milk
from them. We found no sign of offspring anywhere, and photos taken of her
earlier in the day by the site's automatic camera showed neither a cub nor a
yearling (which females may continue to nurse). All the evidence suggested
that Borte had lost her young. Another larger bear appeared in the photos
taken that morning. It looked like a male, whose presence might mean that
she was coming back into reproductive condition and attracting suitors now
that she was no longer actively nursing.

Under optimum conditions, female grizzlies are capable of first breeding
as early as age three. In typical conditions, they aren't reproductively mature
before age four or five. Given marginal habitats with limited food such as the
Arctic tundra—or the Gobi Desert—they may not begin breeding until age
six, or even later. *Ursus arctos* are known to give birth to as many as four cubs.
The usual number is two. Based on accounts from herders in earlier decades
as well as more recent observations, Gobi bears often have only a single cub.
It isn't clear whether this means that the females generally lack sufficient
reserves to carry more than one fetus to term or that they can only produce
enough milk for one cub to thrive even if two are born. It might also mean
that Gobi bear young suffer higher than normal losses from other causes
such as predation. Due to the mother bears' relatively small size, they may

be less able than grizzlies elsewhere to defend offspring from a wolf pack, for example—or from an aggressive male bear.

Kneeling by Borte, I touched the liquid Harry had expressed from her teat, warm and rich-smelling. The toll taken by nourishing a fetus and then producing milk for a growing youngster likely accounted for much of her weight loss since the first capture. Had she given birth before? Had any of those cubs survived? Feeling discouraged, I had to remind myself that even in prime habitats, 30 to 50 percent of the grizzly cubs die during their first year. On the other hand, the mothers in prime habitats will usually have twins or triplets, so the result is that at least one of their babies survives to see the next year. In grizzly bear range like this, though, the odds are probably reduced all around. You would expect females to have fewer offspring in a litter, perhaps just one in most cases. The rate of attrition for the young would be higher, and instead of an interval of two or three years between births, the mother might have to wait three or four years or still longer before she builds up sufficient reserves to successfully support another pregnancy. These are only predictions based on studies in other marginal habitats. There wasn't enough data on Gobi bears to know if they were doing any better than that, or worse.

While my heart was going out to this tough, skinny little bear lying amid our boots and the stones and dust of Thirstland, Borte was apparently metabolizing her drug dose much faster than normal. Without warning, she suddenly raised her head high and staggered to her feet. This happened while Proctor was still straddling her, tightening the last bolt on the new radio collar around her neck, and the rest of the crew was all crowded around logging data or taking photos and video. One second, the Queen lay dead still, helpless and bedraggled, walled in by a huddle of humanity; the next, panicked people were dropping equipment on the ground and fleeing every direction while Borte whirled and swiped drunkenly at the air around her.

She stumbled and went down again, but then struggled back to her feet to slowly wander in circles next to the box trap. After half an hour, she had regained enough muscle control to begin walking away down the canyon. Before Borte went very far, she neared the camera Joe had set up along the way—once again on a stake low to the ground. The last of the daylight was nearly gone now. When the camera was activated to record her approach, it not only clicked but also fired a flash. Startled, the bear bounded away. For a few yards. Then she halted, turned, came back, and demolished the camera, sinking her teeth deep into its mechanical body. Borte might have been the world's tiniest adult grizzly but, by God, she was still a grizzly bear.

[Opposite] Harry and Amgaa support Michael as he checks the grain
pellet supply in a feeder at Shar Khuls oasis. Photo: Joe Riis

05

Baruuntooroi

As of mid-May, halfway through the 2011 spring expedition, Joe Riis and I had solid material for our *National Geographic* story. His photos covered the capture and handling process and documented newly radio-collared animals in the landscape. I'd smelled these animals' breath, felt their musculature, touched their worn claws, and walked in their footprints from bijun patch to gerbil colony. The details were all scribbled into my reporter's journal, though I would hardly need to rely on its pages. The staring eyes of the immobilized bears as I squeezed protective drops into them; being handed a thermometer and told, essentially, to shove it up the butt of a nearly extinct grizzly—images like these were going to stay fully alive in my memory for a very long time.

Joe and I were here experiencing life Gobi-expedition style because of Harry Reynolds. Everybody was here because of him. And Harry Reynolds was here because—well, I wasn't sure. I'd been so focused on trying to figure out these bears and their environment that I hadn't learned very much about the natural history of our leader. To remedy that, I started piecing together his past little by little during long van rides and after dinner in the *ger*.

The son of a Yellowstone National Park ranger, Harry was reared in a little Montana town on the preserve's northern border. He grew up doing what most kids did in that part of the world: hiking, fishing, exploring on horseback, going to church, getting bored in school, and raising a little hell. His father was a good friend of a pair of exceptional wildlife biologists, the twin brothers John and Frank Craighead, who in 1958 turned their attention to a mammal in the Greater Yellowstone Ecosystem that everyone talked about but science scarcely knew. In 1959, ranger Reynolds arranged for fifteen-year-old Harry to join the project.

Along with his fellow research assistants, young Harry practiced pull-ups and other calisthenics that would enable him to climb a tree quickly. Why? Safety. The Craigheads had made the exercises a job requirement, because the subject of this newly initiated twelve-year study was the grizzly bear. Not only was it the first lengthy scientific investigation of the species ever undertaken, it was one of the first major studies carried out for any large carnivore. The Craigheads teamed up with electronic engineers to pioneer the now-routine technique of tracking wildlife through radio telemetry. By the time the project ended, more was known about the ecology of *Ursus arctos horribilis* than about many more familiar mammals.

Catching and radio-collaring the big wild carnivore commonly viewed as the most fearsome in North America earned the Craigheads worldwide attention and acclaim. Yet the information they collected yielded a portrait of a different creature than the one defined for generations by rip-snortin'

[Previous Spread] An old male bear, just out of hibernation, searches for grain pellets at the Baruuntooroi oasis before plant growth gets underway. The reserve lacked funds to supply pellets at the feeding bin there that spring. Photo: Joe Riis

frontier tales and barroom bullshit. Facts got spread around instead this time, not only in scientific publications but also through the pages of *National Geographic*, other popular print media, and television.

Greater understanding is the foundation of greater tolerance, and the resulting shift in the public's attitude toward these bears was one of the main reasons they finally won protection from persecution and heavy hunting. They needed it badly. At one point, no more than two or three dozen breeding females remained in the entire Greater Yellowstone population. Listed as a threatened species south of Canada in 1975, grizzlies have since increased from fewer than 700 in Montana and portions of Wyoming and Idaho to more than 1,800 in those three states.

Gobi Bear Project leader Harry Reynolds. Photo: Joe Riis

Harry continued seasonally helping the Craigheads with grizzly bear research until 1968. He also worked for Yellowstone Park one summer as a packer, hauling supplies with horse and mule trains to remote fire lookouts and patrol cabins. Another summer, he joined a hotshot crew dropped into backcountry areas by helicopter to battle wildfires. At the University of Montana, Harry earned a master's degree studying eagles, their nesting behavior, and their population dynamics. In 1972, he then made his way to Alaska and hired on as a seasonal naturalist in Denali National Park. When autumn arrived, he found work studying grizzly bears for the Alaska Department of Fish and Game. Harry kept that job for the next thirty-four years.

This man's life revolved around heavy-duty bruins and depended on light aircraft. Day after day, he found himself flying to find bears to collar, flying to carry out aerial counts in some swath of countryside, flying because, in the great unroaded expanses of America's largest state, there was usually no alternative. He flew through rainstorms and fogs and snow squalls. He flew through high mountain passes and low to the ground, in order to spot carcasses or shoot sedative-filled darts from an open aircraft door at running bears. He flew to bush camps, lived in them for as many as seven months of the year, waiting out days or weeks of foul weather so that he could fly surveys or occasionally fly home. He flew with the fuel gauge needle bouncing on the top of the empty mark, flew after five helicopter stalls and one helicopter crash, and flew after four emergency landings in little fixed-wing planes and one crash upon takeoff.

The survival rate for Alaskan wildlife biologists whose work requires a great deal of time aloft in small aircraft is not enviable. "Staying out in big, wild country, having opportunities hardly anyone ever gets; I never even thought of doing anything else but wildlife biology for a career," Harry told me. "No. Not even for a minute." Not even for one really hairy minute during any of those flights? I asked. He replied, "If you're going to spend as much time in the air as I did, you have to come to terms with fate, I guess. The decision of 'Do we go up or stay here to wait for better conditions?' is made on the ground. As long as you trust your pilot, it's that person's call. And if the situation turns bad once you're up in the air, there's nothing you, yourself, can do about it. You're not in control of the plane, and you can't change the weather. Okay, I hope we don't go down. But if we fall out of the sky?"

He shrugged. "Well, I had a pretty good life."

Harry is not fearless. But he is imperturbable. I've never seen him act noticeably distressed in the Gobi when equipment failed or the weather scuttled plans or someone botched a task or a van appeared on the brink of plunging into a chasm. He's naturally inclined to be cool-headed, and all the hours he's spent looking at the ground far below through nothing but thin air seem to have reinforced his conviction that fretting doesn't help a damn thing. The other way flying contributed to Harry's steadfast refusal to be ruffled was of course by delivering him daily to meetings with grizzlies. You can't handle more than 1,700 of those animals without developing a serious mastery over wayward nerves.

"The number I like best is 500," Harry said. "That's how many I've caught and collared since the last time I lost one during the process." Back when Harry worked with the Craigheads, the capture and sedation of free-roaming grizzlies was seat-of-the-pants science. Biologists learned what worked best under different conditions by a trial-and-error, "Run-for-it!" approach. They were experimenting with an assortment of veterinary drugs to find out which concoctions would work safely and effectively. Certain compounds were discovered to cause perilous side effects. Most needed to be administered at a precise dosage, which meant that the biologists had to estimate a target animal's weight quite closely. When the subject is a big, broad, toothy beast wearing a thick fur coat, it's extremely hard to keep perception from overruling reality. Upon seeing a 300- to 400-pound grizzly, the average person can be counted on to describe a bear weighing at least twice that much. Then there are the folks who would double that figure again, telling stories of running into a grizz that "musta weighed close to a ton." For even an expert to be off by a hundred pounds or more isn't unusual.

The list of things that can harm or kill these seemingly indomitable creatures during attempts to immobilize them is disquietingly long. Once you've shot a free-roaming bear with a drug-filled dart, the chemicals might not take full effect for five to ten minutes. By then the animal may have sprinted away to parts unknown. It could also have tumbled off a cliff en route as the sedative kicked in. Or tried to cross a river and drowned. Or collapsed with its muzzle down in a shallow pool of melted permafrost on the tundra and drowned that way. Perhaps the bear wobbled over a hill into a thick brushfield, and by the time you tracked it down, it was already recovering from an underdose of the drug and staggering in your direction. Or maybe it never went down at all and exploded from the brush to greet you at full gallop. Either way, the animal may have ended up shot in order to save a biologist's life. Perhaps the grizzly was moving groggily through the woods when it surprised a larger grizzly that reacted by killing it. Maybe the dart held an overdose instead, and your subject was convulsing when you located it. Or chemically suffocating—unable to make its lungs work. Or lifeless because its heart simply stopped. Inside a trap, the lethal possibilities for a grizzly include dying from stress and the effects of extreme heat or cold; succumbing to an overdose; and, again, being underdosed, snapping out of a mildly muzzy state while within a paw's reach of somebody, and getting killed.[1]

Half a century ago, casualties among bears and other subjects were common enough that they added up to a dark underside of wildlife research and management. Improved protocols for handling and monitoring captured animals have greatly lowered the frequency of problems over the years. The most important advances have come in the form of drugs that the animals can tolerate over a broader range of dosages without dangerous consequences. In addition, many of the sedatives used today come paired with a reversal agent, a chemical antagonist that can be kept on hand and injected to neutralize the

---

1   This would be a good place to note that no one who handled Gobi bears during the Project's capture and collaring operations ever carried a gun or any other kind of weapon.

effects of the "knockout" drug if a researcher badly misjudges the animal's weight and administers too much.

Despite the recent improvements, the occasional loss of a subject due to an accident or acute drug reaction remains all but inevitable. Which is why Harry's current tally of 500 straight grizzly bear captures without a death stands as a notable exception. It's probably a world record. I'm not recounting all this to praise him. I'm trying to provide enough background to explain that the reason we were all here in Thirstland was that Harry retired from Alaska's game department in 2005.

In 2004, while serving as president of the International Association of Bear Research and Management (IBA), Harry had accepted an invitation to a meeting with government officials and scientists in Ulaanbaatar.

"The Mongolians were really concerned because Gobi bears were at such a low number and didn't seem to be recovering," Harry recalled. "They had their estimates but couldn't be certain that they actually had more than a handful of these bears left or that they were still producing young. The meeting was to discuss what could be done to save them. Everything was on the table, including taking the last ones out of the wild to try breeding them in captivity.

"The Mongolians were also looking for someone with a lot of experience to help direct studies in the field. Because of my position in IBA, I think they figured I had a good overview of the people doing bear research. Which biologists could I recommend that they talk to about becoming involved?" Harry thought over an assortment of candidates. Who had the right background of fieldwork in remote camps under difficult conditions? Who had plenty of experience with capture and collaring operations? Most important, considering the critically small number of Gobi bears, whom did he trust to ensure their safety during handling? The Mongolians had made it clear that this was an absolute priority. Finally, who would not only want to take on a Gobi bear study without pay but would also be able to shake free from other commitments to start work immediately?

"I did have someone in mind," Harry said. "Me." He had been impressed by many of the Mongolian researchers he met in Ulaanbaatar. Among those whose dedication to conservation he particularly admired was Tuya Tserenbataa, chief science officer (and, later, director) of the United Nations–funded Great Gobi and its Umbrella Species project.[2] Tuya asked Harry point-blank how soon he could organize a Gobi bear project that would yield a reliable picture of the population's current size and range. By June of the next year, 2005, Harry and a crew that included Tuya, Amgaa, Bayasa, and several rangers still with the Project today had set up automatic cameras

---

2 Ecologists define an umbrella species as one whose protection indirectly benefits many other life-forms. It is typically a striking creature, grand, mysterious, powerful, or lovely beyond words, wonderfully odd, or cute and helpless-looking—somehow compelling enough to draw the public's attention and generate support for conserving an entire landscape or ecosystem. The bears, wild camels, and snow leopards of the Gobi all qualify as umbrella species; they are sometimes described as flagship species instead.

at a number of springs and were monitoring traps in the central mountain range, hoping to capture bears to radio-collar.

They had no luck for weeks. Then, on June 22, the team found two bears in the trap at Tsagaan Burgas. One was an adult female twenty-plus years of age. She weighed only 115 pounds. Yet the name they chose for this skinny old female was Mother, because mothers have an exalted status in Mongolian society and this one's two-year-old male offspring had pushed its way into the trap with her. He was given the name Believe—as in "You have to Believe we're going to keep finding and catching bears," "You'd better Believe these bears are producing young," or "I'm beginning to Believe this project just might work out."

The following season, in May 2006, the Project trapped Mother again. After her, the team caught a larger female about seven years of age, a 304-pound male around twelve years old, and a 268-pound male approximately eighteen years old. With modest support from the Ministry of Environment, the Mongolian Academy of Sciences, the IBA, Craighead Beringia South (a non-profit wildlife research and education institute directed by John Craighead's son, Derek Craighead), and funds out of Harry's own pocket, the Project was well underway.

———

AFTER CATCHING ALTAN AND BORTE, HARRY INTENDED TO STICK TIGHT IN the central mountain complex and try to collar more bears. But since Joe and I assumed this would be our only visit to the Gobi, we began making other plans. We had arranged to include an extra four-wheel-drive van and driver in the expedition so that we could travel independently to scout other terrain. We'd made only short sorties so far. Now we felt free to split off from the main party and explore more distant reaches of the immense reserve.

Proctor, Cori, and Odko were keen to join our reconnaissance mission and collect bear hair snagged on the barbed wire around feeders and rub trees at springs beyond the central complex. Gathering samples as widely as possible every year was a way to continue tracking the size and composition of the surviving population. The more often someone from the Project could get to any portion of the reserve to carry out such work and gather data, the better.

The question for Joe and me was which of the two other mountain complexes in the GGSPA to focus on—the western one or the eastern one. They are 175 miles apart at their farthest points. We lacked the time and the fuel to survey both expanses. Our choice was the tallest, driest, and most rarely visited complex, which meant we headed west.

The most distant of the springs was approximately sixty straight-line miles from our Shar Khuls base camp. But there were few straight-line miles en route. Even accounting for the section where we'd dug and pushed the van through wind-borne sand caught in the bends of a wash, we made slow progress. Yet the landscape unfolding before us felt so elemental and ancient that the human habit of parsing time into minutes and then fussing over their loss had begun to seem like a mental disorder. The mountains standing in the distance were made of sedimentary rock formed at least a billion years earlier during the Precambrian period. Tens of millions of years ago, those rocks got crumpled up into the sky as the Indian subcontinent collided with the land mass of Asia. Between us and the nearest Gobi peaks were row after row of low, rounded, utterly barren hills. They were the mountains and ridges that time had already worn down to nubs.

No great glaciers formed in the Gobi during the Ice Ages or earlier epochs to scour and sculpt the terrain. No mighty rivers and their tributaries continually rearranged the topography, either. But through all the eons that they stood undisturbed by those major forces of erosion, the mountainsides were oxidizing, alternately heating up and freezing hard, occasionally fracturing, and thinning as particle-laden air currents blasted through crevices and abraded exposed faces. By infinitesimal degrees, over spans of time we hominid apes can describe but never genuinely comprehend (*Hey, did you get that article downloaded? Yeah, but I had a slow connection. It took forever ...*), how thousands of vertical feet of upthrust stone blocks fell to pieces. They flaked and crumbled until they were reduced to hills all but buried in their own rubble. And those rubbled hills will continue flaking and crumbling until they are once again sediments—sand and silt and dust.

This is not so different from the rise and fall of mountain ranges going on continuously across the globe. But most slopes wear cloaks of snows, soils, tundra, forests, or meadows and, farther down, fields, human dwellings, and road networks. By comparison, virtually every stage of a stone's unmaking is on display across the slopes in the Gobi. Because the lower portions aren't incised by permanently flowing waterways, the eroded gravels spread fairly evenly from the bases of mountain ranges. They continue out at a slight downward angle until they intersect another erosion plain sweeping along at a different angle. The result is vistas of primal earthskin geometries—monumental planes of plains—tilting in varied combinations between ranks of peaks.

All this planetary crust was being polished by a twenty- to thirty-mile-per-hour wind as we paralleled the long Inges Range to the south, then the equally long Atas Range dominated by the massif called Atas Bogd, 8,842 feet high. We passed more *khavtgai*—wild camels—than I had seen since reaching the Gobi. One group was so large that the animals disappeared within the dust cloud raised by their own wide-spreading hoofs. Finally, we started down a broad wash leading to our destination, the springs called *Baruuntooroi* ("Western Poplars"). Bands of argali, wild ass, and more camels appeared to either side. Farther on, a wild camel stood by itself. The tall poplars of the

Wild camels are able to survive on salty, prickly, or woody forage; go weeks without drinking; and travel dozens of miles daily. Like the male on page 14, these two are part of a captive breeding program to bolster the reserves free-roaming population.
Photo: Doug Chadwick

oasis were visible not far away, and this camel, a female, acted reluctant to leave. Ankhaa pointed out that she was pregnant. He guessed that she was fairly close to giving birth.

Wild Bactrian camels are the largest native mammals in the ecosystem. Once widespread across the steppes of Central Asia, they are now, like their Gobi bear neighbors, critically endangered. And whereas *mazaalai* comprise a unique subspecies or variety of the grizzly bear, the wild Bactrian camels are the last of an entire species, *Camelus ferus*.[3] The GGSPA supports three-quarters of the 800 or so still in existence. The western mountain complex and the plains immediately to the north hold more of them than any other part of the reserve and, thus, more than any landscape on Earth.

Our reconnaissance crew used ropes to pull the van the final few yards up a side-canyon in order to get the vehicle and supplies to the ranger *ger* in some hills high above the springs. We were transferring gear and provisions

---

3 Domesticated Bactrian camels are a separate species, *Camelus bactrianus*. Found in a number of Asian cultures, they are larger than *Camelus ferus* and have rounder heads, longer fur, and taller humps. The only other camel species is the dromedary of the Middle East and North Africa, *Camelus dromedarius*. Domesticated perhaps 4,000 years ago, it is somewhat smaller than the Bactrian, less shaggy, and features only a single hump. Its wild predecessors have vanished altogether.

into our new accommodations when Nasaa, who had been keeping an eye on the oasis from a rimrock vantage point, ran up to us shouting in a mix of English and Mongolian. I couldn't understand what he was saying. Somebody else told me, "Camel is having a baby!" Others took up the cry, and we sprinted uphill to the rimrock. As it turned out, Nasaa's message had been badly garbled. Nobody minded, because when we looked where he was pointing, we saw a *mazaalai*, the first I had observed apart from a capture operation.

The full-grown, golden brown bear was sniffing and digging around the base of a rusted feeding bin. As it turned out, the feeder had not been filled this spring. Whether that was due to an oversight, difficult travel conditions, or a lack of funding was never quite made clear. This bear was rummaging for old pellets spilled onto the ground below the bin's troughs. Its efforts didn't appear to be yielding any. Perhaps that explained the animal's listless movements. The bear gave up and wandered off among the tamarisk bushes, where it disappeared into a depression, presumably for a drink. Then it bedded down for a long time.

The sun was close to setting, the wind stayed strong, and the air pushing past us on the heights was cooling down quickly. While I had no experience with Gobi bears' daily rhythms, evening tends to be an active time for grizzlies in general. But the Baruuntooroi Bear stayed still. When it finally stood up again, it left the oasis and started plodding west along the edge of the wash. In full view, the bear looked gaunt, and it moved in a stiff, hunched-up gait, its rear legs swinging slightly out to the side rather than under the body.

In the last rays of sunlight, the gilded Gobi bear made its way slowly uphill to a promontory less than half a mile from the oasis. Near the top, it snuffled at the ground of a ledge while turning different directions. Then it lay down again. A post-sunset luster suffused the land. The glow caught on patches of white fur marking the bear's neck and shoulders, a common pattern on *mazaalai* coats. More white hairs gleamed on the back of the ears when the bear moved its head.

There was something wonderful about this first Gobi grizzly I had viewed at large in the desert. At the same time, my instinct told me there was also something wrong with the Baruuntooroi Bear. Was it stomach cramps? A hurt foot? A hip injury or dysplasia—a condition found in dogs and related to inbreeding? In the end, I told myself that if the animal was as tired as it appeared and possibly footsore, it was likely the result of a demanding journey through bleak terrain to reach this oasis. We were at least twenty-five or thirty miles across the Atas Range from the nearest source of water, and the bear might have traveled directly here from a different spring still farther away.

Night came. B-Bear was still bedded, its head now resting on the ground. I watched until the animal and the promontory ledge it lay on dissolved into darkness, kept watching while the mountains became jagged black walls holding up the canopy of heavens where stars spread like wildfire fanned by the wind, and then found my way home to camp by the light from that blaze.

Long before sunrise, I was back on the rimrock overlook. Joe climbed partway down the cliff bordering the wash to set up his long camera lens closer to the oasis in case B-Bear reappeared. The animal never showed. One wild camel came from the west, striding into the dawn toward the water. Other than that, the liveliest thing in the area all morning was, as usual, the wind. Descending the route from the rimrock back to the *ger* in full daylight, I passed sprouting grasses, wild onion, wild rhubarb stalks, and fairly recent bear scat and tracks. *Mazaalai* had definitely been foraging among these hills and traveling along the route I was on. Following the tracks farther, I continued past the *ger* and then the tent I'd hastily pitched the previous day in a nearby spot free of stones. In other words, I'd inadvertently staked out my sleeping quarters in the middle of a well-used Gobi grizzly bear avenue.

At a salmon-spawning area where grizzlies gather on the Alaska Peninsula, I got to know a brilliant photographer named Michio Hoshino. He camped on a bear trail in Russia's Kamchatka Peninsula a couple years later. That was the last thing he did. A passing grizz dragged him from his tent and killed him.[4]

Compared to *Ursus arctos* on the northern Pacific coast, Gobi bears are markedly smaller, vanishingly rare, reportedly shy, and not known to have ever torn into a person. Hunter Causey, the team's volunteer hydrologist, as familiar as anyone with both Alaskan and Gobi grizzlies, had a tent near mine. Proctor and Cori had put theirs just beyond his. None of them seemed worried. I thanked them for reducing my chances of becoming the first documented Gobi bear mauling victim by three-quarters. We all agreed that predicting what grizzlies of any kind will do is a fool's game but decided to keep our tents where they were for another night.

The farther Proctor and I circled outward from camp, the more rhubarb plants we found on the slopes together with craters where bears had dug up the roots. Overall, knowing that *mazaalai* trekking to Baruuntooroi for a drink had ready access to this handy supply of a key natural food was encouraging. We were less concerned for our safety than about our presence possibly keeping bears away, but we'd be gone from this camp soon. Although the crew especially didn't want to risk disturbing a bear down at the oasis, none had appeared by midday. We decided that this was our time to inspect

4   Bears don't typically behave like that in areas where they're feasting on a salmon bounty. On the contrary, they prove unusually tolerant toward each other at close quarters, and that tolerance seems to extend to wolves, foxes, other wildlife, and people sharing the area.

[Top] Bears rub against trees at oases both to leave sign of their presence for other bears and to scratch itchy spots. The barbed wire on this trunk collects fur samples used to identify bears visiting the site. Photo: Joe Riis [Bottom] Parting the thick, unusually white, underfur of a Gobi bear reveals a camel tick embedded in its skin. Photo: Doug Chadwick

the site. The oasis comprised quite a few acres of reeds and tamarisk among the poplars. As expected, the powdery alkali soil between the plants held a barnyard-thick concentration of dung and tracks—wolf paw patterns atop bear paw patterns; three dainty, heart-shaped gazelle hoofprints and a larger argali print fitting easily within the circular impression left by a camel's hoof.

Wild asses had pawed pits at low points along the center of a single small gully. Most of the pits were merely damp toward the bottom. One held a few tablespoons of muddy liquid. As far as we could tell, the sole useful source of drinking water was a nearby pool barely two feet in diameter. The liquid in it was less than five inches deep. A camel could drink this little bowl dry within a minute, and it would take a lot longer than that for water seeping through the ground to recharge the hole. We searched the length and breadth of the oasis and never came upon another spring. In past years, Proctor and Ankhaa both said, water welled up at different locations within the oasis. For now, however, this single shallow pool appeared to be supplying the whole community of wildlife for many a mile around.

The contrast between the superabundance of animal signs and the absence of live animals wasn't unusual. As I'd come to understand, this was just the Gobi being the Gobi. Bumping into wolves or a snow leopard or a surly male camel emboldened by rutting season hormones would have made a fine "So-there-I-was" story. What we got instead were more camel ticks—whole welcoming committees of heated-up, speed-racer arachnids the size of nailheads. They came the moment Odko, Proctor, and I began inspecting several of the largest rub trees for snagged *mazaalai* fur. In short order, we looked like people dancing to heavy metal tunes playing in our heads: side-stepping to avoid a tick scrabbling toward a shoe, flinging an arm against a thigh to brush away one racing straight up a pant leg, whapping an ear prickled by multiple legs. We heard later that people in the region had been hospitalized with a serious disease transmitted by camel ticks. It turned out to be meningitis. During our time at Baruuntooroi in 2011, all we knew was that the ticks were distracting enough to prevent us from taking any pleasure in going from tree to grand, old, persevering, bear-rubbed tree in one of the few shady environments this desert offered.

For the rest of the afternoon, I climbed from the *ger* to two different high points from which I could look over new country to the north. My plan was to scan the area with a handheld directional antenna in the hope of locating a radio collar dropped somewhere in the western portion of the reserve by a bear collared the year before. I switched on the receiver I was carrying, set the frequency dials to pick up the radio's telltale beeping, and listened carefully. But not expectantly. If the collar lay in a canyon or under a ledge or simply on the opposite side of a hill, the straight-line VHF signal would be blocked, and I was overlooking multitudes of canyons, hills, and peaks. The search was a needle-in-the-haystack enterprise, but that was not enough reason to stop trying.[5]

Having picked up only random crackles of static on the receiver, I devoted the evening and early night to perching again on the rimrock above the oasis. From there, I sent out telepathic signals to B-Bear and any others of his kind: *Come for a drink, I beg of you. Let me glimpse just a bit more of your life. I might never return.* That didn't produce any better results than the radio. Later that night, Cori went batting, setting up her mist net over the little lone pool of open water. That didn't work either, for the moon rose nearly full into the clear desert sky. The bats were able to detect the fine threads of the mist net with ordinary vision and evade capture.

Early the next morning, I hiked once more to the vantage point. And I did see a bear. Close. For a few moments. After that, the object I was staring at revealed itself to be a combination of pre-dawn darkness, a *mazaalai*-size shrub, and my imagination as I remembered all the edible plants and bear signs I'd recorded along this route the day before. The oasis proved empty of hoofed or clawed mammals. Once the sun arced high enough to burn away the last long shadows, I returned to take down my tent and get ready to roll on to the next water hole.

FROM BARUUNTOOROI, WE STARTED OUT BACKTRACKING TO THE EAST TO reach a point at which we could cut south through a gap between the towering Atas and Inges Ranges. Before we turned, though, the van's engine quit. The driver, a private contractor hired in UB, tried to start it again so many times that I feared the battery would expire next. Half an hour later, he had the carburetor out and in pieces atop a cloth on the front seat. He couldn't spread them out on the ground to work on because the wind across the huge plain was blowing so hard that it was loaded with grit. The rangers had counted on being able to resupply our water barrel and jugs from the deep pool of an oasis across the mountains, so we weren't carrying much. We were stuck on the wrong side, in the exact Middle of Nowhere, with a blow-you-sideways gale, eight or nine scrubby saxaul bushes, and umpteen billion shards of stone for company. Above the inside of the van's windshield, a photo of the Dalai Lama smiled beatifically down on the disassembled carburetor parts.

5 A light plane, the best means for covering vast tracts of the GGSPA to detect a VHF radio signal, wasn't an option. There were no air charter services available in most of the Mongolian Gobi and no operating landing strips near the reserve. Had a plane, landing strips, and refueling stations all magically appeared, together with magical money to fund air surveys, we would still have been restricted from flying over terrain near the Chinese border, and all three mountain complexes the bears inhabit fit that description.

Sometimes, the only way to get a supply-laden van to the top of a slope
is to round up enough team members to pull it. Photo: Joe Riis

An hour passed, then two. While I know it sounds trivial to point this out, each of us eventually came up against the fact that there is no place to hide from a gale on a Gobi plain when you have to pee. It's a problem mountain climbers are familiar with: You dare not try whizzing into high winds, but you can't turn your back on them either, as your body's blockage of the powerful air currents creates a vacuum that brings the liquid showering back in toward you, and you can't pee sidelong without wetting your downwind side. As the minutes stretch into hours, you've got a personal fluid mechanics problem to solve by experimentation—plus another reminder not to take anything for granted out in this desert.

By afternoon, the engine was running once more, and we had crossed the mountains to arrive at Bogt Tsagaan Ders, a water source within an enormous basin surrounded by small hills. The oasis was treeless but quite large, consisting of a quarter-mile wide expanse of the tall *Phragmites* grasses everyone called reeds. As promised, a deep, still, blue-green pool at least ten feet across and fifteen feet long waited at one end. The characteristic double-track trails made by the repeated passage of bears led from the water to a feeding bin on a slight rise above the oasis. Among the tracks was a set of small pawprints left by a juvenile—an always-welcome sign of ongoing reproduction and early survival. The automatic camera showed adult bears visiting the previous month. As at Baruuntooroi, however, the feeder held no grain pellets. When I asked why, it came to light that none of the bins at oases

The old Mongolian fort next to the Khukh Khuls (Blue Reed) oasis. Troops were stationed here in the early twentieth century to deter the Chinese from the south and the Kazakhs from the northwest. Photo: Doug Chadwick

in the western mountain complex had been stocked this spring, primarily due to a lack of funds.

The track we followed toward the next oasis was edged in one place with seven piles of stones. They marked the graves of Mongolian soldiers killed while on patrol here in the 1930s by a larger force of Kazakh raiders. The rangers began to describe different versions of how the men died, and Odko interpreted: "It wasn't a fight, maybe. One story is that a Kazakh woman visited the camp at night and cut everybody's throat. A different story tells that the soldiers were captured alive, and then the Kazakhs cut them open and pulled out their insides."

The fort where the seven soldiers had been garrisoned with other troops was located next to the springs known as Khukh Khuls (Blue Reed), where water welled up in a series of clear pools along a wash. Bright green, closely grazed grasses and sedges colored the banks. Just upstream, the surface of the wash was bone-dry but crowded by tamarisk and nitre bush rooted in the subterranean seepage. By Gobi standards, this was an accommodating niche. The building itself wasn't much larger than a single-story, elongated farmhouse. Built of mud bricks in the first part of the twentieth century, it had later deteriorated after being abandoned. Missing its roof and the upper third of the walls, it had the look of a ruin dating back centuries rather than decades.

The sign left by gazelles, ibex, asses, camels, wolves, and bears traversing the area suggested that these animals treated the disintegrating fort and the piled stones marking out courtyards no differently than other minor geological features. I tried to imagine the years when troops ate and slept and drilled and whiled away the time on these same grounds, a long, long journey from the nearest market and fresh provisions. The soldiers would have kept livestock. To say that they would also have taken advantage of any source of wild meat is probably an understatement. Mongolians have a long and enthusiastic tradition of hunting for fur, hides, and sport as well as for food, and the men stuck here on long tours were surely grateful for any diversion. Judging from the number of old bullet casings around, it seemed a safe bet that although Gobi wildlife was becoming scarce in many places today, it was doing a whole lot better in this one spot now than when the troops lived here.

From Khukh Khuls, we looped back into the bulk of the western mountain complex. A winding wash led us into a seemingly interminable canyon whose sides loomed taller and taller as we approached the center of a major chain of peaks. We crossed that range and a section of flats, only to begin following the course of a deeper, longer, more serpentine canyon through a taller range. Ankhaa spied movement above us on a steep stone face and called a halt. Horned animals. More emerged from the shadows of a cave and followed the others across the cliff. From our perspective, none of the ledges appeared wide enough to provide room for four hoofed feet. Babies raced close behind their mothers as the herd started climbing to put more height between themselves and us. How they found enough traction from slight cracks and protrusions on the sheer walls to propel themselves upward at that pace was hard to fathom.

It's possible that we had just discovered Gobi Anti-Gravity Ibex, a kind of cousin to the Gobi Bigfoot and Gobi Death Worm. What is indisputable is that the creatures we beheld had genetically, through generations, prevailed over the demand to stay earthbound in a conventional way. And they were all-too-quickly gone from sight. Ankhaa spotted three male ibex a few canyon bends farther on—a small bachelor band. They carried horns the length of their legs yet were able to more or less float up the side of a palisade, casually showcasing the fusion of strength, grace, and experience that defines world-class climbers.

In the core of the mountain range, Ankhaa called again for the driver to stop as we neared an oasis. Among the adult bear tracks left in the gravel and sediment of the canyon floor, he had noticed something else: Footprints of what he described as "baby bear." Not a new cub born over the winter but, judging from where Ankhaa held his hand above the ground to indicate height, perhaps a yearling or a two-year-old—a juvenile small enough that it would still be traveling with its mother.

In my mind, Ankhaa was a master naturalist. While he was especially attuned to animal signs, nearly all the rangers qualified as experts, too, not as a result of formal training but due to years of experience reading the Gobi's fine print. Knowing where and when and how to look had become second nature for them. More than anything else, it was their pointing fingers that brought an intimidating and empty-looking desert to life for me—again and again until I could begin to sort out the myriad wildlife survival games underway here.

The next day, we were back at home in the main field camp near Shar Khuls. Harry said we hadn't missed out on any captures. All he had to offer in the way of bear news was that the automatic cameras showed one *mazaalai* hanging out at the Tsagaan Burgas springs, while another bear had shown up at Tsagaan Tokhoi, ripped away the logs wired into place to block off the troughs of the feeding bin, and eaten its fill of the pellets stored inside, ignoring the bait in the trap.

Two days later, we discovered that the area's bears had been up to more than that. Joe had left an automatic camera and flash near the edge of a fair-size water hole dug by wild asses at the Khotul Us oasis. Our check of the area found the flash knocked over and the camera missing. It hadn't gone far. It was resting at the bottom of the pool, badly crunched. After retrieving what was left of it, Joe extracted the digital card that stored the photos. He dried that out, and it proved to be in working order. The final images showed a young bear coming to the water hole. Rather than bending down to drink, the grizzly plopped right into the pool, sat down, and had itself a big splashfest that sprayed drops across the camera lens.

This looked like a very happy grizzly doing exactly what one of its Rocky Mountain cousins would do after coming upon a natural bathtub. Here in the Gobi, this had to be one of life's special pleasures. Unhappily, Bath Bear looked over its shoulder and noticed the flash going off. The animal reacted by leaping out and away. Apparently, it reconsidered once beyond camera range. There is an image of the grizzly returning, after which both the flash and camera paid dearly.

The remainder of the 2011 spring expedition brought no captures and no more Gobi bear stories. I was dealing with an eye that had begun turning an angry red. The problem could have come from handling samples of fur and dried dung or any number of other items. More likely, the cause was

Oh, the joy of a desert pool that wild asses pawed deep enough
to serve as a Gobi bear bathtub. Photo: Joe Riis

continual irritation from strong, drying winds and the dust particles they carried day and night. The infection wasn't terribly painful. Just the same, I viewed the final events of the trip with that eye mostly closed to try to keep the condition from worsening.

On May 20 emerging with a cup of milk tea from the Shar Khuls *ger*, I noticed Ankhaa was working on the GGSPA van again, repositioning a bent tie-rod. Harry once watched him replace the busted lifter valve on a piston by beating a large nail into the appropriate shape. Most of the crew was headed off soon to check all four traps in the central complex and close them for the year. You could feel the Gobi summer heat coming on after midmorning now. Our food supply was down to wild onion, fry bread, the last of the dried camel meat, and raisins left over from the bear trap goodie supply. We had been well fed, but it really was time for us to get ready to leave.

First, I planned to spend this final day hiking by myself from camp to a distant peak of orange rock strata that rose alone out on the plains to the east. I'd watched many a sunrise break over the formation and many an evening turn the stone walls from orange to pink or, once in a while, a deeper coral hue. Hence the name: Red Mountain. I set out toward that landform and walked straight at it for hour after hour over the gravels of the plain.

In his 1940 book *Mongol Journeys*, Owen Lattimore wrote:

Between the dawn and the sunrise we again adjusted ourselves
as the order of the sky paled and we returned to the order of the

earth. We had been traveling in the dark; how much had the land changed under the soft stride of the camels? This was the time to pick up contours again, to look back at what we had ridden through in the dark.... Morning and evening are the best times to do this, when the light is level and shadows definite. The range of temperature is wide on the Mongolian plateau; when the sun gets high there is a dazzle of mirage, in winter as well as summer. Even when there are shadows to give shape and sharpness to hollows and heights, there is no accustomed scale of magnitude for the man whose eyes have the habit of seeing the world in relation to trees, houses, and firmly drawn roads. You must learn a new way of seeing. Until you do, you may ride confidently toward a height of land that seems only a few miles away but takes hours to reach; or you may set your direction by a far hill that breaks and refocuses as a little knoll a few hundred yards away, while in the golden light new pools of blue shadows, new slopes of reddish brown, new dun levels of plain and new purple distances flow and spread into a changing landscape.

It is the same afoot as by camelback, just slower and closer to the ground. Although we'd only been gone from the central mountain complex a few days, I noticed that the wild rhubarb's big basal leaves had grown larger, the stalks taller, and the flower clusters at the top a more vivid red. The golden buttons were still in bloom, glowing everywhere in profusion. Freshly dug holes of gerbil colonies interrupted the desert floor every so often. I didn't see many animals on this final outing; a hare, some wheatears and wagtails, small toad-headed agama lizards. Looking for wildlife wasn't the point of this walk. The point wasn't even to walk. I stopped often just to sit in the Gobi's quiet, clarifying immensity. The point was to say good-bye.

———

ON THE WAY OUT OF THE GGSPA FROM SHAR KHULS IN THE VANS, WE rendezvoused with Puji, who was traveling, as ever, on his motorcycle. He'd been waiting for us to catch up so he could say farewell before peeling off in a different direction to reach the reserve's headquarters while we continued north toward Ulaanbaatar. We sat together and chatted a long time while others interpreted. The longer he talked about the patrol work he would resume after we left, the more I realized how puny my travels through the desert during our stay were by comparison. In a typical month, Puji covers routes that add up to about 600 miles. During ten-day tours, he said, he generally goes with another ranger. On runs that will only keep him out a week or less, he rides alone. He's had bike problems that forced him to walk for help many times. Once, when he underestimated the extra gas he would need, he spent the next two days trekking more than seventy miles without water.

Here's a fuller job description for this soft-spoken, self-assured, and self-sufficient man who served in the Mongolian Army before joining the GGSPA staff: Keep vigil over the middle third of the reserve, including the entire central mountain complex. Check on local conditions, water sources, and wildlife; note anomalies in order to report them back at headquarters. Keep an eye out for trespassing herders who drive domestic livestock into the core of the strictly protected area to grab extra forage; issue warnings. Keep the other eye out for illegal miners; make arrests, issue citations, try not to get hurt.

Stuck sitting in a van for two days during the return drive to Ulaanbaatar, Joe and I found plenty of time to mull over the pressures facing *mazaalai* and other wildlife in the reserve. We had originally signed up to produce a *National Geographic* story that would introduce the world's rarest bears and the threats to their survival to a broad audience. Well and good. The question we were asking ourselves now was how else we could help. We talked over possibilities with Proctor and Harry, who bring global perspective to the subject of bear conservation. In addition to his work as a wildlife ecologist specializing in North American grizzlies, Proctor was an advisor to the Bear Specialist Group of the International Union for the Conservation of Nature. For his part, Harry remained actively engaged with the International Association for Bear Research and Management, a nonprofit group of more than 550 professionals from fifty different nations, after having twice served as the organization's president.

Mongolia's Ministry of Environment and the Gobi Bear Project had already taken steps to try to improve life for *mazaalai*. Yet the rangers still needed more basic logistical support, Proctor and Harry agreed—upgraded motorcycles, another van or two, and a greater gas allowance so they could patrol more often. Grain pellets infused with more nutrients ought to be produced, preferably locally, and they ought to be distributed dependably to all the feeders each spring and again each fall rather than merely when funds allowed. Some of the water holes might be improved by digging them deeper. Perhaps a solar pump could be set up to increase the flow at a couple of sites. These weren't complicated steps to be taken, but they all required more money. The catch was that the Project was trying to figure out how to persuade the Mongolian government to boost the budget for this world-class wildlife reserve, while the government looked to the Project to somehow raise the necessary additional funds.

And the ninja problem? Getting on top of that called for more rangers as well as more vehicles and fuel. Illegal mining was a growing concern. "The bigger worry here," Harry said, "may turn out to be legal mining. Not long ago, a mining company was lobbying really hard to get the government to open part of the reserve to commercial gold mining." For a while, it looked like the corporation had enough political support lined up to push that change through the Mongolian Parliament, but the motion fell short of votes—that time.

Few countries did business with Mongolia before the Soviets pulled out in the early 1990s. For years afterward, the country's economy was nearly moribund. Mongolia's main export remained goat wool—cashmere—and the total value of the trade was small. In the first decade of the twenty-first century, the situation changed in a huge way. With gold prices spiking above $1,500 per ounce, other precious metals following the same upward trajectory, and coal in heavy demand as well, companies from neighboring China were queuing up alongside those from Australia, the United States, and elsewhere to lavish attention on the long-overlooked nation now nicknamed "Minegolia." In addition to encouraging mineral development on general use lands, Mongolia's government began removing acreage from some protected natural areas to make them available for mining as well. Gobi Gurvan Saikhan National Park, a short distance east of the GGSPA, had already seen a significant chunk of its southern reaches excised for gold mining interests.

In 2006, not long before the mining company seeking gold in the GGSPA began lobbying the government to allow them into the reserve, the Gobi Bear Project had radio-collared a large male that the crew named Yokozuna—the title bestowed upon athletes in the top tier of Japanese sumo wrestling, which is widely followed in Mongolia. At the time, this was only the fourth Gobi bear the Project had captured—a 304-pound twelve-year-old. Yokozuna started giving off GPS signals from the portion of the reserve targeted for the mining operations, and Harry made sure that officials with the Ministry of Environment saw the data. That wasn't the sole reason the government chose to turn down the mining company's request, but solid proof that Yokozuna— and by inference, other *mazaalai*—relied on the area definitely helped.

"At these prices for gold, mining companies will be making another run at part of the GGSPA," Harry said. "It's only a matter of time. They'll wait for the next election and a change in government. Get a few more politicians in Parliament on board...."

We reached Ulaanbaatar in the middle of the night. After the spare, dark landscapes of the Gobi, the city, with it streetlamps and neon signs illuminating long, straight concrete canyons made me feel as though we had wheeled into some colossal arcade game. The next morning, Harry learned that patrol rangers had come upon the bear we saw at Baruuntooroi. It was still by the springs, and it was dead. The rangers said they were going to examine the carcass more carefully, but they thought the primary cause of its demise was old age. This male's molar teeth were worn all the way down to the gumline. He probably emerged from his den in poor condition before the weather warmed enough for plants to begin sprouting. Prior to making the trek to Baruuntooroi, he might have sought out grain pellets from other feeders. As long as he stayed in the western mountain complex, there wouldn't have been any to find. Although vegetation was growing well in a number of areas by the time we met him, the long winter fast and early spring food scarcity had left him starved, too weak to carry on given the underlying loss of vigor due to advanced age.

This was an elderly bear. Elderly bears die. The news shouldn't have been especially tough to absorb, but the loss nagged at me. I looked for consolation in the fact that B-Bear hadn't died young; that even a healthier B-Bear may have been too old to take part in the competition to mate and pass along genes anymore; that a B-Bear with a stomach stuffed to contentment with supplemental food pellets might still have keeled over because his time was up. Maybe a couple of *mazaalai* babies had been born that spring somewhere in the reserve. Yet all I knew for sure from my visit was that the female Borte had lost her infant and now B-Bear was gone. Two fewer grizzlies remained in the tiny population. Departing for the States, I was leaving behind an extraordinary group of creatures that might be more vulnerable than ever.

My thoughts about coming back for another expedition began to turn from hazy intentions toward resolve.

06

Prayers and Offerings

In my Montana home is a bathroom like most Americans' bathrooms, complete with a reading rack stuffed full of magazines and a book or two. One difference is that the wall above the rack holds a page from poet Gary Snyder's book of essays, *The Practice of the Wild*. The page ends with this passage:

"Creatures who have traveled with us through the ages are now apparently doomed, as their habitat—and the old, old habitat of humans—falls before the slow-motion explosion of expanding world economies. If the lad or lass is among us who knows where the secret heart of this Growth Monster is hidden, let them please tell us where to shoot the arrow that will slow it down. And if the secret heart stays secret and our work is made no easier, I for one will keep working for wildness day by day."

Snyder's words have been up there for many years. Months go by when I scarcely notice them any longer. But sooner or later, I read them and turn the words over in my mind yet again.

Since the long-ago days when all the *Homo sapiens* in the world numbered in the tens of thousands, people kept taking as much as they were able to from nature, whenever and wherever they could. But toward the end of the nineteenth century, when the human population reached 1.5 billion, the consequences became too pervasive to ignore. Nations finally began enacting rules to conserve living resources. For the first time ever in most places, game laws limited how many birds and big animals a person could kill in a given period.[1] National forest reserves and wildlife refuges were established. A number of areas were also set aside as national parks, though the boundaries were often drawn more to encompass scenic features than biological components. Planners weren't thinking in terms of ecology and ecosystems. It would be decades before most people even heard those words.

By the early 1970s, cracks were beginning to appear in the bedrock belief that modern industrial progress and a better quality of life were one and the same thing. The global population had more than doubled to 3.5 billion. Many cities and whole nations were trying to cope with serious overcrowding. Pollutants were toxifying people and other species at unacceptable levels.

Growing public concern over the degradation of our life-support system led to sweeping new environmental laws to stave off the worst of the threats. When it came to nature conservation, however, the emphasis was still on safeguarding a relatively narrow selection of creatures and settings—the ones that people found most compelling. Earlier campaigns had led to heartening last-minute rescues of iconic species such as America's bison and trumpeter swans. Now the call was to do the same for a longer list of charismatic creatures in peril, from tigers and great whales to the delicate Karner blue

---

1 Genghis Khan instituted one of the very earliest conservation measures in the thirteenth century. He restricted hunting outside the winter period in order to protect game animals during the birthing and mating seasons and ensure a more stable supply of wild food.

butterfly (discovered, named, and beloved by the novelist Vladimir Nabokov). Save this species, save that wildland, keep running from crisis to crisis as they come to our attention. The idea was that this ongoing emergency room drama would carry our wild inheritance along with us into the future. Really? Even as we continue to proliferate and convert the globe's remaining wildlands to meet our needs?

Not a chance.

By 2012, just four decades after reaching the 3.5 billion mark, the number of *Homo sapiens* had doubled once more, surpassing 7 billion. I mentioned this figure in the first chapter and am not shy about repeating it. Very little of what I learned as a wildlife biology student about how to conserve nature was relevant to dealing with the impacts of that many people. The world's coral reef systems *are* for the most part damaged, dying, or dead. Most of the commercially harvested fish species around the planet *have already* become scarce. In fact, most everything big and amazing and supported by a backbone, from river dolphins to snow leopards, four-foot-long Chinese giant salamanders to the great apes with which we share all but a few of our genes, *is* dwindling fast, if not already on the verge of disappearing. To merely describe in neutral terms what *is* happening to life on Earth makes you sound like a doomsayer.

There have been tremendous die-offs on a global scale before, but not since human civilization began. So what exactly is one person out of the

On some of the longer van journeys to check distant portions of the bears' range, a curious mixture of Mongolian ballads and American rock music can be heard. In fact, there's no escaping it. Photo: Joe Riis

[Previous Spread] A cairn erected to commemorate the visit of a Dalai Lama who stayed at the Shar Khuls oasis in a previous century. He came through the Gobi to visit Mongolian monasteries farther north. Photo: Doug Chadwick

billions now around supposed to do in a biosphere where a preponderance of natural landscapes, tens of thousands of species, and whole ecosystems are unraveling in real time? *When normally cautious climatologists keep warning about the feedback loop of global warming, which continues to strengthen as more heat-trapping greenhouse gases in the atmosphere cause air and sea temperatures to rise?* When all environments and the creatures that depend on them are suddenly at risk?

My answer is this: *When you see nature falling to pieces, start trying to put some parts back together.* Travel, hike, climb, get dirty, fall in love, have fun, rest up, make some money, call your mom, try to take care of yourself. Do all that. But for goodness's sake, keep working to fix what we've broken. Recruit others to do the same. And refuse to stop. Even when you feel the ground tremble from the Growth Monster's approaching footsteps, don't quit. *Especially* when you feel the ground tremble from the Growth Monster's footsteps, don't quit.

IN 2012, I WENT BACK TO MONGOLIA FOR ANOTHER SPRING EXPEDITION, this time as a volunteer, paying my own way. The plane touched down in Ulaanbaatar the first day of May. Joe Riis was off photographing wildlife in other places, Cori Lausen was preparing for bat research in the tropics, and Michael Proctor had grizzlies to catch and collar in British Columbia. But Bayasa, Odko, and Ankhaa met Harry and me at the airport, and Amgaa joined us the next day in the city. Fine spring weather held sway over UB, which felt noticeably busier than the year before. New buildings had been completed along the main streets, and some of the dreary old Soviet mausoleum-style architecture had undergone face-lifts. Mongolia's newfound mineral wealth was equally apparent in the number of expensive new cars around. None of them was going anywhere very quickly, for the downtown had become the scene of a continuous traffic jam. People striding along the sidewalks through the exhaust fumes and talking on their cell phones were making better time than the prestigemobiles.

Primarily due to the influx of money from mineral development, Mongolia's Gross Domestic Product (GDP) had risen at a rate of 17.5 percent in the fourth quarter of 2011. The nation's fledgling stock market soared. Through the first quarter of 2012, the GDP stood at 16.5 percent, still far and away the fastest pace of economic growth for any nation in the world. Thereafter, the economy cooled down a bit, but the increase in the GDP figure continued to be several times higher than that of most so-called developed countries such as the United States.

The boom times came with complications. Many citizens felt that too much of the incoming revenue stayed stuck in the top echelons of government and business rather than filtering down to improve the lives of ordinary citizens. An election had recently been called, and Mongolians voted in a new president. His predecessor was in jail on charges of corruption, many of them related to mining agreements that critics claimed were sweetheart deals. The ex-president's supporters took to demonstrating in public squares to have him freed. Politics in Mongolia were looking a little messy. Yet that can be taken as a healthy sign in a democracy, as can the fact that Mongolian authorities allowed the protests to proceed without interference.

In addition to learning about Gobi bears, the Project also needed to learn more about the most recent Mongolian administration's commitment to conservation. Amid current economic and political pressures, how high on the state's must-do list was helping the small group of desert-dwelling bruins near the Chinese border? Scientific knowledge is critical in planning ways to aid wild animals. Passion is invaluable. But funds from the Mongolian government to supply the GGSPA with patrol vehicles, fuel, supplemental bear food, and other key items remained at inadequate levels. If officials did come up with more tugriks (Mongolian money) for Gobi bear conservation, we wondered, how did they want to see the budget spent?

Przewalski's horse, a subspecies native to the Central Asian steppes, is considered by many to be the ancestor of the domestic horse. *Equus ferus przewalski* began to disappear quickly through the first half of the twentieth century. As of 1958, thirteen Przewalski's horses remained in zoos. The animal went extinct in the wild not long afterward, but offspring from the few captive horses were shipped to other zoos, and the facilities jointly began a breeding program designed to maximize whatever diversity was left in the gene pool. The population increased well enough that in 1992 a group was reintroduced to the wild in Mongolia, where the last free-living herds had roamed.

You can find the released group's descendants not far from Ulaanbaatar in the hilly steppe country that was designated Khustain Nuruu (also called Hustai) National Park in 1998. A second group was introduced to Great Gobi Strictly Protected Area-B, situated along Mongolia's border with China, about a hundred miles northwest of the much larger GGSPA-A, the Gobi bears' home. Over the winter of 2009-10, a severe blizzard, the dreaded white *dzud*, buried the GGSPA-B terrain beneath snow and shattered the herd. It has not recovered. By contrast, the group in Khustain Nuruu is thriving, and

Mongolia has been able to skim members from that population to stock an additional site at the northern edge of the Gobi.

Mongolians are justifiably proud of recovering Przewalski's horse, which they call *takhi*. A number of people in the government saw that as a model for saving Gobi bears. During our meetings in the capital, officials would invariably want to discuss snatching a few of the remaining *mazaalai* to be bred in confinement, believing that the group would safely increase there and one day produce a surplus for reintroduction to the wild. Several years earlier, the Ministry of Environment had gone so far as to use funds donated by sources outside the country to begin construction of a large concrete structure in the Gobi to serve as a captive bear breeding compound. It was never used. A majority of biologists, including those affiliated with zoos, advised against putting the plan into practice except as a last resort.

It isn't that grizzlies in general have trouble producing young in captivity. They don't breed as readily as horses, but they get the job done. Since Gobi bears have never been held in zoos or any other enclosures, unforeseen problems could arise for this particular subspecies in a confined environment. But even if all were to go smoothly, two major issues would remain.

First, with perhaps no more than ten fertile adult females in the wild, removing just two to a facility would likely mean fewer young born into the remaining population, lowering chances for the reserve's bears to maintain or increase their numbers. Second, bears growing up in the GGSPA learn the secrets to survival by traveling with their mothers for at least a couple of years. How would bears born and raised within the walls of a relatively featureless compound and then released into the stark, water-starved, mazed enormities of the GGSPA find the widely scattered oases? How would they know where the grasses and wild onions first green up in springtime, or where the rhubarb or the summer berry bushes grow most thickly? How would individuals lacking the home-range knowledge of the resident bears make their way from a release site to other habitats able to sustain them without wandering too long in parched and foodless directions?

The not-to-worry view is that newly freed animals should be able to survive by relying on the instincts and senses they were born with. But hoping that will happen instead of dehydration, starvation, and death is not a valid plan. It is an experiment, and Gobi bears were already the subject of an ongoing experiment; namely, being provided with supplemental food. Now that steps were being taken to improve the nutritional content and distribute pellets at the oases more often than before, it was especially important to see what effects this might have on the population. Removing animals for captive breeding might be worth the risk at some point. In the meantime, most bear experts brought into the discussion felt that the emphasis should stay on gathering more information about the lives of Gobi bears in their native range.

Harry didn't hold back from expressing his doubts about captive breeding at this point. At the same time, he felt strongly about respecting the views of his hosts. These were the Mongolians' bears, after all. The GGSPA was the Mongolians' reserve. They had invited him here to help direct field studies and advise, and there is a fine but crucial line between advising and trying to call the shots. "Every so often," Harry told me, "a politician will stand up in Parliament and ask, 'Why do we have foreigners running wildlife projects here anyway?'"

Harry thought that was a fair question. In practice, not many foreigners were in charge of conservation-related studies in the country, and he didn't think many should be. While collaboration between Mongolians and outsiders with certain kinds of expertise is valuable, the survival of the bears and other Gobi wildlife ultimately rests with the Mongolians themselves. This was why Harry visited offices at the Mongolian Academy of Sciences and the Ministry of Environment to discuss future plans every time he passed through UB. It was why, when in the field, he always asked the Mongolian rangers and scientists what they thought the next day's agenda should be and how it ought to be carried out. It was why he paid for Bayasa to travel to the United States to do graduate work at the University of Wyoming, much as Proctor found grant money to bring Odko to British Columbia so she could hone her research techniques at the Wildlife Genetics International laboratory; why Harry and Derek Craighead helped establish a Gobi Bear Club at several different schools in the two provinces whose territories include a portion of the GGSPA; and why Harry was now delaying our 2012 departure for the desert another day so that he could present a talk on Gobi bears at the Academy's Institute of Biology.

The audience turned out to be just three kids, their teacher, a couple of curious biologists who wandered in from other rooms in the old plaster-patched building with sagging wooden floors, and two women I didn't have a chance to greet before someone dimmed the lights and Harry launched his first slide. Compared to the roaring daytime hubbub of UB outside, the effort seemed cloistered and a little forlorn.

Then the two women introduced themselves. I found out that both were teachers working for a nongovernmental organization called Nomadic Nature Conservation. Visiting rural areas, they held community classes for children and adults and spoke about common herding practices that were leading to the overgrazing of grasslands and their streamside vegetation. About three-quarters of Mongolia's land area is categorized as agricultural acreage. Of that, close to 98 percent is open range for livestock, Mongolia being too high, dry, and cool for growing most crops.

With the country's history of nomadic pastoralism going back thousands of years, folks in the countryside are pretty certain that they know what they are doing when it comes to raising domestic animals. They do, but the traditional methods aren't serving well for a human population that has increased over the past century from 650,000 to three million tending a livestock population grown to an all-time high of 50 million head.[2] Too much of the rangeland gets eaten down to the height of turf on a seldom-watered golf course, while the shrubs and trees that once lined rivers and streams have been stripped away, leaving trampled banks bleeding silt into the channels.

The teachers were introducing grazing strategies designed to limit overuse and maintain the health of pastures. Those same techniques designed to benefit pastoralists and their herds would also ensure forage for native animals and streamside nesting habitats for the birds. As opportunities arose, the two women recruited members of herding families to document changes in project areas, monitor the local flora and fauna, and learn more about Mongolia's wildlife in the process.

By the end of the afternoon, I had convinced myself that the homegrown Mongolian conservation movement was making headway. Nevertheless, as our vans crept through traffic jams in a haze of smog on our way out of the city the next day, I had the same questions as I did when leaving UB for the Gobi the previous year: How were a bunch of scrawny, thirsty bears tied to a distant stonescape going to compete for the attention of the ever-swelling number of Mongolians focused on paychecks, cool consumer goods, and the stimulation to be found 24/7 amid the hum of the modern urban hive? How do you talk to a government minister about the truest wealth being Earth's splendored array of life without sounding like a mush-headed idealist?

━━━━━━━━━

IN UB, I'D STOPPED IN TO VISIT BAYARJARGAL (BAYARA) AGVAANTSEREN OF THE Snow Leopard Trust. It was during my travels with her years earlier, when I was reporting on snow leopards, that I first learned about a much rarer carnivore from her assistant, Tserennadmid (Nadia) Mijiddorj. A vision of Nadia standing high on a mountainside stays as fresh in my mind as

---

2 In the year 1900, humans and their livestock made up about 2 percent of the total living weight, or biomass, of mammals worldwide. Today, we and the mammals we raise to eat constitute 90 percent of the total. This figure does not describe a trend. It describes a massive and nearly complete takeover.

[Top] Big sky country, Gobi style. [Bottom] Downtown Bayantooroi, the village where GGSPA headquarters are located north of the reserve's actual boundary. Photos: Joe Riis

the wind that made it hard to hear her soft voice when she said, "They are called *mazaalai*."

After I updated Bayara on this season's plans for the Gobi Bear Project, she pointed to a map on the office wall and told me, "During my last visit to villages in the Gobi-Altai, I heard from people about a hunter who saw a *mazaalai* in the mountains here." She made a circle that took in an area about fifty to seventy-five miles beyond the northeastern boundary of the GGSPA. When? "Not too long ago. I think in the last year or two."

Harry had heard of sightings east of the GGSPA, in Gobi Gurvan Saikhan National Park, and south of the GGSPA, in China. Some of those observations were several years old, and none came with documented proof, but such reports couldn't be ignored either. To an optimist, they suggested that Gobi bears not only wandered from time to time through areas beyond the reserve but might also, under the right circumstances, take up residence there one day.

The easternmost of the three main mountain complexes that serve as the bears' core homeland within the GGSPA takes its name from Tsagaan Bogd (White Mountain), the tallest of the peaks there. The tiny settlement of Ekhiin Gol sits just inside the reserve's eastern boundary. Although it is several dozen miles north of the *Tsagaan Bogd* complex, residents of the village had definitely seen a Gobi bear wander by within the past year. It was not hard to understand what might have drawn a *mazaalai* there from the mountains. Ekhiin Gol was built next to a true, blue lake—the single largest body of open water in, or anywhere near, the reserve. Only about a dozen miles farther east, in the low hills outside the reserve, lies another oasis, where water flows on the surface of a tamarisk-edged channel for more than one hundred yards.

During the period of Soviet control, authorities decided that the generous supply of water from the Ekhiin Gol spring and lake should be put to use growing vegetables for villages in the Gobi region. The fields that were planted yielded produce, but transporting those goods to small, scattered markets from a locale as remote as Ekhiin Gol proved impractical and prohibitively expensive. People initially drawn to the scheme left the area, and the irrigation systems fell into disrepair.

Harry and I departed the reserve's Bayantooroi headquarters on May 8 with several of the rangers who had worked with the Project in 2011. We were also joined by a couple more who had been part of the team in earlier years. One was the senior ranger Boldoo. The other was Nyamaa, the tall, strong, big-bellied ranger-biologist who loved to eat and liked to goof around and shared with Odko the kind of infectious laugh that regularly had the crew passing the miles in a hilarious uproar. Listening to them on our way to begin this year's trapping season in the eastern mountain complex dominated by Tsagaan Bogd, you would have thought bumping across Gobi barrens breathing dust inside an overheating van was the most fun a human could possibly experience.

We got as far as Ekhiin Gol the first evening and decided to spend the night there. These days, the village resembled the movie set for a ghost town. Most of the houses stood boarded up and abandoned; winds swirled alkali dust through empty streets. The central building was a huge gymnasium sided with rough-cut planks. Through the broken windows, I could see basketball hoops inside at both ends and the remains of a volleyball net drooping between posts midway along the court. A couple of ramshackle community pit toilets tilted outside at the edge of a depression next to heaps of partly burned trash. Ragged-haired dogs rooted through the residues, eyeing me warily as I passed.

We had dinner in the home of Nyamdavaa (Baboo) Davaadagva, a young ranger responsible for operating Ekhiin Gol's little weather station and patrolling the eastern third of the reserve by motorcycle. In the course of the evening, one member of our Project team got hopelessly drunk and had to be carried off to bed in a nearby empty house. I slept in the next room, periodically awakened by the man's bouts of coughing. After one especially loud episode, I decided that I might as well go stroll outside under the stars. There was a universe full of light overhead, and my thoughts took off dream-walking all over the place while the night winds roared and set loose boards clattering up and down the haunted streets.

In UB, I'd felt hemmed in by humanity-gone-viral. To have moved so quickly from the Anthropocene to the steppe of rolling grasslands with only an occasional distant *ger*, then on to an ancient desert stripped to stone, and ending up in this post-apocalyptic–looking village where the modern world had failed to take hold was disorienting, to say the least. It felt like traveling in a time machine with unreliable controls.

The present-day world was circling closer. Shortly before entering the reserve's boundary from the north, we had passed a camp of gold miners. Theirs was a small-scale operation with men digging pits in the desert floor and shoveling the debris into a dry segregator. This machine operates on the same principle as a placer sluice, but instead of using water to swish away the lighter material, the generator-powered device shakes the debris to sort out the heaviest chunks, which can then be inspected for gold. Less than twenty miles east of Ekhiin Gol, a wide dirt track now ran through the corridor separating the GGSPA from Gobi Gurvan Saikhan Park. Truckers relied on this road to travel to and from the large area removed from the park's southern section so mining companies could go after the gold there.

Portions of Gobi Gurvan Saikhan hold tall dunes like those known as the Singing Sands. Other portions, watered by springs or the melting of mountain snows or both, support meadows. Generations of herders raised camels and goats in those grassy niches. When the park was established in 1993, the government let the inhabitants remain in small settlements and continue grazing livestock. Similarly, after Great Gobi Strictly Protected Area-A was protected, in 1976, residents of Ekhiin Gol and their livestock were allowed to stay in the reserve. You'd be hard put to find a couple dozen human souls at home in the village now on a given day. But you don't have to travel many miles north before you find the stone corrals and campsites of other herders, who come from towns to the north of the GGSPA. They have permission to enter the reserve and to run stock in its northern portion from late autumn until early springtime, while the bears are snoozing.

A majority of Mongolia's parks and other nature preserves allow at least seasonal grazing in what is usually termed a limited use, or buffer, zone. If you ask about the possibility of restricting such activity to provide more forage for hoofed wildlife and to stop the killing of predators—mostly wolves—by herders, officials tend to stare at you as though you just suggested changing the name of favorite brands of vodka and beer from Genghis to Fred. The practice of nomadic livestock herding pervades Mongolian culture. It shaped the traditional dress, songs, stories, and lives of the people in this land.

If it seems odd that neither Mongolian national parks nor even strictly protected areas such as the GGSPA are, in practice, strictly protected, keep in mind that in the U.S. of A., you can hunt, fish, trap, graze livestock, and drill for oil on national wildlife refuges; commercially fish, harvest seaweed, and collect aquarium specimens in our national marine sanctuaries; and mine in officially designated national wilderness areas where you could get fined for dropping litter or cutting down a live sapling to make a ridgepole for your tent. In Alaska, you can even hunt big game and trap furbearers in national monuments, national preserves, and some national parks.

Most every nation vowing to protect nature compromises to some degree according to its history and cultural norms. The special challenge for the GGSPA and its wildlife is the addition of illegal miners to the mix of people using the reserve for purposes other than conservation. When we stayed at the GGSPA headquarters en route to Ekhiin Gol, we met with the new director, Dorjgotov (Gotov) Ayursed, a frail-looking man in his forties with nearly translucent skin, who had taken over from Miji. He explained, "The

The white (sometimes called pied) wagtail, found throughout the region, was most common around springs and our campsites, probably attracted by the greater abundance of insects. Photo: Doug Chadwick

ninja problem started in 2009. We have had more than 600 ninja encounters up until now [May of 2012]. Their numbers are a difficult thing to track. We can't say for sure whether they are increasing or decreasing, but the problem is nonstop. They are everywhere. We find their tracks. We see ninjas on the wildlife cameras at springs. Some drove heavy excavating equipment into the reserve last year. What money we have for fuel has to be spent patrolling for ninjas instead of wildlife and doing the usual work."

From Ekhiin Gol, we went on to the eastern mountain complex and pitched our tents in a little valley called Alaguneet (or Alagan Neet). The focal point of this camp, which would remain our base for the month, was a rectangular wooden hut built as part of the 2003-2007 United Nations Development Programme project, Conservation of the Great Gobi Ecosystem and its Umbrella Species. Used ever since as a patrol outpost by the reserve's rangers, the building was in good shape. Later in the day, though, we noticed that the wood on two corners was pocked and splintered in places. A closer look revealed exploratory tooth and claw marks. A grizzly standing on its hind legs had been inspecting the structure. The rake marks still higher up might have been left as conspicuous signposts, like those *mazaalai* make with their upstretched paws on poplar trees.

We took the bear's engravings as a note of welcome and set about opening and baiting the metal box traps waiting at four different springs in the area.

A shrine along the road to the Gobi-Altai. The color blue is used to signify Mongolia's traditional reverence for the powers that reside in the sky. Blue also symbolizes the Buddhist faith adopted later in the country's history. Photo: Joe Riis

En route between two of them, we passed the northern face of the great peak Tsagaan Bogd rising above a formidable collection of other walls and crags. The plain sloping from the base of the range was covered not only with gravel but also with rough stones from the size of bricks to boulders. Precipitation increases slightly from west to east in the GGSPA, which could be one reason this easternmost of the three main mountain complexes holds several springs only a few miles from each other. The greater rainfall and runoff may also have been responsible for the clusters of rhubarb and wild onion flourishing between the stones strewn along the mountain's base.

Where the lower end of the plain ran up against another range of mountains, the ground leveled out. When you turned to look back upslope from there, the lines of sight seemed to steadily gather until they suddenly soared upward together to the Tsagaan Bogd rampart. Rocks from the flats had been stacked to form several chest-high cairns. They were the kind of monuments found alongside travel routes and atop peaks and passes throughout Mongolia and much of central Asia as well. Herders and wayfarers have been piling up stones this way since time immemorial. Some serve merely as route markers in the landscape, but many were also built to honor the special qualities of a place.

In Mongolia, cairns are often wrapped on the top with blue ribbons. A mound can represent the old religion of shamanism, which involves reverence for the deity Tenger and the immanence of the Blue Sky where he abides. Or it may symbolize the newer religion of Tibetan Buddhism, which Mongolia adopted beginning in the fourteenth century.[3] Passersby will add small stones, natural objects like bones or horns, or, these days, shards of glass from one of the ubiquitous vodka bottles lying around wherever people stop on a travel route.

When Ankhaa pulled the van to a stop and we got out to walk over to the line of cairns, I thought the purpose was simply to have a closer look at them while we stretched our legs. But no. Odko emerged from the van carrying a container of milk tea and packets of sweet bread. Good—a snack break. Wrong again; the provisions were to be shared more widely. Odko distributed the bread among the crew, and each person began carefully placing pieces among the stones in the cairns. Next, the milk tea was passed around. The team's members took sips, then dipped their fingers in the cup and flicked drops toward the heavens, as they would do when ceremonially given vodka. Odko occasionally filled a cup to the brim and tossed the contents outward in a high arc toward Tsagaan Bogd.

3 Mongolians don't seem to make a point of separating the two belief systems. A Buddhist chorten or stupa, many of which ornament Mongolia, resembles a more formal version of the ancient stone cairn shape. About 60 percent of Mongolians describe themselves as Buddhist. During the 1930s, communist leaders undertook a brutal campaign to purge the religion. Lamaseries were razed and thousands of believers, including an estimated 18,000 monks, were put to death, foreshadowing the genocidal horrors inflicted on Tibetan lamas by the Chinese state later on. A small proportion of the Mongolian population, primarily ethnic Kazakhs in the western part of the country, adhere to Islam, and they, too, suffered religious persecution under communist rule.

"For the mountain?" I asked.

She thought a moment and replied, "It is for the mountain. We do it for the sky too. For the bears and all the animals. Everything. How can I explain? It is for the nature in this place."

I arranged pieces of my bread on the nearest cairn and flicked milk tea skyward along with my thoughts for the mountains and plains and the lives among them. Still, the occasion wasn't a solemn one. It felt light and free. I was completely comfortable being in this band of travelers talking silently with the natural world around us, wishing it well, each of us hoping at the same time that we would somehow get some extra mojo going for ourselves and our work by doing this. A bit of luck. A little more strength.

Grizzly bears examine the world in good part through the use of their mouths, paws, and claws. The animal that left the wood etched and punctured at the corners of the hut was likely extra curious about this big, strange wooden object with leftover scents emanating from it. Even if the bear mostly just wanted to break in on the chance of finding food inside, it was still, in its own fashion, trying to figure out what would work, how to force what it wanted to happen to actually come to pass. Is that so different from what humans are doing when they make prayers and offerings?

We understand a fair amount about the world as facts. All the while, we also sense that there is as much or more that we don't understand. Grizzlies bite with their mouths and shove and probe with their paws, drag and roll objects around if they can, peer inside, smash them open for a better look, watch and imitate their mothers and siblings, and so forth. It's how bears learn. We continue to try to know things through our senses, by trial and error, by communicating with others, by logic and deduction—and through charms, prayers, offerings, and every brand of holy cajoling we can invent. Another flick of milk.

"A group of us climbed that peak a couple years back," Harry mentioned as we made ready to return to the van. "You should take a day and go to the top while we're here."

"I'd like to if we have time."

"It looks tough from this angle, but there's a route on the western side that's not technical at all. Just a long walk."

Gazing at the summit again, I promised myself I would get there.

Trying not to feel insignificant in the enormity of Thirstland. Photo: Doug Chadwick

A

B

E

F

G

H

J

L

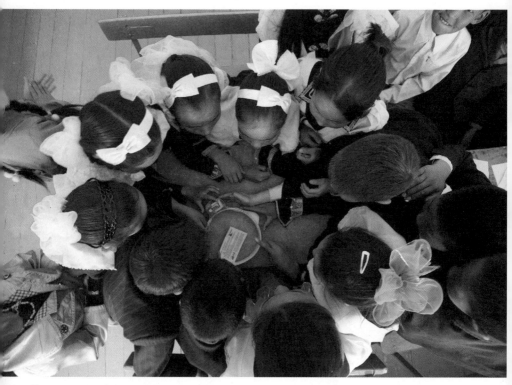

Q

A   At one of the sites underlain by springs and generously defined as an "oasis", Odko peers into the sole source of drinking water—a small, muddy pool enlarged by the pawing of wild asses. Photo: Joe Riis

B   This bear den burrowed into a tamarisk thicket included a body-length pit dug three feet deep into the silt, sand, and fine gravel floor of a dry runoff channel. Photo: Doug Chadwick

C   A heavyset Gobi bear, probably a male, captured by an automatic camera anchored to the wall in the narrowest part of a canyon. Photo: Joe Riis

D   After helping camp cook Geerlee Namkhai prepare fry bread, Amgaa waits patiently inside the underground *ger* at Shar Khuls for her to finish cooking a batch. Photo: Joe Riis

E   The GGSPA Director's formidable mastiff dog isn't guarding the entryway to a guest *ger* at GGSPA headquarters so much as waiting for someone inside to toss him another table scrap. Photo: Joe Riis

F   Ankhaa (center, holding daughter's hand), his wife (left), and mammalogist Ariunbold (right), chat at the ranger's family *ger* near GGSPA headquarters before Ankhaa departs on a bear research expedition. Photo: Joe Riis

G   Wingless grasshoppers appear as spring warms, sometimes in impressive numbers. Judging from remains in dung piles, bears add these protein-laden insects, along with darkling beetles, to their diet as the opportunity arises. Photo: Joe Riis

H   Like some uprooted thornbush, a long-eared hedgehog lies curled into a defensive ball after somehow setting off one of the research traps intended to be triggered only by big, heavy bear feet. Photo: Joe Riis

I   As the Gobi bears and the security of their last stronghold go, so go the region's wild asses, critically endangered wild Bactrian camels, rare snow leopards, and the rest of this varied animal community holding on in one of the most extreme and least spoiled environments on the planet. Photo: Doug Chadwick

J   With funding from the Ministry of Environment, GGSPA staff built this solar array at a western mountain complex oasis to power a pump that boosts the water flow from a spring. Photo: Doug Chadwick

K   Odko (left) and Unuruu, a translator, freshen up before breakfast at Shar Khuls. Photo: Joe Riis

L   Looking out from the school playground in Bayantooroi. Photo: Joe Riis

M   Schoolchildren in the Gobi Bear Club in Bayantooroi compare drawings of their favorite wild neighbor. Photo: Joe Riis

N   Other members of the club get a feel for the satellite radio collar the Project uses to track the bears. Photo: Joe Riis

O   And a beaming schoolboy shows off his Gobi Bear Club badge. Photo: Joe Riis

P   A woman prepares milk tea for a weary Gobi Bear Project crew on the long road back to Ulaanbaatar. Photo: Joe Riis

Q   A youngster playing in the dusty center of Bayantooroi pauses in the sunset to acknowledge the photographer. Photo: Joe Riis

07

Interruption

Early one August morning, I was at home in northwestern Montana organizing field notes from a Gobi expedition when I heard my son Russell talking to someone in the front hallway. It turned out to be my friend Tim Manley, who works for the Montana Department of Fish, Wildlife, and Parks. He's the grizzly bear conflict manager for this part of the state—the guy you call when one of these animals is causing problems, which might mean it's ripping up your livestock or just that you're new to Montana, saw a big-ass bear amble across your driveway, and freaked out.

The only grizzlies worrying me at the moment were on the opposite side of the world in the Gobi. Tim was just stopping in to say hello on the spur of the moment since we hadn't caught up with one another in a while. His busiest times with conflict bears come in the spring and fall. Food in the upper reaches of the Rocky Mountains can be scarce then, and many grizzlies move to lower elevations in search of meals. This puts them closer to the ever-expanding activities of people in the valleys and foothills.

Almost inevitably, a grizz ends up crossing the line into human territory, mostly outlying cabin sites and rural settlements. And then Tim gets the call because somebody left out garbage, a bird feeder, or dog food. Or neglected to put a strand of electric fencing around a chicken coop, goat corral, or hog pen. Or didn't pick the apples and plums from trees in the yard before the berries in the backcountry froze and dropped off. The list of foods that can draw in big bears is about as long as the list of things humans like to put in their stomachs. We both qualify as impressive omnivores.[1]

Once a grizz has been rewarded with easily sourced meals around humans, the animal is likely to return for more. Some of Tim's calls come from people who have managed temptations around their home properly but end up with a shaggy omnivore on the porch because a neighbor has been leaving out unsecured food.

I'd worked for years with bear managers such as Tim, other agency officials, conservation groups, and magazine editors to help get one simple, essential message across to the American public: PLEASE DO NOT FEED THE BEARS!

Where citizens purposefully provide food to bring bears closer for viewing and photography, the animals quickly make a strong association between easy meals and the presence of humans and become more comfortable around them. It's exactly the same story when food is offered inadvertently near campsites or homes. The more often bears become habituated this way, the more frequently opportunities arise for an aggressive, annoyed, or merely startled animal to hurt somebody. Actual attacks by bears are exceedingly

---

1 Granted, bears will scavenge a moldering animal carcass a human wouldn't touch. On the other hand, I can't picture a grizzly savoring blazing hot chilies or wasabi. We also eat rotted foods (beer, hard booze, cheese, soy sauce, etc.), though we prefer to call them "aged" or "fermented." Like bears, many human cultures include insects in their diets. Once in a great while, a grizzly eats a human. But on occasion, people eat people, too.

A Montana grizzly bear mother and her cub, who appears to
be working over the leg of a mountain goat. Photo: Steven Gnam

rare. The far more common result is an aggressive, annoyed, startled, or just uncomfortably nervous person shooting the animal—or calling in authorities to dispatch it. Across much of the species' range, the primary cause of grizzly bear deaths other than hunting and poaching is conflict caused by the sustenance people make available. Which explains the second common message used to try educating the public about the problem: A FED BEAR IS A DEAD BEAR.

Then I found myself in the Gobi Desert, where our motto could have been: LET'S GO FEED THOSE BED-HEAD BEARS!

The supplemental food program for *mazaalai* was begun out of desperation when the average annual precipitation in the reserve between 1993 and 2007 dropped from one hundred millimeters (four inches) to fifty millimeters (two inches), stifling the growth of native vegetation. After the long drought ended, officials continued the bear-feeding effort in hopes of boosting survival and reproduction during times of normal or better moisture. From the beginning of the program, however, shortfalls of funds for the protected area meant that only a few of the bins got filled some years.

In addition to contributing some money and working with the reserve staff to make the supplemental food supply more reliable at existing feeders,

[Previous Spread] A painting of a mother Gobi grizzly bear and her cub—complete with
the white blaze of shoulder fur often seen in this subspecies—on the side of the metal
feed storage bin. Photo: Doug Chadwick

the Gobi Bear Project helped get feeders in place at more water sources. Rangers had been stocking the bins with grain pellets once a year during early springtime, the critical period when bears emerge from their dens after having lost as much as 30 or even 40 percent of their weight over winter. Beginning in 2012, the plan was to start replenishing the bins in autumn as well. That's the season when grizzlies enter a phase termed hyperphagia (sciencespeak for cranked-up eating), foraging overtime in an attempt to quickly pack on as many pounds as possible. For a hibernator, fall fat is like the logs cut and stacked in a cabin's woodshed. You want to lay in all you can, because if you burn through your fuel before winter is over, life can turn grim in a hurry.

The better nourished a female grizzly is, the earlier the age at which she can begin producing cubs, the more milk she is able to provide them, and the more quickly she will come into breeding condition again after the offspring separate from her, usually by their third year. If a population has declined to a remnant group, and the fertile females among them number less than a dozen, as in the Gobi, the most practical short-term fix you can offer while you try to figure out a long-term solution is to see that those female bear bellies are filled with food. You save the natural-versus-artificial debate for later.

It was unsettling for me at first to make the mental switch from NO FEEDING BEARS to PRO FEEDING BEARS. But not too difficult. Putting out supplemental grain for Gobi grizzlies doesn't lead to problems for permanent human residents in the reserve because there aren't any, save for the handful of folks hanging on in Ekhiin Gol. Very few people dwell anywhere close to the bears' current range, and tourism within the reserve isn't permitted. Rangers linger around the feeders only a few times a year, and then just long enough to fill them or merely check on the area. As a result, the bears have little chance to make a positive association between the artificial food source and people. The other practical reason a feeding program can be carried on here is that even though the pellets are basically the same kind given to livestock by herders (a mix of grains such as wheat and barley, called *horgoljin*), the wild hoofed animals visiting oases don't compete with the bears for this chow. Whereas grizzlies tend to be curious and enthusiastic opportunists, the area's native ungulates—camels, wild asses, ibex, etc.—appear much more leery of experimenting with unfamiliar foods. Moreover, any that do sample the pellets may end up with digestive problems because their guts lack the microbes needed to help digest domestic grain.

The Project further expanded the artificial feeding program by placing smaller, easily portable bins at several water sources far from any others. These feeders are ordinary fifty-five-gallon fuel barrels with a slot cut out near the base to dispense a continual flow of grain pellets as mouthfuls are removed. Some barrels were set up at sites slightly beyond the population's current range to see if they might draw bears out into more of their former homeland.

Tim Manley understood the Gobi bear feeding program. One autumn, I'd helped him collect apples and road-killed deer to provide supplemental food for a mother Montana grizzly and her cubs. She'd come down off the mountainsides where the wild berry crop had been a near-total bust that year and was trying her best to put on enough weight raiding fruit trees and garbage in a rural agricultural area before hibernating for the winter. She wasn't going to leave before then. If she did, her underweight cubs would probably starve to death inside the den before the snows began to melt in spring, and she might too. By supplying a banquet of extra food, Tim was able to draw the bears to a dense copse of woods among the fields and hold the family there out of sight of any local residents. Between the three grizzlies, several hundred pounds of deer meat and apples disappeared into bellies without bothering a soul. Then mom led the way back uphill and went to sleep high among the peaks.

Summer, when the mountainsides grow edible plants in profusion, is Tim's calm time outside the winter hibernation period. What he'd been doing instead of coping with people-bear conflicts was trying to catch a few grizzlies in typical habitat for research and monitoring. He also hoped to capture a healthy young female with no history of getting in trouble so she could be relocated into the Cabinet Mountains farther west in the state and help boost grizzly numbers there. Even after grizzlies were protected from hunting as a threatened species south of Canada, enough illegal shooting had continued in the Cabinets, with their extensive network of logging roads, to drive the bears' numbers down to a critically low level. Increasingly isolated, the population now included fewer breeding-age females than Mongolia's last group of *mazaalai* did.

As we talked at the kitchen table, I learned that Tim had caught a female the previous day high in the Whitefish Range and fitted her with a satellite radio collar. She was a perfect candidate for releasing into the Cabinet Range to augment the surviving population. When he telephoned his colleagues with the news, though, he was told not to bother bringing her. The summer's record high temperatures and low rainfall had culminated in raging wildfires all over the West. In the Cabinets, high winds had just changed a 2,000-acre burn into a 12,000-acre inferno and was claiming more territory by the minute. Road travel was shut off, and people in the area were being evacuated.

"She's waiting inside the culvert trap where I caught her," Tim said, "so I'm just going to drive up this morning and kick her loose." He could have released the female on-site immediately after hearing that he couldn't deliver her to the Cabinets. But she took a longer time than is usual to recover from the immobilizing drug, and he hadn't felt it safe to send her off groggy into the dusk. Beyond the risk that she might somehow injure herself in that condition, there were four other grizzlies that Tim knew of in the vicinity. Like the female, they had been drawn to the road-killed deer he set out at the site for bait. Things might go badly for a strangely behaving, woozy young female if she encountered those bears, particularly a 600-pound male that had moved in to claim the meat pile.

The high basin where the culvert trap rested wasn't a long distance from my home, but it wasn't a short distance away either. I'd traveled with Tim many times when he went to deal with bears for one reason or another. He knew I liked to tag along on all things grizz, and I knew he liked a bit of company as well as another set of eyes where he had reason to expect bears close by.

"Need a hand with anything?" I asked.

"You guys would be welcome to come," he said.

"Let me grab my bear spray."[2]

"Sure, if you want. But I've got four or five extra cans in the rig."

———

WE DROVE UP THE PAVED HIGHWAY FOR HALF AN HOUR PAST A DOZEN LAKES and then turned off onto a sprawling network of logging roads. They took us through national forest lands, state lands, and property owned by a timber corporation. All of this acreage held a patchwork of blocs cut for lumber. But as we neared the ridgelines many a switchback later, the forest grew thicker with the dark green spires of Engelmann spruce and subalpine fir rising from an understory of huckleberry, serviceberry, beargrass, and shrub alder. These subalpine woodlands, too, had been logged, but not as heavily, and once the cutting was finished, some of the timber roads were closed off with a steel gate to restore a measure of security for the bears and other wildlife.

Tim had the key, and we drove on uphill.

Smoke from the multitude of blazes as far west as Washington's North Cascade Mountains made it feel as though we were moving through a strange, warm mountain fog suffused with the smell of campfires. After crossing the

———

2 Bear spray consists of a canister that shoots capsicum, or hot chili pepper extract, in an oily mist for about twenty feet to deter an aggressive animal. The stuff works. You'll know why if you get a snootful youself; imagine suffocating and also having a heart attack while someone keeps blowtorching your eyes and nose.

Having just finished eating an entire adult white-tailed deer by himself, this 600-pound
Montana grizzly is not trying to figure out how to lift his belly off the ground, it just looks that way.
Photo: Tim Manley, Montana Dept. of Fish, Wildlife, and Parks

ridgeline and descending into a pocket-like basin on the other side, I could
see the culvert trap on an old logging skid road overgrown with tall grass.
Tim drove past it and parked the truck in among some fir trees and pointed
to a heap of small limbs piled at their base. This was where he had put the
deer carcasses. He asked Russell and me to stay in the truck for a minute and
opened his door. Before his feet hit the ground, he was shouting out greetings:

"Hey Bear! Hey there, Bear!"

Nothing.

With my pepper spray can unsheathed and handy on the dashboard, I
swept the forward area with my eyes while Russell kept watch out the back
window.

"Ho Bear! Ho, anybody out there!"

Nobody.

Satisfied, Tim walked over to one of the trees and removed the digital
card from the motion-triggered camera wired to a tree trunk. He walked back
to the truck and plugged the card into his laptop. Up on the screen popped
nighttime photographs and video clips of an immense, heavy-bellied male—
the 600-pounder—tearing meat off one of the carcasses. More video showed
him sitting nearby, breathing hard and looking more than a little stuffed. We
could see through the front window that almost nothing remained of the
bait pile, to which Tim had added an entire deer body the day before. Back

on the screen, the male was tilting his head up and opening his mouth with an odd expression, as if not even he could quite believe how much he had eaten. Most likely, he was only giving off a great belch.

"That's the guy," Tim said. "I knew he'd be back. You can see why I didn't want to turn our girl loose yesterday in the shape she was in with him around guarding the food."

We exited the rig and followed Tim to the back of the truck. Grabbing the rim of a barrel riding in the bed, he tipped the container over, and out spilled yet another bloody, road-killed deer he had picked up. We added it to the bait pile. Next, Russell and I strung a line of barbed wire from tree to tree around the heap of meat so that Tim might be able to snag a fur sample when Big Guy returned. The leftover wire and Tim's gore-soaked work gloves went back into the truck, and we moved over to the female in the culvert trap.

She was a truly pretty bear, glimmering gold and silver in the trap's dim interior, quiet and soft-faced but fully alert, watching with eyes that caught the outside light and shined it back toward us. All we had to do was attach a rope to the top of the big aluminum door, run it over a pulley above, and hook the other end to a winch on the truck. We sat safely back inside the rig while Russell operated the winch control to raise the door. The female stayed still, silhouetted against the bright new opening. She waited almost half a minute, taking in the overgrown road before her, perhaps trying to fathom this sudden, strange turn of events. Then she bolted out and raced straight down the skid road for a couple hundred feet before veering into the woods.

Done. She wasn't the last bear we saw that morning, though. A black bear ran out of the brush and along the road ahead of us briefly as we drove back down the mountains.

The West's accumulation of forest fires had shrouded northwest Montana in an acrid haze for weeks, and I hadn't got in my usual amount of late-summer hiking. In fact, between the choking smoke and my writing work, I had scarcely been out. This unexpected trip brought the familiar feel of the upper-elevation forests back in a rush, as if a big pulse of wind had suddenly swept in and carried the smoke away. Even after a summer of unrelenting heat and drought, these Montana bears were walking the uplands knee-deep in grasses, shoulder-deep in brush, shaded by conifers whose pungent sap spiced the air despite the smoke. The ground stayed soft and yielding. Water was still running in rivulets and collecting in streams and ponds. Practically everywhere I looked, the movement of a grouse, songbird, squirrel, or chipmunk caught my eye.

Back in the Gobi, shrubs mark the channels where water from infrequent rains runs through an immense gravel plain in the western mountain complex. Photo: Doug Chadwick

The contrast between the plush, animated contours of the grizzlies' habitat here and the bleak homeland of *mazaalai*, where my thoughts had often been during those housebound days, suddenly seemed much sharper than I remembered. It made me realize how much my perception of the Gobi had changed since my first visit. Though there were always moments when the place made me feel as though we were scouting for life on Mars, the longer I hiked across the stonescapes of Thirstland, the more normal that had begun to seem.

Becoming accustomed was only natural, and I was glad to gain enough of a sense of familiarity with the desert setting that I no longer felt dislocated and vulnerable all the time, the way I had in the beginning. However, this unplanned morning foray with Tim Manley and Russell pushed some sort of re-set button in my head. All at once, I was seeing afresh what a wonder a grizzly bear in the Gobi really is—an existence so extraordinary that at one time I could not have even imagined it, much less pictured myself at the base of a towering desert mountain, flicking drops of milk tea toward the sky and offering prayers for those animals' lives.

08

Odd Poo

The shadiest spot for a mile in any direction from Alaguneet, our 2012 base camp in the eastern mountain complex, was the north wall of the bear-clawed patrol hut surrounded by our tents. Strung on the outside with dangling sausages and various body parts of goats and sheep, that wall was our meat locker, shared with a small but determined squadron of flies. It was also where the crew stacked empty vodka bottles. Within the first week of our stay, the heap grew impressively high.

Vodka is Mongolians' drink of choice. There is even a brand called *Mazaalai*, the Mongolian name for the Gobi Bear—naturally, a bottle made its way to camp. Photo: Joe Riis

After dinner, as the stars brightened and the temperature plunged, the Mongolians would pile into one of the vans to tell jokes and stories while playing cards with the overhead light on, readying another vodka bottle or two for the pile of empties next to the hut. I remember Bayasa telling tales from his expeditions with the Conservation of the Great Gobi Ecosystem and its Umbrella Species Project. "So after we finished and I wrote the report," he said one evening, "some people were looking at me like I did something wrong. Why? I did a good job. What happened is that the computer program I used automatically changed the word *saxaul* to *sexual* every time. So some habitats had an abundance of sexual, and the camels were going to where there was good sexual, and I liked to analyze sexual."

The late-night voices carried to my tent hundreds of feet away after I made my exit. It was as if a bunch of schoolkids were having a campout in the

[Previous Spread] Petroglyphs depicting the area's large mammals—here, argali and possibly a wild ass—are found etched into the cliff walls close to oases; many include hunters with bows. Photo: Doug Chadwick

yard next door. The noise swelled and subsided with the rhythms of a cascade. Somewhat to my surprise, falling asleep to the sounds of laughter like water in the middle of a desert turned out to be an easy and pleasant thing to do.

So as not to give the wrong impression: This was the least lazy crew I have ever been with. When the Project team had to do something important first thing in the morning, it got done first thing in the morning. If folks didn't need to start rolling right away, they slept in and then got busy doing everything that needed to be done before the end of the day. The Mongolians liked to work, always anticipated the next task, and labored hard to accomplish it. Everyone did his or her part. No one shirked, nobody grumbled. Complaining didn't seem to be part of the culture in rural areas and was definitely not part of the ranger culture. Staying up late and having a good time definitely was.

———

THE DAY AFTER SETTING UP CAMP AT ALAGUNEET, WE HAD MADE OUR FIRST check of the digital cards from the motion-activated cameras at each of the four oases where we were preparing traps for the season. The photos revealed that bears had been at all of the sites, seeking pellets placed by rangers earlier in the spring. Harry also knew from photos taken the previous year that the eastern mountain complex oasis called Mukhar Zadgai had been visited by two bears in the autumn of 2011. The pair looked to be about three years old and were probably siblings that had become independent of their mother over the summer. With luck, they would survive to maturity, adding two more breeding adults to the population. They had made it through the winter at least. We knew that because the Mukhar Zadgai camera had caught images of them together again this spring. One of the siblings was visiting the feeder the night before we arrived. At another oasis, the camera had recorded chukar partridges, hares, ravens, curious argali sheep, a lynx, and two or possibly three different *mazaalai* at separate times the previous week. The smallest of the bears had a distinctive white ring around its forequarters and neck and looked like a young animal; born within the last three or four years.

We found recent scats at all four oases as well. While Odko searched for fur samples on the barbed wire strands and the rangers tested the traps and cameras to keep everything in working order, I made it my mission to collect samples from the scats containing remains of meals from the wild, rather than from the grain pellet bins. I could tell from a quick inspection that sprouting wild onion was among the most popular fare so far this spring. Examining the strands of vegetation in one sample, Amgaa nodded and said, "Also *Stipa* grass." Then he walked closer to the water source and began digging into the ground. I thought he might be searching for roots or bulbs that the bears eat in the springtime, but he began putting the spoonfuls of the soil into folded sheets of paper and labeling them. When Odko passed by, she stopped to interpret. "He says he is taking samples for the Institute of Biology. They want to find out what microbes live in the ground here. Nobody has done that yet in this part of the Gobi."

Bioprospecting is a flourishing field of research, since laboratories now have instruments capable of sifting through all kinds of material to detect invisible life-forms by traces of their DNA. What Amgaa was doing, spooning up Gobi dirt, didn't look like a treasure hunt. Yet one of his envelopes might include a Gobi oasis bacterium or microscopic fungus with a unique and previously unknown chemical compound. While ninjas were out there somewhere excavating for nuggets, some microscopic organism Amgaa scooped up with a spoon could prove to be of infinitely greater value to humankind as a medical cure.

I left Amgaa to his mini-mining operation and continued digging through scat. One appeared to be made entirely of ant parts. Another dropping was ropy, tapered at the end, and full of the long hair of a hoofed animal. At first, I thought the dung had come from a big wolf. Tracks and scat from these canines were ubiquitous around oases. I hadn't considered the possibility of this scat being from a grizzly. Harry told me he hadn't seen any Gobi bear scat with the remains of big animals since the Project began. He also saw intact carcasses that passing bears had ignored entirely. Nor did the bears show any interest in the meat Harry had tried using for bait in the traps during the first year of the Project. That was very ungrizzly-like behavior. But, then, mazaalai are not very typical grizzly bears.

When I began to pull the dung apart, though, more and more particles of digested grain appeared among the hairs. Hold on; wolves don't touch the supplemental food pellets. This was bear poop. A mazaalai had plainly been dining on a large mammal not long before it came to get chow at the feeder. Did mazaalai scavenge more often than Harry and others realized? Would most of the bears turn to scavenging at times, maybe when other food was scarce? Or did only certain bears make the switch? Grizzlies are highly individual in terms of their temperament, experiences, and learned behavior. Studies of them elsewhere showed that the percentage of meat in the diet varied not only from one bear to the next but also between the sexes, with males being more predatory and carnivorous than females.

This was just a turd. It was a confusing one, though, and therefore shit worth contemplating. In science, being confused is an opportunity to admit that you don't understand something and to start asking questions. The obstacle is that part of human nature urges us to avoid confusion and stick with the answers we already have, working to make them fit. The more you heed that inner voice, and the more you assume that the answers you have must be right, the lower your chances of learning something new.

The epistemological question of how people decide what they know and don't know is endlessly intriguing; the practical question at hand, though, concerned just how much carcass scavenging Gobi grizzlies do. If the *mazaalai* rely heavily on this food source, then their fortune becomes linked to the welfare of the resident wild camels, argali, ibex, and black-tailed gazelles, not to mention the *khulan*—the wild asses that create and expand water holes. Even if only a few bears eat carcasses, under limited conditions, this could influence the health and size of the population as a whole over time. So if you want to conserve Gobi grizzlies, you may need to be paying close attention to anything that affects numbers of hoofed species in the same southern portion of the reserve. And if you believe that the day will come when the bears can expand into different parts of the GGSPA and beyond into other former range—and you have to believe that, or else you're just curating them like a relic from a bygone time—the outcome might depend on how the native ungulates are doing in the re-colonized territory.

The platitudes about everything in an ecosystem being hitched to everything else are as true as ever. You lift up an odd piece of poo, and you find within it connections to the future of an entire wildlife community.

———

AFTER A QUICK—AND FRUITLESS—EARLY-MORNING CHECK OF THE TRAPS ON May 11, we traveled from Alaguneet through the mountain complex until we emerged on the southern side and came to a broad dirt track paralleled by a series of telephone poles. Running roughly parallel to the northern boundary of China, miles farther south, this was the border route, and it was patrolled by soldiers stationed at widely separated outposts. We turned onto the track to drive westward and made good time for a while. Then we turned off it and went bumping back into the mountains again. The purpose of the trip was to set up a feeder at a spring. A camera placed there in 2011 had captured photos of nearly all the reserve's big mammal species coming to drink.

The surrounding hillsides were scored with wildlife trails. Their patterns resembled webs pulled at one end, with the strands converging upon a single point—a clear pool issuing from an alcove in the rock wall at the base of a cliff. A dry wash wound past the cliff, and on its opposite edge stood what

I, at first, took to be two stone cairns. They were actually small turrets con-structed so that a person could sit hidden inside. Whether these observation blinds had been built by hunters before the reserve was declared or later by poachers was difficult to guess.

Next to the spring, the team built a level rock platform. We placed a fifty-five-gallon drum upright on that shelf and anchored the barrel against the cliff wall with wire and pitons. Then we filled the container with grain pellets and clawed some out from the opening cut near its base to make sure the rest would dispense easily as a hungry bear started to eat. The place was too remote to use as a trap site that could be checked as part of a daily circuit. We were simply making more food available for bears using this part of the reserve.

Once the bin was set up we continued west on the border track, then blazed a route south, still closer to China, to search for a lost radio collar. It had dropped off the neck of Altan, the young adult male caught the previous year at the Khotul Us oasis in the central mountain complex. Homing in on the last GPS coordinates broadcast before the satellite radio's battery died, we reached a high vantage point and pulled to a stop. Ahead lay a maze of hills with all kinds of meandering little arroyos and silty basins tucked within the folds. It could have taken days to search. In a way, that was an attractive thought. We'd been seeing *khulan* and argali on the side hills, and we knew

Team members search for the radio signal from a dropped collar. All too often, the device comes off deep within a labyrinth of mountains, hills, and twisting canyons. Photo: Doug Chadwick

from Altan's cluster of GPS locations that at least one *mazaalai* found this convoluted terrain to its liking.

However, we had open traps to return to in the eastern mountain complex. The collar contained an auxiliary transmitter that was still sending out a standard VHF radio signal with a range of several miles. Bayasa was able to pick it up with a receiver attached to a handheld antenna. Excitement spread across his face as he waved me over to listen. "I think we will be lucky soon," he said. "These are strong." The pulses—cheep! cheep! cheep!—seemed to be coming most clearly from a draw to the southwest. Joined by Nyamaa, Bayasa took off trotting up and down the hills' contours, waving the antenna back and forth and adjusting his course to keep in line with the signal's strongest chirps.

When I finally caught up with the pair, Nyamaa looked at me with a mournful expression and shook his head. Bayasa tried to do the same but gave away the game by breaking into a grin. He brought his hand out from behind his back and revealed the collar he'd been hiding. They had found it in a small basin. We walked together back to that spot. Judging from the number of diggings Nyamaa pointed out, Altan had been plundering a trove of wild rhubarb when the collar detached. The site was only a little more than twenty-six miles from Khotul Us—as the desert raven flies. As the grizzly bear walks, Altan would have covered twice that distance, working his way through the labyrinth of mountains and canyons before his travels brought him here.

We were now south of the central mountain complex. Even without a single flat tire or breakdown, we weren't going to get back to Alaguneet, on the north side of the eastern complex, until late. And before we could leave, we were obliged to present papers at a border patrol station a long drive west on the boundary road. With perimeter walls and a whitewashed round tower topped by turrets, the outpost resembled a scaled-down, low-budget version of a French Foreign Legion fort set somewhere in the Middle East. The number of visitors, travelers, lost wanderers, and suspected illegal border crossers that the guards here saw in a month probably averaged close to zero.

The officials took their time going through the motions of checking our passports and special permits for operating in a strictly protected area. Their wives brought tea into the room where we waited. That was soon followed by bowls of noodle soup. We appreciated the hospitality. At the same time, we knew that we were gently being held hostage to provide the fort's residents with a distraction from the daily routines of life on a lonely desert frontier.

Bayasa and Ankhaa offered news from Bayantooroi and our Alaguneet research camp, and the talk turned to *mazaalai* here on the rim of China.

Had any of the border guards seen one while on their motorcycle patrols? Harry wanted to know, Bayasa interpreted: "The commander says he has been stationed at this outpost for four years. He does not know of anybody coming upon a bear, but someone reported tracks maybe last year or the year before." After an hour of conversation I couldn't follow, we were taken on a brief tour of the grounds. We said our good-byes, and as we bounced away along the border road, Harry told me he had heard a secondhand account of border guards at the next station, far to the east, using a vehicle to run down a Gobi bear and lasso it. Once they caught the animal, they thought better of what they were doing and cut the rope to let it go.

It was getting close to midnight by the time we wound through the mountains and descended the gravel plain spreading out from the foot of Tsagaan Bogd. En route, we drove by the feeder and trap at Suujiin Bulag, where one of the two young bears presumed to be siblings had been photographed shortly before we came to set up camp. We made it back to Alaguneet around midnight. The next morning, a check of the Suujiin Bulag camera revealed a nighttime picture of our van passing the trap. The photo just before that showed one of the young grizzlies nosing around near the box. Our late-night return from the border station had scared it off.

———

BABOO, THE EASTERN RESERVE PATROL RANGER, HAD COME TO JOIN THE TEAM at Alaguneet and carry out the morning trap checks. But on May 12, he turned his motorcycle over to Bayasa to make the rounds. At midmorning, Bayasa sped into camp to say we had a bear in the box at Altan Tevsh (Golden Bowl/ Golden Box), the oasis in a canyon just over a ridge from Alaguneet. "A big bear," he announced. It wasn't—judging a *mazaalai's* size within the shadowy confines of the trap from a distance was never easy—but the animal was at least an adult. As Harry approached to estimate its weight in order to prepare the right amount of immobilizing drug, the bear was quiet and wary, keeping low in the cage. Harry withdrew, calibrated the dosage, and returned to the box. Within milliseconds after he struck with the jab-pole, the animal had morphed into a grizzly tornado, trying to tear apart the open grating to get free and violently smacking into the walls. BOOM! WHAM! The bear had the trap of thin sheet metal rocking from side to side now, up onto one edge, then the other, until we feared the box would tip over and release the catch on the door or bust its hinges. Harry had to jab the captive with another dose of drugs. The bear finally lay down, struggling to lift its head until it wouldn't move any more. Even then, it continued to growl.

Although this *mazaalai* proved to weigh only 155 pounds, it was a prize—a female Harry believed wasn't known to the Project: young, healthy, and in prime breeding condition with years of potential for making babies ahead. Her nipples were somewhat enlarged and roughened, suggesting that she had already produced cubs in an earlier year. We carried her outside the trap to collar her in its shade. She came out of the drug slowly and eventually staggered over to the nearby spring to lap at the water for a very long time, pausing in-between drinks to rest her head on the ground. Her muzzle sometimes dropped into the edge of the shallow flow that ran intermittently on the surface for a couple dozen feet.

Dauntless, this young, just-collared female weighing scarcely 150 pounds, kept advancing toward the crew-filled van while we beat a retreat down the canyon. Photo: Doug Chadwick

Having once darted an Alaskan grizzly from an aircraft and found the drugged animal dead where it had collapsed facedown and drowned in a shallow tundra puddle, Harry was growing uncomfortable with the current situation. "Odko," he said, "can you tell Ankhaa to drive the van closer? We need to get this bear up and moving." She passed along the message and Ankhaa motioned for everyone to get inside. The engine noise caused the female to raise her head from the pool. She struggled to get up on all fours, succeeded, and tried to charge at the incoming vehicle, staggering as she came. Ankhaa was smiling and shaking his head as he backed the rig away, happily defeated by a bear that weighed less than he did. Apparently satisfied as well, the female returned to the water to drink. A quarter of an hour later, she started up the steep canyonside, sniffing at plants and pausing every

Patrol ranger Altanshagai (Shagai) Nanzad (left), ranger-biologist Nyambayar (Nyamaa) Yanjin (middle), and driver Dondogdorj (Donduuk) Ramjin (right) relax among piles of supplies in a little patrol hut. Photo: Doug Chadwick

now and then to take in her surroundings. Though unsteady on her feet and reduced to turning in wobbly circles at times, she seemed determined to reach the ridgetop. She did.

Seeing her continue over the crest and disappear from view was the opposite of a farewell. It was more like a beginning. If DNA from her fur samples confirmed that this individual had not been previously recorded, we could safely assume that the population was one bear larger than we had known before—one all-important young breeding female larger. And the stream of GPS coordinates coming in from her new, lightweight satellite radio collar would add one more set of data to inform researchers about *mazaalai* travels, habitat choices, and survival, making these bears a little less mysterious with each passing day.

SINCE THE CAMP SELDOM BECAME VERY BUSY IN THE EARLY MORNING, I HAD the twilight before dawn to myself. I would walk out alone into the stillness of the desert to greet daybreak on a hilltop or pass. From there I could hike in any direction I chose for another couple hours, simply wandering in an elemental wilderness, exploring landscapes richly lit by the sun's low angle with my senses tuned up and my eyes wide open and nothing to distract me from absorbing every detail. I felt on the edge of being lost to the world and, because of that, I felt free. By the time I found my way back to scrounge break-fast in the crowded hut, I'd already had a good day. Every time. The bears had brought me back to this place, but the wild immensities they roamed exerted a powerful pull of their own.

It turned out that I also had plenty of hiking opportunities after break-fast—day after day passed without another bear capture. I did see Altan again. Not in the flesh but on a photo taken May 18 at Mukhar Zadgai, another of the four trap sites we were monitoring daily this season. Although he had dropped his collar, he could still be identified by the colors of his ear tags. Just as golden-brown as when he was captured at Khotul Us, he had notice-ably grown in size. He was one of at least six *mazaalai* currently showing up at those oases but avoiding the temptation to enter the baited metal boxes. When we had checked Mukhar Zadgai earlier in the week, Harry pointed out that the peregrine falcon nest on the cliffs above the oasis had three adults together in it, a highly unusual combination for these aerial hunters. And now the first Gobi bear I had ever touched was paying a visit.

<hr/>

DURING A DIFFERENT BEARLESS DAY, BABOO AND AMGAA SET OFF EARLY together on a motorcycle to search for the radio collar recently dropped by Borte, the second bear we had caught the year before. They had a round-trip of more than a hundred miles before them. The last GPS coordinates the men were homing in on might prove misleading if those signals had been bouncing off steep topography. The signals could also have been thrown off—corrupted, as researchers say—as a result of interference by frequencies emanating from other sources. This had happened from time to time before, the prime suspect being military bases in China's portion of the Gobi.

We didn't expect the men to return before midafternoon. The day turned heavily overcast with a developing windstorm. Any other place with a sky as leaden as the pall over our heads would have been soaked with rain before long. But this region only got swept by stronger winds. When Amgaa and Baboo didn't show up, the crew assumed that the collar wasn't where the last coordinates indicated it would be, and the guys were prolonging their search. Dusk fell with the windstorm continuing to gain strength and the motorcyclists still missing, so Harry and Ankhaa tried to make contact with them via satellite phone. No luck. It was after dark when someone first called attention to the distant sound of an engine.

Baboo and Amgaa came into the hut carrying the collar. They had found it at the Tsagaan Burgas oasis, the water source closest to Khotul Us, where

Borte had been caught. Nestled beneath white willow and tamarisk brush, the collar was precisely where the GPS coordinates promised it would be. From there, the men went south to the border road, generally the smoothest dirt track in the entire region, so they could make good time getting from the central mountain complex to the eastern one before cutting through the upland canyons to return to our camp. First, though, Amgaa explained, they had stopped in at the guard station and watched satellite television. Who wouldn't want to hang out watching soap operas and sumo wrestling for three hours someplace where the windy, waterless sprawl of Mongolia's Gobi turns into the windy, waterless sprawl of China's Gobi? The men were pretty sure they could find their way back over the maze of mountains in the dark.

Several years before we placed the collar on Borte in 2011, Harry had given her a collar that failed to yield much besides corrupted GPS locations. This second collar was made by a different company. Stored within it now were thousands of digital coordinates that could finally give Harry a picture of her seasonal movements and overall range. When Amgaa and Baboo presented their prize, Harry kept that collar clutched in one hand and with the other repeatedly gripped the Mongolians' arms by way of thanks.

While the wind yammered outside the hut, vying for attention, we talked and told jokes late into the night. As usual, the guys—including the biggest ones, Ankhaa and Nyamaa, who often wrestled one another when things were slow around camp or while taking a break from a long van ride—sat with an arm resting around a companion's shoulder or leaned back against someone else's chest or belly. I'd once asked Harry what he most liked about Mongolia. He often spoke of how much he loved the big, open landscapes, but when he replied this time, he said, "It's the unaffected way people behave here, the lack of pretense, and the camaraderie. It's like...." He struggled for some time in silence to find the words he wanted and finally said this: "I'm not big on the idea of reincarnation, but if I were, I'd say I must have lived here in a previous life."

How so?

He lifted both arms into the air and said, "It just feels right."

A field research camp is a special community unto itself. You might save the animals you're studying; you might not. Still, there's magic in the fact that the everyday problems and social expectations of the world at large count for little or nothing here. You bond in a special way with your camp-mates through shared efforts. There is no one else for help with little things, safety in dangerous conditions, humor, sympathy, fresh ideas—whatever is needed. A camp has no overstuffed places for affectation and fakery to hide in; things are too close to the bone. This far beyond the rest of society, there is really no point to being anything other than your genuine self. It is an honest, clarifying way to live. It just feels right.

———————

ON YET ANOTHER WAITING-FOR-A-BEAR DAY, MAY 18, WE MADE THE SUUJIN Bulag oasis the last stop on a morning trap-checking circuit. From the baited box and closed-off feeder, we went uphill to the spring and re-filled the camp's water barrels from a clear pool amid the *Phragmites* reeds. Ankhaa then drove the van father upslope over the rubble at the base of Tsagaan Bogd for maybe half a mile to the mouth of a big wash coming out of the massif. There, five of us left the van and set off on foot for the summit. Harry would stay behind along with Odko, who, as a woman, was not supposed to climb any peak designated a *bogd*, which meant it was recognized as a holy place.

I remembered Odko telling me, "Some people believe there are spirits in the highest peaks, watching over the animals and the people and the land." Power does coalesce up there, whether you think of it as a supernatural thing or a mixture of super-strength winds and weather and the sort of terrain and views that make mere mortals feel all-seeing once they reach those heights. But I never heard a good explanation for why women were not allowed to climb a *bogd*. I'd have thought that any spirits swirling around Tsagaan Bogd's peak would welcome someone like Odko, who also watches with care over animals, people, and the land. But my beliefs were impertinent here. Odko respected the tradition.

A couple of the Project team members who had been in UB before coming to the Gobi brought a hacking cough along with them. They got over their cold, but not before Baboo caught it. He, too, was staying behind today, and at first I wondered if I shouldn't have done the same. I had been achy and feverish for several days before the climb. As we started up the canyon, my lungs were still raw from coughing, and my legs tired easily. Trudging over the wash's loose gravel and grit felt like walking in soft sand.

We hadn't gone more than a mile from the canyon's mouth when Amgaa called me over to a cliff band at the edge of a turn in the wash. At the base of the lowest belt of rocks rested a fairly fresh scat surrounded by scrape marks. They were from a snow leopard. For me, that cat counted as one of the spirits that dwell atop *bogds*. It had the power to make me forget feeling lousy and get on with pushing for the top.

Our Alaguneet camp was about a mile above sea level. The summit of Altan Bogd stood just a little over 8,200 feet. As Harry had promised, the climb wasn't the sort that required special skills, only a measure of endurance and as much water as I could carry. For miles we gradually ascended the mountain's western flank simply by walking up the broad wash of the canyon floor. I found more leopard scat and scrapes, both old and relatively new. The wash was clearly one of the cat's regular travel routes toward the Suujiin Bulag water source and the hoofed animals it attracted. Once we cut away from the wash to begin climbing, we quickly left the hoofprints of camels and gazelles behind. Farther up, the ridges turned spiny, and the cliffs on the north side became long, sheer drops. The trails of the wild asses thinned out, and we soon left their last tracks below as well. From there on, all the remaining signs came from argali and ibex. Lots and lots of ibex.

By Gobi standards, the upper elevations were lush, transformed by the slightly greater amount of moisture the heights receive in the form of rain, snow, and direct condensation from clouds snagging on Tsagaan Bogd. After climbing up and over some jagged ridgetops to reach the mountain's shoulder, we found ourselves walking through small meadows solidly filled with grasses, sedges, and low-growing brush, a sort of desert alpine tundra between the rock formations. I wasn't carrying very much in my daypack, but I began lagging regardless. Amgaa came over and motioned for me to let him take my daypack. I gave him a water bottle and a couple of other items from it to carry. "I'll take the rest," Bayasa said, snatching up my bag from the ground before I could return it to my shoulders—and waving me off when I reached to take it back. "I don't have anything in my own pack," he lied. Nearing the summit, I was moving hand over hand, not so much because the steepness of the rocks really called for it but because I was close to exhaustion.

Sick.

Overheated.

Parched.

And then filled with delight when the last few steps transformed me into a mighty, all-seeing son-of-a-gun. Unimaginably big views of China opened to the south, where the giant mountain gave way to foothills, which gave way in turn to a near infinity of pale desert and pure white alkali pans. In the other three compass directions, the world was made of mountains beyond mountains beyond mountains. I sat on the summit and made two candy bars magically disappear into my gut.

It was early afternoon. Hard, unfiltered sunshine fell straight down on this crinkled part of the globe and found no swaths of vegetation to light anywhere. No green fields. No roads, no villages. Our 360-degree perspective took in thousands of square miles of raw, rough, dry planet skin looking the way it had for millennia. The name itself—Gobi, "a waterless place"—took on extra meaning, for it was all bedrock, gravel, sand, and dust.

The weathered metal side of a feeding bin displays an old symbol
formerly used by Mongolia's Ministry of Environment to encourage
the protection of wildlife. Photo: Doug Chadwick

Here was the *mazaalai's* realm, their refuge from the crowded world over the horizons. Black shadows from a few scattered clouds rippled across the endless folds of mountain ranges and sailed smoothly over the white desert pans deep in Chinese territory. Atop Tsagaan Bogd, the dominant color was blue. The revered eternal blue sky enveloped us above and on all sides. Blue ribbons left by earlier climbers and pilgrims were wrapped around the natural rock formations and the stones in cairns. Symbols drawn on the stones with blue paint told of people who had come from afar to pay their respects at this summit.

The wind rolled against us, pushing hard. Simply standing was like trying to stay upright in surf. The landscape seemed to come rushing in from all directions like a colossal shout. Modern Mongolians hold this mountaintop sacred, and the Stone Age people who came before them probably did as well. Whatever your origins, you would have to own a shriveled soul to rest upon this summit and not understand why.

AROUND THE TIME OF OUR ASCENT OF TSAGAAN BOGD, SOMETHING WENT wrong in two different traps. Maybe it was the setting of the treadle plate raised off the floor, or maybe the tension of the cord linking the plate to the catch on the raised door needed adjustment. Whatever the source of the problem, bears went inside each of those traps, and nothing happened apart from the animals leisurely feasting and then strolling back out into the desert. But on May 21, we caught another bear at Altan Tevsh, the same place we had caught the young adult female. This second captive was also a female and about the same age. Like the first, she waited quietly in a corner of the metal box, as if feeling vulnerable and hoping not to be noticed when we arrived in the van. And like her predecessor, she sprang at Harry with a roar when he approached. When he moved still closer, she started trying to rip apart the open grating on the trap's side.

Harry needed to give this animal a second drug dose, too. He had just finished explaining to me how grateful he was for the immobilizing drug he was using. Mammals tolerated the immobilizer extremely well without side effects, he explained, even if the dosage exceeded the amount recommended for a subject's actual weight. When he opened the trapdoor and we dragged the bear out to work on in the open, however, his expression changed to one of serious concern. The bear's breathing was abnormally faint and shallow. Harry bent down and put his ear close to the animal's mouth to listen. The crew silently gathered round, counting the animal's breaths before deciding what to do next. Inject an antidote? There wasn't one for this particular drug because of the wide latitude of dosage animals were able to accept. Try artificial respiration by moving the arms and legs up and down? That might be called for, but for the time being, Harry would just wait and keep a careful count of her labored breaths.

I walked a short distance away down the canyon wash and stopped at a bend where the canyonsides came close together. An all-but-forgotten generation of people in the Gobi had etched petroglyphs into the shiny black desert patina of the cliff faces. There was no headwall closing off the canyon farther up the wash. I think the name of the oasis, Golden Bowl (or Box) referred to this pinch point just below the spring. The GGSPA held an assortment of petroglyphs. Most of them were near oases, and nearly all of them adorned the walls at or near a natural ambush site like this one. Cut into smooth facets of stone at about head-height, they portrayed the circular-horned argali, scimitar-horned ibex, camels, asses, and men with bows and arrows. Curiously, they never included *mazaalai*. Perhaps the bears were always too rare, too risky to hunt, or simply weren't tasty enough to inspire the hunter-artists.

Placing my hands on the stone next to the renderings of animals and bowmen, I didn't think about the artwork as a hunting log. I chose instead to see it as a testimony to the enduring connection between human lives and those of other large, intelligent beings. People ate them, tracked and watched them, learned from them, and shared many of the same plant foods and all of the main water sources. Generation after generation admired these mammals, depended upon them, were grateful to them, dreamed about them, and surely drew spiritual strength and meaning from them. And now, back at the trap site, there was a team of worried hunter-gatherers of information whose minds were utterly focused on the existence of a wild creature.

I stood with my eyes squeezed shut, pushing against the cliff wall as if I had to keep it from toppling into the wash, making silent wishes with all the force I could muster. I don't believe this sort of thing makes a whit of difference, but I don't think we know enough to be absolutely sure that it doesn't. Also, there wasn't much else I could do. After a while I walked back toward the group. Well before I got there, I could hear the bear growling. That isn't always a sound you want to hear when you're close to a bear, but in this case it was a wonderful sign.

Everybody in the team was soon up and walking around the animal, preparing to measure and collar it. This female was slightly younger than the first—seven years old at most. She weighed 145 pounds. From the smooth, unworn appearance of her teats, Harry could tell that she had not previously given birth. He said that this was not unusual for a grizzly inhabiting a harsh, marginal environment. Many in the Arctic were as old or older before they first bred. Our captive seemed to be in good physical condition and could be expected to begin producing young within the next year.

Like the first female captured, this one made her way to the spring to drink as soon as she regained her footing. Interestingly, she then returned from the water to the trap and thoroughly investigated it, over and over, as if mystified and trying to put together what had happened. We waited next to the van about 150 feet away. Watching through binoculars, I thought the female's head looked oddly flattened on top. Harry agreed, saying that the hairs on the forehead sometimes become worn down or completely rubbed off during the winter months in a den.

"Notice anything else?" he asked, keeping his voice barely above a whisper. Before I could answer, he did: "The claws. They're the longest I think

[Top] Overgrazing by livestock allowed in portions of the reserve weakens the prospects for the survival and recovery of Gobi bears. Photo: Joe Riis [Bottom] The most serious threat is posed by mining, both in the form of illegal gold-digging ninjas and persistent lobbying by industry to open the area to mineral development. Photo: Doug Chadwick

I've seen on a Gobi bear. What's she been eating? It doesn't look as though she's been digging at all."

As if becoming aware for the first time that she had company, the bear began walking directly toward us. We jumped in the van and eased away. She kept coming, all 145 damn-the-consequences pounds of her. We drove farther down the wash, and she kept right after us. With its carrying rack, the top of the van was nearly eight feet off the ground and almost three times as long as she was. She was three feet high at the shoulder, still weak and stumbly, and intent on having it out with this giant metal contraption, never shying to one side or even pausing when its engine growled. How could she not be intimidated in the slightest? What internal fires cook up audacity of this order?

But as far as our fierce little loopy female could tell, her plan was working. She had us in full retreat. A couple hundred yards down the wash, she decided at last to let us be. Turning into a side-canyon, she disappeared behind a thicket of caragana and *Zygophyllum*. Good on you, Ms. Gobi Bear. We'll add yet another to the number of *mazaalai* born since the Project began and now thriving as an adult. Perhaps after Odko tests the DNA from samples of your fur, to be sure you haven't been counted before, we'll be able to add yet one more reproductive-age female to the population's total. Thanks to you, we just raised the number of different Gobi bears collared in the study so far from thirteen to fourteen.

This capture of a second female just entering her prime breeding years took place on what turned out to be the last full day of the 2012 field season. Although we had matched the Project's average of two bears per spring, the real reason we were closing down field operations somewhat early was that Harry had learned via sat phone that the president of Mongolia was expecting to meet with him. We needed to get back to UB within the next week to fit into the president's schedule.

———

DURING THE FINAL DAYS BEFORE OUR DEPARTURE FOR UB, I DEVELOPED AN eye infection, just as I had the previous year. I thought the flu-like cold might have worn me down enough to make me susceptible to other microbes, but there was more to it. Walking to my tent from the hut one night with the temperature falling rapidly toward freezing, I clicked on my headlamp and was surprised and happy to see that it was beginning to snow. The flakes weren't large but, rather, more like a fine mist of ice crystals. That would have been in keeping with the two spells of rain we experienced during the trip. Both were minor drizzles of drops scarcely big enough to wet the ground.

The difference this time was that the sky was cloudless. Stars shone brightly all across the sky.

What I briefly took for snow was the typical amount of dust in the air when winds were gusting, which was about four days out of five in the spring-time. In the headlamp's beam, the particles flashed and spun like troupes of spot-lit dancers crossing a stage. Most of the particles were clay. Some appeared to be gypsum crystals; others looked to be tiny flecks of mica. Still others were probably crystals of alkali salts from the desert pans. To be sure, my eyes were equally under assault inside the vans whenever we were driving with the wind at our tail, enveloped by the dust plume the vehicle raised. And everyone's eyes took a beating during the dust storms that darkened the world like a solar eclipse. However, when you're looking at a clear sky and the sharp outlines of faraway mountains, marveling at the visibility offered by the dry desert air, you don't consider the load of near-microscopic mineral debris that your eyes are constantly contending with, not to mention your nose and lungs.

I resolved to find some antibiotic eyewash as soon as we reached Ulaanbaatar and to never visit the Gobi again without a good supply of eye drops. But when we did reach the capital, close to midnight two days after catching the season's second bear, my eye was already feeling slightly better, and all I had on my mind was the usual post-camping fantasy of a long, hot

A toad-headed agama camouflaged among the Gobi gravel. They are the most common lizards in GGSPA, and Gobi bears occasionally include them in their diet. Photo: Doug Chadwick

shower. Naturally, the hotel's hot water system wasn't working. Harry and I filled a black plastic camp shower bag with a mixture of cold tap water and hot water from the machine in the lobby that dispensed water for coffee and tea. Back in our room, we hung the bag from the showerhead and finally got some of the dust out of our pores.

Among the first beneficiaries of our improved hygiene was the GGSPA's former director, Batmunkh (Miji) Mijiddorj. Now living in UB and advising the Ministry of Environment, Miji was kind enough to visit us at the hotel and discuss the Project. He was interested in what the latest expedition had accomplished, and Harry was always eager to gain more insights from Miji, who had studied the bears on his own for so many years before the Project began. As for me, I had a notebook with a list of questions to ask, beginning with Miji's findings about *mazaalai* food habits. He was preparing a scientific book about the bears. It was in Mongolian, but he intended to have the book translated into English at some point.

With Bayasa acting as an interpreter, Miji told me, "The number one bear food is *bijun* (wild rhubarb), then *Nitraria sibirica* (nitre bush) berries. After that come berries from *Ephedra*, young *Phragmites* (the oasis grass, commonly called a reed), *Alium* (wild onion), and *Stipa* (the widespread grass). *Oxytropis* (*O. aciphylla*, a dwarf shrub in the legume, or pea, family and rich in nitrogen) is also a valuable food. Insects form the next most important group in the diet. Number one is the wingless grasshopper, then beetles. After that, lizards and small mammals. Oh, and chukar and some small birds."

I wanted to know what he had found in the way of large-mammal remains in the bear scat he had collected. Gerbil colonies provided most of the meat from mammals, he said. But yes, he had identified wild camel, wild ass, argali, ibex, and black-tailed gazelle—the whole array of hoofed fauna—in *mazaalai* scat as well. Though their remains made up only a minor percentage of the bears' overall diet, scavenging large mammals was by no means an unusual behavior.

The other surprise came when I inquired about the stone corrals I had seen north of Ekhiin Gol in the GGSPA. It looked to me as though the vegetation was seriously depleted or missing altogether in some sites. Was this effect localized or widespread? How many herders had permits for grazing in the reserve's so-called buffer zone? I expected to hear a number like twenty-five to thirty. According to Miji, the correct number was 250 to 300 herders. They bring in 50,000 to 75,000 head of livestock to forage just outside the reserve and are regularly allowed to enter the northern third of the strictly protected area.

Miji was careful to point out that domestic animals are only allowed to graze within the reserve from October through March. Since this is before the spring growing season starts, the effects aren't as severe as they would be if the herds were stripping off the new growth. What he didn't say is that the head count for livestock adds up to many times the total number of wild grazers in the GGSPA. In this nation of pastoralists, you don't expect an official to come out and declare that the impact on the native plant community from that much livestock is clearly excessive and harmful to the vegetation. Yet it is. This was a dry and hungry landscape before the tame animals were encouraged to monopolize the buffer zone for part of each year. If the government was sincere about encouraging Gobi bears to one day expand back into that major segment of their former range, the level of use by herders was going to have to be reduced.

Our appointment with the president had changed to a meeting with Mongolia's vice president, then switched to a lunch with one of the president's top policy advisors. The man's name was Lundeg (Puru) Purevsuren, who assured us that the new president was a strong supporter of the environment. Indeed, he was a candidate for a United Nations Champions of the Earth award that year. Puru contrasted his boss with the past (and recently jailed) president, who had opened a number of strictly protected reserves to mining in the course of his tenure and given out something like fifty new mining permits during his last days in office.

"It was time to slow down," Puru told us. "The mineral development was too much, too fast. Too much of the money was going out of the country, and we needed to begin getting more control over development. It's good to have these protected areas for the future." Not only was the current president serious about improving conservation, he had selected an ecologist named Jamsran Batbold to be the State Secretary in the Ministry of Environment. Mr. Batbold earned his doctoral degree comparing the genetics of marmot subpopulations in a region that included parts of Mongolia and neighboring Kazakhstan.

With the president's blessing, Batbold was already planning to declare 2013 Mongolia's Year of the Gobi Bear. He was determined to boost awareness of *mazaalai* and help bring them to the fore as a national symbol of conservation. My own plan for 2013 was to return to the Gobi, hoping to learn more about what the bears themselves were doing. I didn't need any extra incentive, but it was heartening to think I'd be doing that during a year intended to officially celebrate these animals. If their greater habitat came to include enough people's consciousness, they would find themselves with enough allies in their fight for survival to re-take ground in the desert.

━━━━━━━━━━

ONCE, I HEADED EAST FROM A PROJECT CAMP ON AN AFTERNOON STROLL following a path laid down by generations of wild camels and wild asses. The route split at the cutbank of a gully. Then the fork I took split at the base of a steep conical prominence. I circled right, deeper into the foothills. Looking back after a while, I was careful to note that the section of the gully I'd crossed was banked with pinkish stone, and the conical hill stood out sharply as bright orange next to a series of rounded black hillocks. These were my markers. A half-hour farther along, I looked back again and saw a scene crowded with other pink stone formations and other conical orange hills next to black ones. The whole place, including the terrain ahead, was lighting up with colors as the sun arced lower in the sky. In addition to the pink, orange, and black features, there were peaks and hills shining yellow, tan, brown, purple, or red in the late light. Some of the bare, rubbled mounds took on a metallic green cast that made them seem coated with lichens or moss from afar. It was big rock candy mountain county viewed through a kaleidoscope—a wondrously polychrome pattern, infinitely repeated in every direction. Fractal topography.

To keep oriented, I fixed on a hillock of pure white quartz gleaming like a lighthouse lamp and made that my destination. It wasn't far. I went a bit beyond it to explore along the bottom of a twisting ravine. When I climbed back out, expecting to find my white beacon waiting, I found two. Both stood farther off than I expected. I was midway between them and couldn't decide which was the first I had seen. Nor could I recognize the series of hills I had come through any longer. I wasn't lost. But I was disoriented enough that I suddenly felt hollowed out and chilled. Wildlife paths led everywhere. I couldn't find my footprints on any of them. To reach camp, I would have to pick exactly the right sequence of hills out of countless similar-looking possibilities.

Since I originally planned to walk only two or three miles, I hadn't packed much. However, I was carrying water and a compass. They would get me back. Not through the puzzle palace of eroded mountain slopes, though. I would go due north until I broke out onto the huge plain in that direction and then hike west paralleling the base of the range. This was going to be very much the long way home, but it was a way home, and that's all that mattered.

The evening faded. Once finally out on the plain, I walked westward for what felt like longer than necessary to intersect the canyon mouth leading back in to camp. I kept thinking that the next defile coming out of the range had to be the entrance. None was. This was my mind playing tricks, anticipating too much too soon; I was aware of that. Even so, there did come a point after which I became seriously worried that I had missed the canyon in the deepening twilight or, worse. What if within the massive maze of these mountains there was another range grading out onto a different plain, and I was on the wrong one, truly lost after all?

Six or seven canyons later, I was at my tent. It wasn't terribly long after dark, and I hadn't come close to giving up. Still, I could never figure out how my original course through the countryside became so obscured by hills and mountains that I hadn't taken into account on my outbound journey. Sometimes that walk seemed like a metaphor for the Gobi Bear Project. You look round to take a fresh fix on the route toward your research and management goals, only to find the perspective somehow changed by all these socio-econo-political bumps and unexpected drop-offs crowding into view, obscuring the way. This is not the kind of terrain you've been trained to analyze as a scientist. Nevertheless, it's the real world, the lay of the land, and you have to either navigate through it or figure a way around and hope the new course won't lead you farther astray.

Our 2011 expedition had given me reasons for optimism and reasons to despair but not enough perspective to picture how the odds could be changed to favor hope. The 2012 season introduced me to a great many new factors in the equation: To the eastern mountain complex portion of the bears' range. To new water sources and new terrain where *bijun* and wild onion and *Stipa* grass were growing well, but also to new places within the GGSPA overgrazed by livestock. To the realization that *mazaalai* eat large mammal carcasses at times and are thus more closely linked to the area's wild ungulates than I had been aware of. I'd also been introduced to more reports of ninjas, but also to a number of new bears through their tracks, photos taken at the oases, and the two young females we trapped.

Like Altan, caught the year before, both females were not only born during the severe drought that lasted from 1993 through 2007 but born in the final years of it. The accumulated effects of the prolonged dry spell on plants and animals were as bad as they would get by then, and the females

A mother with two cubs born in her den over the winter were photographed in April 2013 by an automatic camera set near a feeder. This may be the first image of Gobi bears that young.
Photo: Courtesy of the Gobi Bear Project

knew nothing else during their earliest years, when they were as small and vulnerable as a Gobi bear can be. They did more than endure those years. They overcame them and got bigger, left their mother, continued to get bigger and stronger, and started life on their own.

To have placed my hands on those females and found myself talking reassuringly to them as they lay at my feet, aware but incapable of making their muscles work ... this created a connection that's hard to express, even though putting together words is supposed to be my job. To then be run off as the first female charged a several-ton van filled with eight or nine people who each weighed at least as much as she did was an honor as well. Merely being close to that much crazy tough determination gave me an infusion of confidence in the Gobi bears' future. If I put my emotions aside and reviewed the situation strictly on the basis of logic, the path to recovery for the rarest of bears still looked risky from every angle. Yet these animals' survival abilities, combined with efforts on their behalf by the Project and the GGSPA staff, were beginning to give more cause to be encouraged than discouraged. Good enough. *Yawi awi.*

09

Big
Bawa

On the way back to Mongolia in April 2013, I traveled by air from Seattle, Washington, to Seoul, Korea. Somewhere in the plane's cargo hold was my ditty bag full of eye drops for this year's expedition. Spring is the windiest season in the Gobi, and I'd learned the hard way that I'd need something to counter the effects of the nonstop barrage of desert dust on my eyes. Looking down from 30,000 feet at luminous streaks of clouds, I pictured us flying at that very moment through some of the fine particles whipped up into the stratosphere by Gobi whirlwinds and gales.

Everybody, especially in the Northern Hemisphere, gets a taste of Central Asia one way or another. A quarter of all the desert dust circulating in Earth's atmosphere comes from the Gobi Desert and its close neighbor to the west, the Taklamakan Desert, which lies almost entirely in northwest China. Carrying phosphorus, nitrogen, calcium, and iron, those big Gobi airstorms go on to fertilize phytoplankton—the single-celled algae that produce much of the planet's oxygen—all the way across the Pacific Ocean. One study was able to measure the extent to which the phosphorus, vital to plant growth, increased the productivity of tropical ecosystems on the Hawaiian island of Kauai. In North America, the elements in Gobi dust enrich forests and fields from California to coastal British Columbia and eastward to the slopes of the Rockies, where I make my Montana home. I promised myself to try to remember this the next time brown grit rimed my nostrils and turned my eyes red in Thirstland.

Harry and I had rendezvoused at the Seattle airport. While waiting there, we caught the news on television. North Korea's Revered Leader for Life, Kim Jong Un, the baby-faced son of former Revered Leader-for-Life Kim Jong Il, was more pissed off than usual at South Korea; so pissed, in fact, that he was supposedly lining up nuclear bomb-tipped missiles aimed at Seoul. Not the best time to be headed there for a layover in transit to Ulaanbaatar. The flight across the Pacific was eleven hours long, offering ample time to envision radioactive debris circling the globe along with Gobi dust.

We no sooner touched down in South Korea's capital than we heard that Mr. Un was upping his rhetoric, ranting on about how he was just a finger-twitch away from cleansing the evils of South Korea with atomic flames. Another head-fake from a tantrum-prone leader? We sincerely hoped so, for we learned that due to high winds in the valley where Ulaanbaatar is situated, our flight to Mongolia was now delayed for twenty-three hours. Predictably, Harry, the Guru of Imperturbability, shrugged and said, "If a nuke hits, well, it's been a great run," and suggested we get one of the little rooms at the hotel inside the terminal.

[Previous Spread] Big Bawa among the *Phragmites* grasses at
the oasis where he was radio-collared. Photo: Joe Riis

Assuming that nuclear Armageddon was put on hold, Earth's nonhuman life forms would still be disappearing at a thousand times the normal rate. This isn't me calamity-mongering. It's me being a reporter, stating a fact. Biological Armageddon was already underway. The question was what the Gobi Bear Project could do to help limit the fallout in a little-known section of the driest region in Mongolia. In a couple days, we would begin learning from officials what Mongolia's new administration had in mind for *mazaalai* now that the government had proclaimed 2013 the Year of the Gobi Bear.

For the time being, though, Harry and I were stuck in Seoul's glossy airport terminal, living the limbo life of re-scheduled travelers. The air outside was too smoggy to see through very far. It was hard to tell what, if anything, existed beyond cargo trucks and airplanes moving back and forth on the tarmac. Inside, we wandered aimlessly along polished corridors walled with boutiques. Picture two hominids with reflexes and senses honed by several million years of evolution walking for hours through habitat consisting mainly of very expensive purses. Every combination of animal skins, synthetic fabrics, colors, and baubles the human mind was able to conceive of had gone into the creation of thousands of these bags displayed like hallowed artifacts on illuminated shelves.

Continuing down trails through the Kingdom of Uberglitz, where weary wayfarers are magically transformed into weary wayfarers toting more shopping bags, I thought about why Harry and I liked the Mongolian countryside so much. Part of it had to do with the way the inhabitants of *gers* keep all the household's effects tucked into a few small, brightly painted cabinets set next to the walls of the circular tent. That leaves the center open for family and guests to sit around the stove and share meals and conversation. The rest of folks' lives take place outside and is equally uncluttered. Tent life in the Gobi feels much the same. At the end of a field season, I'm always amused to find clothing and supplies from my minimalist cache in the duffels that I'd never used at all.

We arrived in Mongolia and rendezvoused with Ankhaa, who had once again driven a van from the distant Bayantooroi headquarters. Photographer Joe Riis flew in to rejoin the crew. The next morning, we met with Dr. Batbold, Secretary of the Ministry of Environment (renamed the Ministry of Environment and Green Tourism). Other administrators, academics, and representatives of several nonprofit Mongolian conservation groups were present as well. Among them was N. (Tumen) Tumenjargal, a private businessman who had founded a group called MAMA with the goal of boosting the quantity and quality of the grain pellets for *mazaalai*. To make it harder for one dominant animal such as a big male to claim the supplemental food supply at a water source, Tumen was also helping put feeding bins in secondary locations at several oases where a single feeder was already in place.

Harry gave a presentation about grizzly bear biology. Where does this species, found across much of the Northern Hemisphere, fall to its lowest known density? he asked. Not surprisingly, the answer was: in Mongolia, and more specifically, in the southern third of the GGSPA. The last stronghold of *Ursus arctos gobiensis* holds just 1.5 to 2 bears per 1,000 square kilometers. For comparison, Alaska's salmon-rich Admiralty Island has about 370 per 1,000 square kilometers. Harry then showed a map with the movements of one of the *mazaalai* males the Project had radio-collared. That single animal's home range took in 5,000 square kilometers. The challenge before everyone at this table, Harry reminded his audience, is to save a unique subspecies with extremely low numbers very thinly spread over an immense expanse of austere habitat.

After the meeting, Batbold invited Harry to return the next day for a private get-together. Harry did, and during that session asked what the Secretary would like from the Project. Batbold had a straightforward answer: He expected a compilation of the study's data and, based on those findings, a list of suggestions for management aimed at recovering the bear population.

In turn, Harry said he was interested to hear more about what new steps the government was taking in the Year of Protecting Gobi Bears. First, Batbold replied, there were public events and school programs planned in the capital, news releases, and television coverage, all directed toward introducing more of the public to *mazaalai* and making these animals an icon for the protection of Mongolian wildlife in general. As for programs in the bears' home, the Ministry intended to experiment with cloud-seeding to increase rainfall in the mountains when conditions looked promising. Two new wells would be drilled to create additional water sources in the bears' habitat. Some existing springs would be improved and their flow directed into concrete pools to provide more reliable reservoirs for wildlife to drink from. Money would be available to work with MAMA to build ten new feeding bins and improve the nutritional quality of the grain pellets with vitamins and rich oils. Fifty new motion-activated cameras were being purchased. They would be deployed along travel routes in key habitats by a student group from the National University of Mongolia. Finally, the Ministry would call upon experts to create maps of Gobi bear habitat in 1940 and in the present day; the two could then be compared to gauge the effects of local human activities and climate change.

"The Ministry has always been interested in Gobi bears," Batbold continued. "In the Year of the Gobi Bear, I wanted to make an especially strong effort
to pursue research and conservation. As Mongolia focuses more attention
on Gobi bears, we hope this will begin to draw interest and financial support from the international community." Then Batbold added, "Our Action
Plan calls for spending 159 million tugriks on the bears this year." Yes! That
amount was equivalent to $114,000 in U.S. dollars at the time, the biggest
single financial commitment the government had ever made to *mazaalai*
conservation.

ON THE WAY OUT OF UB ON APRIL 17, THE CREW, AS USUAL, MADE A LAST-MINUTE
stop at a grocery. When we left the store, we walked into a snow squall. A day
later, it snowed again in the countryside around the small village of Erdene,
which stood like a remote encampment lost among the folds of the Gobi-Altai
Mountains. This place, half a day's journey north of the GGSPA, was the
home of Puji, our indomitable moto-ranger. Our traveling crew included a
young GGSPA ranger, his wife, and their toddler daughter. Puji's wife gave us
all dinner in the family's *ger* while the family's son played with the little girl.

When we went by van into unknown terrain in the central third of the
GGSPA looking for a lost radio collar, a reported possible water source, a

Young Mongolians at a village store, which in this spare desert setting feels like a grand
emporium stuffed ceiling high with a dazzle of goods. Photo: Joe Riis

cluster of GPS locations suggesting a key feeding site, or the like, Puji usually led the way on his bike to reconnoiter the lay of the land and pick the best route. Whenever the crew negotiated a series of gullies or slalomed through a maze of hillocks resembling giant petrified haystacks, unable to keep a fix on distant landmarks and casting about for new bearings, Puji would appear in the distance, rocketing up the impossibly steep slope of a tall hill within view. He'd brake at the very crest, perch sideways on the bike seat, fire up a cigarette, and wait there in his camo fatigues and wraparound sunglasses. *This way*. He was our scout, sentinel, and signpost. Now, it was a delight to see Mr. Kool Hard Guy at home among family and neighbors with a con-tented cast to his face.

After a few rounds of vodka and toasts to the success of our forthcoming season, it was time to leave the warmth and light of the *ger* and rattle on toward the GGSPA headquarters at Bayantooroi in the gathering dark. Puji wasn't joining, since we weren't working in his patrol area this year. Seeing us off, he told us that parts of the reserve had received a lot of precipitation over the winter. For a while, Edrengiin Ridge, the next range north of the central mountain complex, had two or three feet of snow on its heights. Down here in the valley holding Erdene, the flakes were starting to come down faster and faster, and we had one more tall range yet to cross.

In the foothills we passed a lonely stone herder's hut with adjoining stone corrals. They were full of goats taken in for the evening. After a quarter hour of

Lost in a snowstorm, practically buried beneath flakes, the white goat kid was returned to its owner, a herder already caring for another struggling new member of her herd in a mountain range on the way to the GGSPA. Photo: Joe Riis

driving higher up the slope of the range, Ankhaa spotted movement beneath a mound of fresh snow and stopped. He jumped out, brushed the snow away, and found a newborn goat kid, lost and freezing to death far from the gathered flock. We took the young animal into the van's heated interior. Held against someone's chest and covered with a coat, the kid showed encouraging signs of life as it warmed. "Okay," Odko said, interpreting for Ankhaa. "We go back." Reversing course, he drove down to the lower foothills and delivered the weak but increasingly alert youngster to a woman who emerged from the stone hut. When she greeted us, she was already holding one goat kid. Now she had two infant goats that needed help to thrive, but our thawed-out passenger at least had a chance.

The passage through the high country was treacherous in places and tested the van's high ground clearance as the vehicle busted through deepening snowdrifts. Snow kept falling. The terrain kept rising. Finally, the van's headlamp beams leveled out and then pointed down the southern slopes of the range. A river whose wide floodplain was filled with overflow ice posed the final barrier between us and Bayantooroi. Ankhaa and Amgaa walked out through the snow onto the ice to test its strength, searching for a route that might get us across without breaking through into the water. Watching the two figures from shore through the falling white flakes, I drew my coat's collar tightly around my neck to keep the wind from blasting more snow against my skin. After picking a route, Ankhaa started driving. By the time we reached the other side in the van, our feet were soaked and cold from having to push the rig free from spots where a wheel broke through the thin top layer of ice into a slushy sinkhole.

What kind of desert is this anyway?

People I ran into Stateside expected to hear tales of dodging heatstroke and deadly snakes in an ocean of scorching sand. The Gobi's different. It has grizzly bears and snow leopards—a clue to the weather. In UB, Miji told us that an automatic camera recently photographed one of the cats coming in for a drink at Altan Tevsh, where we had caught both *mazaalai* females the year before. I think the association of the Gobi with snakes comes mainly from *The Long Walk*, a popular book by Slavomir Rawicz, originally published in 1956 and later made into a movie, *The Way Back*. Rawicz's story chronicles the escape of prisoners from a brutal Siberian work camp and their 4,000-mile journey south by foot through Central Asia's drylands, Tibet, and on over the Himalayas to India. When the party crossed the Gobi, it was besieged by writhing hordes of large, lethal snakes. This was an incredible adventure—literally incredible, as in not believable, though it claimed to be a true memoir.

No one has been able to verify Rawicz's account. Of more immediate interest to me, none of the GGSPA rangers had warnings or tales about snakes. In all the miles I covered by vehicle and foot, I saw two. Both were nonpoisonous racers, pencil-thin and little more than a foot long.

We arrived at the GGSPA headquarters in the middle of the night. The next morning, Gotov, GGSPA's director, explained that while 300 millimeters (almost 12 inches) of precipitation had fallen on the mountains to the north, most of the reserve got no more than 100 millimeters (4 inches) the past year. That was only a normal amount, but normal was good, considering that droughts seemed to be coming more frequently. Gotov went on to say, through Odko, "The rangers put out a large amount of grain pellets last fall. To increase the protein, we added dog food." It was in the form of dry kibbles containing some meat by-products. North American grizzlies like that sort of dog chow well enough that some end up in trouble for snitching it from porches or storage sheds. We knew that *mazaalai* eat insects and small mammals along with an occasional lizard or bird. Though they don't appear to prey on large mammals, we and others had found evidence that they scavenge those animals' carcasses. Gotov now told us, "They ate the grain pellets, but they left the dog food," adding to the mystery of just how, when, and where meat fits into these bears' mostly vegetarian diet.

Far to the north and south, mountaintops stood shining with fresh snow above a faint haze of Gobi dust. Down in the broad plain around Bayantooroi,

Recovering from the sedative, a just-collared female Gobi bear rests by the uplifted trap door. The equipment containers near her were abandoned by the fleeing research crew when she first stood up—far sooner than expected. Photo: Joe Riis

springtime had arrived. The poplar trees planted in the reserve's courtyard were budding. Wagtails and sparrows perched on the branches. Out of the wind, the temperature grew hot by early afternoon. While the rest of us bought extra supplies in the village and rearranged gear, Odko enlisted members of the school's Gobi Bear Children's Club to fold pieces of colored paper into the shape of little envelopes. These were for holding the individual samples of Gobi bear fur she hoped to gather at the oases and analyze back in her genetics laboratory. "I didn't bring enough envelopes from UB," she said and nodded toward a cluster of schoolgirls doing the work on a tabletop. "So I found help. I already like these better."

We headed south the next morning in two vans. As always at this stage of the journey, the vehicles' load included full gas drums that leaked a little and burlap bags full of fresh goat and sheep parts, making our caravan a sort of combination of a rolling slaughterhouse and incendiary bomb. Near the base of the first set of mountains in the reserve, our group split into two. Harry, Nyamaa, and some of the rangers would travel all the way to Alaguneet and open the same four traps we had operated the previous year in the eastern mountain complex. Odko, Ankhaa, Nasaa, Joe, and I would travel to Baruuntooroi on the opposite, western end of the reserve. Our itinerary called for surveying the spring there, then moving eastward, checking every other oasis in the western and central mountain complexes en route before we rendezvoused with the group at Alaguneet. Our parting ceremony required vodka, naturally. Standing in a circle and leaning into the wind, each recipient took a turn flicking drops skyward along with invocations for safe travel and good luck for all, then tossing down a swig of liquid fire.

"We didn't start a journey with vodka one time," Harry observed as the shot glass made the rounds. "And we didn't catch any bears. You see? This stuff works."

———

THE FIRST AND ONLY TIME I HAD VISITED BARUUNTOOROI, WE PASSED QUITE a lot of wildlife as we neared the oasis. But the single bear I saw there was the gaunt, listless, old male who moved as if walking pained him. He looked to be on his last legs, and that turned out to be the case. This time, we came upon black-tailed gazelles, wild camels, and a band of twenty or so wild asses. We also stopped to watch three argali rams at almost the exact spot on the cliffy hillside where we had encountered argali two years earlier. I didn't expect to see a bear, and we didn't, but the automatic camera lens had captured images of two different *mazaalai* using the feeder between March 2 and 12. One was a large male, and he was the very picture of health—plump, especially for having just emerged after months in a den, and apparently getting plumper by the day on supplemental food.

Ankhaa stood staring at the feeding bin and shaking his head. "I filled this with food early this year," he told Odko, who translated for us. How many bags? "He says he doesn't remember. Three or maybe four." Each bag contained eighty pounds of pellets. The feeder was now completely empty. But it had served its purpose of supplying nutrition in the critical weeks before vegetation started growing this spring.

When Tumen, the founder of MAMA, visited Baruuntooroi with the rangers while distributing the pellets to this and other oases at the end of winter, he had seen a mother bear with two juvenile cubs that he estimated to be two years old. We found fresh tracks and scat among the sprouting rhubarb and wild onion close to the Baruuntooroi *ger*, where we stayed overnight. Some of the tracks were small enough to have been from a juvenile. At the end of the 2011 expedition, learning that the struggling old male I watched at this oasis had died sent my spirits on a downward slide. Now, they were rising by the same amount. A plump-looking spring grizzly was noteworthy even in good habitat. Here, it meant that between natural food sources and the troughs of the metal bins, at least some of the *mazaalai* were finding enough nutrition in this desert to do more than survive. They were able to stay in prime condition. By the same token, Tumen's sighting of the female with a pair of two-year-old offspring offered eyewitness proof that the population had recently produced babies, always a cause for optimism. More than that, the juveniles had made it through the early years of life, a period when between a third and a half of the young grizzlies in mountain ranges with much richer habitat than this desert typically die of natural causes.

For the next two days, we drove from oasis to oasis and from one patrol *ger* to the next, checking cameras, noting wildlife signs, tightening the barbed wire strung around feeders, and collecting *mazaalai* fur. Months earlier, Baboo had arrested a group of men in a truck poaching firewood farther north in the GGSPA. They were targeting the largest saxaul bushes, which grow to the size of small trees in places. Now, while en route, we encountered fresh truck tire tracks leading into a cluster of low mountains. Ankhaa felt sure that a big vehicle this deep in the reserve was not after firewood. It had to belong to a gang of ninjas with mining equipment. He wanted to take off after them but thought better of it. He was, after all, driving a Project van whose passengers included civilians. When we reached a high point in the terrain, he would try using his two-way radio to try to get through to head-quarters and report the location of the trespassers' tracks.

Every other place we passed was undisturbed except by wildlife. The settings looked exactly as I remembered them. With few areas of shifting sands and the rest of its features hardened to withstand the sun and cold and wind, this desert seemed almost fixed in time apart from the cycles of the seasons. Almost. One of the automatic cameras Joe wired to the cliff wall on the side of a wash was found months later far down the channel, carried there by a flash flood that had roared through the canyon several feet deep strewing boulders and brush in new patterns for miles all along the channel.

Harry and the usual crew, who had been joined by Baboo, the twenty-five-year-old patrol ranger based in Ekhiin Gol, greeted us at Alaguneet on April 23. The news was no news. There were no bear pictures on the cameras at the oases and no fresh sign of bears. In a reversal of the usual pattern, the eastern mountain complex appeared to have received less precipitation than the other complexes. Most of the vegetation still lay dormant. Perhaps the *mazaalai* were using areas where the spring growth was farther along. Returning to this segment of the GGSPA for the capture season was beginning to look like an inauspicious choice.

Harry had nevertheless activated the radio collars he was carrying in order to test their ability to transmit once we affixed them to bears. Three worked perfectly, but the fourth device would only send its GPS signal. The collar's other transmitter, which sent a VHF (Very High Frequency) signal, wouldn't turn on. Its lower power emission carried only a few miles at most, but its regular cheeps were the key to tracking both an animal's movement when we were nearby and the collar's location after it dropped off.

Harry used every programming trick he knew to tell this balky collar's software to start up the VHF signal. Finally, he called the equipment maker on his satellite phone and was advised that an interior device called the reed switch sometimes gets stuck. What to do? The tech specialist told Harry to grip the collar—which cost $2,500—firmly and smack the section containing the satellite and VHF radio transmitters on the ground. Harry shrugged and gave the thing a WHAP! against the wooden floor of the patrol hut. He switched on the radio receiver. His dubious expression re-formed into a smile, and he turned up the volume so everyone could hear: Cheep! Cheep! Cheep! All fixed.

But it would help if a bear, any bear, showed up at one of the four springs with newly baited traps.

"We'll give it a try for a while longer," Harry said after dinner. "If we're not seeing any activity at the sites, we'll pack up and move over to the Shar Khuls *ger* and open the traps in the central complex."

I left to sleep in my tent, glad to be done with all-day van journeys for a while. Waking early for my first full day in Alaguneet, I performed my ritual of pissing on the thirstiest-looking plant I could find within pre-caffeine shuffling distance. I returned to sip thermos coffee by the tent while watching dawn's glow brighten behind the ridges to the east, then set off on a hike. The desert was utterly still. There was no wind, nary a breeze, not a bird in flight or an insect moving in the cold. The camp was just as quiet, the Mongolians having stayed up late making a party out of their reunion after a few days apart. I climbed to a low pass and paused at the cairn placed as a marker. Wondering how long ago the cairn was first built, I added a stone and then walked on to the canyon where the Altan Tevsh spring welled from the ground.

The gravel in the wash showed no *mazaalai* prints. I continued through the bend in the canyon where the wall displayed petroglyphs of ibex and camels and edged along the last outcrop for a peek at the trap by the feeder. The door was still up. Nothing moved except sunlight slipping farther down the canyonside. I had the feeling of being on a stage or movie set where something was supposed to happen, but I had got the time of the performance wrong. Upon returning to camp, I noticed the light hitting a corner of the hut so as to illuminate claw and teeth marks—a bear had once again come to chew and scratch the wood. The marks were in more or less the same area as those we found in 2012. This time, there were even a few tufts of fur for Odko to collect as samples.

We set out later in the morning in two vans, one to get water from the pool at the Suujiin Bulag spring, the other to check the two remaining oases with traps farther north. The first van was leaking oil from the differential. Ankhaa planned to fix it later in the day. The other van had a broken starter jury-rigged to operate until it, too, could be properly repaired. It took any number of tries to get the thing to fire up. Before separating, we had to stop by the big cairns at the foot of the rubble slope below Tsagaan Bogd and make offerings to the mountain spirits. Whereas the early morning was a study in silence, coveys of chukars had since taken over the stage, walking, flying in short whirring bursts, clucking, and *pitchoo-wichoo*-ing on all sides. They added a background chorus to our ceremony of asking the powers atop the peak to help all the life here thrive.

This beseeching business really worked well. Why don't I do it more often? The trap at Muktar Zadgai didn't simply have a bear; it was *filled* with a bear.

We wouldn't know the age or sex for sure until the drugs Harry injected it with kicked in, but this was one hefty *mazaalai*. By the time the animal succumbed to the sedatives, the sun was high and the day, a rare windless one, had grown awfully hot. We dragged the bear out and laid it close to the side of the metal box so that most of its body rested in the trap's narrow rectangle of shade. A normal body temperature for a grizzly bear is around 101 degrees F. Using a rectal thermometer, Harry got a reading higher than that and immediately directed several of us to bring water from the spring, which came out of the ground chilled that time of year. Moving quickly, we hauled jugs of it back to splash onto the bare skin around the captive's groin—it was a male—and the "armpits" where his front legs met the side of his chest, just as one would do for a human threatened with hyperthermia. Next, we poured water onto the bear's coat and rubbed it in through the outer hairs and dense underfur to be sure it reached the skin. Before we quit, we had essentially given our captive a coldwater bath.

There was a lot of bear to wash. The crew arranged a rope harness around the male and attached it to the lower hook of a weight scale. The upper hook was then tied to a pole about five feet long. Two rangers, one at each end of the pole, lifted it into the air. A little way. Two more crew members grabbed on to help. It was still a struggle to get the bear high enough off the ground that his head and legs swung freely in the air. Others on the team crowded in to lend an arm. The scale only read up to 150 kilograms. That wasn't quite

Because *mazaalai* can neither burrow into hillsides in the Gobi stonescape nor amass insulating fat due to their meager diet, they rely on thick outer fur and dense underfur to provide insulation while hibernating through the cold winter, often partly exposed in caves. Photo: Doug Chadwick

enough. The mass of our bear pulled the marker half an inch beyond the last number. Harry estimated the animal's weight at 155 to 160 kilograms—at least 350 pounds.

The largest bear previously documented in the study was the male named Yokozuna, after the champion sumo-style wrestlers. This was the bear that helped dissuade Mongolian authorities from opening up part of the reserve to gold mining years earlier. The locations from Yokozuna's collar left no doubt that his range extended into the proposed mining area. A bear the size of the new male might well range between all three mountain complexes, too. The way I saw it, the most important thing he had to tell us and the Mongolian government was that the desert reserve, left uncompromised by development, could grow truly big, fat, strong, and healthy *mazaalai*. And that boded well for the future of the population as a whole. Look at him!

The Project held off naming the two bears collared in 2012. Team members decided that honor should be reserved for people in the towns nearest the GGSPA, Gobi Bear Children's Clubs, or perhaps a prominent politician who might be inspired to promote guarding the protected area from potential threats. This male would be named in the same fashion. But I already had my own name for him: Big Bawa (bawa being how the general term for bear, *baavgai*, is pronounced.)

Not long after Big Bawa began to shake off the drugs' effects, he made a staggery run at the van. Although we were expecting it, the result was still chaos when everyone who was standing beside the vehicle or perched on a nearby rock tried to climb in through the side door at once. The van's iffy starter finally cranked the engine into life, but before we could gain any speed, Big Bawa's claws were scratching at the rear doors while people frantically tried to close the windows. Which was a lost cause. The inside latch rarely worked unless someone went outside and pressed the window hard against the frame, and that definitely wasn't going to happen at this point. As the van wheeled farther away, Big Bawa turned and ran back toward the trap. "Aw no, not again," Joe said, shaking his head. Big Bawa attacked one of Joe's remotely operated cameras set close to ground level. After chewing a while on a few thousand dollars' worth of optics, the male unerringly homed in on Joe's second camera in a different location and crunched another few thousand dollars' worth of digital photo equipment. Then he walked off to the big oasis pool below a cliff for a good long drink.

Both camera bodies were trashed. That made five lost to druggy *mazaalai* in the two seasons Joe had joined the Project. The positive news was that at least one of the lenses Big Bawa bit looked as though it might still be operable. On the other hand, Joe was down to one working camera body, and this was the first bear of the capture season. Big Bawa was last seen wandering through the *Phragmites* grasses spreading outward from the open water. Despite his size, the dried blonde stalks and seedheads were too tall and thick for us to keep him in view. We just had to hope he wouldn't come rushing back out while Joe gathered up the remains of his camera gear on the open ground near the trap.

There was vodka all around that night at Alaguneet to celebrate the capture. A toast to our mothers and fathers and friends and one big chub of a *mazaalai*.

The rangers checking trap sites the next day saw a wolf and an ibex by Muktar Zadgai but no hint that Big Bawa was sticking around. He had traveled on, and we were once again without any fresh sign or automatic camera photos of *mazaalai* at the four springs with traps. The only bear we knew of in the area was one of the females caught at Altan Tevsh the year before. By calling his wife in Fairbanks, Alaska, on the sat phone, Harry could have her read off the latest GPS locations from the female's collar as they were downloaded onto the computer at their home. The current coordinates showed the female in a same set of hills where she had denned during the winter. Two days after catching Big Bawa, Harry elected to go search for that den and examine it. He also wanted to try locating the female by homing in on her VHF radio signal with a handheld antenna. Getting a glimpse of her was not the main goal. If we could just manage to get close enough within the puzzle of ridges and knolls, we might find tracks that would tell us whether or not she had young at her side.

The place we were looking for was miles away to the northwest. We drove there, pausing for two hours while Ankhaa rebuilt the carburetor after the engine quit. After arriving, we set off on a hike through the hills. The route, if sketched, would resemble a tangle of dropped yarn. We were still picking our way across a succession of promontories as night descended. All we'd found were diggings for rhubarb, the fairly recent tracks of one adult bear, and older tracks that might have been from the same animal.

I skipped my morning hike the next day. The early wind shaking the tent was cold enough that I put on a hat and gloves as well as my down coat. I needed to pump more water from the camp barrels into my drinking bottles and the jug by the tent and reload my daypack with trail food. I was taking my time with these minor chores, looking around and wondering what the day would bring when Harry came hustling out of his tent. He appeared to be dancing some kind of freeform jig, hopping and grabbing at one of his pant legs and shaking it. A moment later, he was pulling his pants down in front of the hut while a bemused group of Mongols looked on from the doorway.

"Shit! Something stung me hard," he said. I was thinking, *camel spider*, as Harry probably was. These arachnids are actually a pseudoscorpion rather than a spider. While they aren't venomous, their bite can inflict a painful wound that often becomes infected. The worst part is imagining the bite. We'd all seen these alien-looking creatures putting their multiple slice-and-dice mouthparts to work scissoring into a lizard and sucking the victim into a shriveled husk. Instead, as Harry turned the pant leg inside out, he revealed a true scorpion clinging to the fabric.

"Little bastard got me right in the crotch the first time, and it just stung my leg." The scorpion started across toward the other leg. Three seconds later, Harry's pants were off and lying on the ground. Yet now that Harry at least knew what had been attacking him, he turned calm. Joe was leaving with the crew on a water run to Suujiin Bulag, but he ran to his tent first and returned to leave an Epi-Pen (injectable dose of epinephrine) with Harry, just in case. Harry called Miji in UB on the sat phone to ask his opinion of what to do next. The former GGSPA director wasn't home, so Harry called Amgaa, the Project scientist with the most experience in the Gobi, and asked his advice. Amgaa advised vodka. I learned this when Harry walked up and offered me a shot in a tin cup. It was the middle of the morning.

"Scorpion medicine?"

"Yup."

"But I didn't get stung by a scorpion, Harry."

"Well, you could be."

"Right. Cheers."

In no time, everyone had come around for an oral dose of the scorpion sting medicine.

Harry told me, "It's sort of like all those times flying when we hit the kind of turbulence that makes you wonder when the wings are going to rip off. I'd tell myself that if we die, it won't bother me a bit, because I'll be dead. That doesn't mean my asshole wasn't puckered up like it could hold onto the seat all by itself." After another few minutes went by and he still hadn't felt the start of any virulent reaction to the scorpion's jabs, Harry decided that the little beast might have grabbed him with its pincers rather than stung him with its poison-packed tail. That, or the arachnid's poison glands were dry. Either way, Harry became his usual unruffled self, going off to write and bring his field notebook up to date.

The traps had all been checked. Nobody was discussing plans to investigate anything else. It was turning into a catch-up day in camp. I trekked out toward Tsagaan Bogd and spent the better part of an afternoon poking along the mountain's base just chuckin' with the chukars and watching toad-headed agama lizards race from rock to leafless shrub as the day grew hot.

Shamans from outlying villages are among the people who come to pay their respects at the foot of Tsagaan Bogd. Some go on to climb the mountain and commune with the spirits more directly at the summit. Baboo, the eastern mountain complex moto-ranger, told me one evening that he now considered himself a shaman. If I understood Odko's translations correctly, Baboo's transformation began after he crashed his motorbike somewhere and broke his leg. He went to a shaman, who told him, "You have a spirit following you. It is the spirit of an eighty-one-year-old man who lived 800 years ago. Go to a doctor in UB, and your leg will heal in twenty-one days." According to Baboo, it did. He said that everyone was amazed, but he wasn't. He had discovered that he could consult directly with this spirit, which sometimes took the form of eight yellow horses. Other spirits can re-shape themselves as ravens and eagles, he told me. "The spirit that was following me is now inside. I can speak to it, and it can speak through me."

Baboo explained that there are white spirits, which heal and guide, and black spirits that ward off bad luck and trouble. "To be a healer," he continued, "I would have to train for years under a religious leader from the Blue Sky tradition. I don't know if I will do that. Maybe. But as a shaman, I can help people in other ways today. My main responsibility is to protect children and my relatives."

Fittingly, Harry made the decision that evening to give the GGSPA's largest known bear a name after all. It was to be Dagvaa, after an Ekhiin Gol ranger who worked with Harry during the early years of the study. This man, whom Harry grew fond of, was Baboo's father. He had passed away. While giving the bear the name Dagvaa was well-intended, it was later made known to Harry that the gesture was problematic. One wasn't supposed to refer to a deceased family member directly by his or her name, for the powers of the spirit world are deep and complex and not to be casually summoned. Accordingly, Dagvaa the animal went back to merely being Bear Number 15. But to me, he remained Big Bawa.

Odko broke off translating long enough to mention that she was very close to her grandparents when they were alive and that she still talks with them often. Whether this resembles the way Westerners sometimes speak when visiting the grave of someone they loved and continue to love or is a give-and-take conversation, I didn't inquire. When planning a trip, Odko added, she consults a shaman to learn if there might be problems ahead. For instance, before she went to study snow leopard genetics in India, the shaman reassured her that things would go favorably. He also gave her a red ribbon to wear around her wrist. It was an extra precaution. "To keep … badness away," Odko said.

When trapping operations were based in Puji's patrol territory and he joined the team, I'd sometimes see him rolling "knucklebones"—the dice-size metacarpals and metatarsals from a goat or sheep that had been part of the crew's meat supply. He would cast the cleaned bones onto a board and silently study them at length prior to setting off on a long scouting mission. As a biologist, I viewed this augury, like other forms of divination, less as superstition than as a means for the mind to access its deeper sectors. In Puji's case, his conscious brain might be probing for information about impending weather, developing mechanical problems, or hints of unusual human activity in the area unconsciously picked up by his senses and tucked away in memory banks. Perhaps contemplating the bones was an indirect way for him to talk to his body as well—to assess his own biorhythms and state of readiness. The ritual made me think of something else Odko said: "Sometimes I feel there is a much bigger world around us than the one we know." Is there anyone, young or old, American or Mongolian, herder or scientist, who hasn't felt the same way?

———

AFTER A FEW MORE DAYS WITHOUT ANY BEAR SIGN AT THE OASES, THE TEAM closed down the traps and split up again. Harry, Joe, and most of the crew left for the Shar Khuls camp to prepare for a trapping effort in the central mountain complex. Baboo motorcycled back to Ekhiin Gol. Nyamaa, Nasaa, and I followed him there in a van. After stopping for lunch at his home, we continued east to the spring just outside the reserve, set up a fifty-five-gallon barrel feeder, and stocked it with grain pellets. Bears had occasionally been reported in the Ekhiin Gol area, and Miji told us that during his tenure as director of the reserve he periodically heard rumors of the odd bear roaming terrain still farther east in the population's historical range. By providing supplemental food in transitional areas such as the spring where we placed the barrel, the Project hoped to lure some *mazaalai* beyond the GGSPA on the chance they would go on to reclaim some of that eastern portion of their former homeland, much of which was now protected as Gobi Gurvan Saikhan National Park.

Between Ekhiin Gol, where we spent the night, and the camp at Shar Khuls stood sixty miles of low mountains, hills beyond counting, gullied bad-lands, and featureless plains. Rather than use the roundabout route they knew would eventually take us there, the rangers decided to find a shortcut. Before long, they were studying their handheld GPS units intently and frowning. They weren't exactly lost in the Gobi, but I can't say they weren't perplexed in the Gobi. Nyamaa and Nasaa took turns directing the driver, a young man from UB named Lama who had never been in this part of the country before. If the van lipped out on a fall-away ridge, we would try a different route, then another when we found ourselves bogging down on a slope with more sand than packed dust beneath the gravel. How about the line of hills over there? Who knew they would lead out into a boulderfield where the maximum speed possible was two miles an hour? Maybe if we backtrack and try slipping around that line of mountains over there? Nyamaa sang and hummed to himself the whole time except when discussing route changes with Nasaa.

If I ever stop going to *mazaalai* country, these all-day, thrill-a-minute van rides in the heart of Long Gone will be the thing I miss the least. Finally, in the hottest part of the afternoon, I made out the profile of Red Mountain far in the shimmering distance. Camp was only a few miles beyond that. Then the van stopped running. I didn't speak enough Mongolian to understand what the problem was. My guess, from the English words the rangers knew, was that the engine had run too long without cooling down. Had it fried? Not quite. Forty minutes later, Lama was able to coax the thing back to life, and we reached the Shar Khuls *ger* just before a leaking rear tire went completely flat.

"Oh man, you missed it," Joe said by way of greeting. "Yeah," Harry added, "we just saw a snow leopard, four wolves, and a giant ibex. And an argali, a fox, and a big Gobi bear." Their tone let me know they were messing with me. They had seen those animals, but only as images on the automatic camera when they went to check Tsuvluur Us. This was the spring where the team had placed a barrel feeder the year before, on the south side of the central mountain complex. They were welcoming me with the heartening news that this water source continued to be well used by wildlife in general and was now offering extra food to at least one *mazaalai*.

Toward evening, the reserve director, Gotov, arrived with Boldoo from Bayantooroi, bringing two renovated traps. Puji came motorcycling back from a late check of Khotul Us, the farthest of the four central complex oases the crew would focus on for capturing bears once the additional traps were put in place. Big surprise: a multiple reunion like this called for vodka. The director had also brought fermented camel's milk. An impromptu party took shape, and the entertainment was traditional wrestling. Nasaa never took a match against Nyamaa, who towered over him and must have outweighed him nearly two to one. But as far as winning people's respect for persever-ance, Nasaa came out on top. I think he inspired Joe—Superslender Gobi

One of the automatic cameras deployed at the feeders caught this mother bear defending her subadult youngster from a larger bear. Photo: Courtesy of the Gobi Bear Project

Joe, as he was known during his memorable but extremely brief wrestling career—to give Ankhaa a try. Within seconds, Ankhaa had grabbed one of Joe's arms and flung him to the ground. Gobi Joe did not persevere. His arm socket was still sore two days later when Bayasa and his father, Amgaa, arrived at camp. With more vodka.

I recognize that this is beginning to sound a bit too much like a drinking safari. But two bottles of vodka ceremonially passed around a circle of fifteen people in between toasts and speeches over the course of an evening hardly amounts to a bacchanal. The traps got set up and checked daily, and other oases in the area were surveyed for sign while Odko and whoever went along that day collected fur samples. In the cool of early morning before the rest of the camp stirred, I got in my dawn ramble, sometimes with Joe. We fit in evening forays too, traipsing through the canyons or out onto the broad plain to the north. If there was a hitch in the operation, it was strictly from lack of cooperation by the bears.

The first excitement at the traps came after a freight train wind rumbled through overnight and shook a raised trap door until it fell shut. A crew arriving the next morning in a light breeze enjoyed a few moments of thinking a *mazaalai* might be inside. Twice after that, tingles of expectation gave way to the sight of a long-eared hedgehog (*Hemiechinus auritus*, a one-pound ball of spines with the head of a gremlin) that had unaccountably tripped a trapdoor shut. Once, according to the automatic camera, a fairly big bear went all the way in but somehow avoided stepping on the treadle and triggering the trap.

Here, then, were fifteen people, a genuine crowd for this chunk of the Gobi, doing everything they could to capture a second bear for the season, all to no avail. The crew had been through periods like this before. While getting skunked day after day was disappointing, I didn't sense any frustration growing among the team. Just the same, I dropped my shtick of striding into the *ger* at breakfast and announcing, "Hey, gang. It looks like it's gonna be another clear and sunny day!" By 9 a.m., we were looking for shade. The thermometer reached the upper 80s (F) by midday. It was startling to think that in just another few weeks, the temperature could be rising as much as 30 degrees (F) higher.

The hot days were bringing out tremendous numbers of wingless grasshoppers this year. They were everywhere underfoot. The bears might have been eating so many of these pudgy insects that the grain pellets and sweet treats in our metal boxes no longer seemed as tempting. Ticks were also thriving in the warmth. At some of the oases where we helped Odko search for fur on the barbed wire wrapped around the trunks of rub trees, our presence would spark multiple stampedes of camel ticks (the larger—and much faster—of the two species in the area) from the surrounding grasses and brush out toward our legs. When I went to bathe or clean my clothes at the stream coming from the Shar Khuls reed beds, I always did my washing a few yards back from the bank to keep from contaminating the flow. But now I had to do my washing fifty yards away on a bare hillside to escape the tick surge whenever I ventured to the water to refill the bucket.

One warm night inside the *ger*, a camel spider emerged between cracks in the floorboard. The Mongolians, who had extensive experience with the creatures, all went for the door. These pseudoscorpions are predators from the dawn of terrestrial life. Their long legs come with fine filaments extending far to the sides, sensitive to the faintest movement, which triggers an instant attack. Watching a camel spider use its prehistoric array of mouthparts to spear a grasshopper, excavate its head, and begin dining on the body from the inside, Harry offered this observation about the animal kingdom: "Man, once they get more than four legs, they develop some nasty habits."

Counting microbial forms, 99.999 percent of the organisms on the planet have few or none of the traits that allow humans to empathize with them. The irony is that while each of our bodies is made up of trillions of human cells, at least that many microbes inhabit our guts, our mouths, our pores, and every other piece of us in multitudes beyond counting. The meta-irony is that the 0.001 percent of Earth's life-forms that do possess traits we admire—elephants, great apes, the great wild cats; dolphins; the creatures in which people recognize shared qualities—are taking the worst hit from human activities in the Anthropocene.

You'd think we would try harder to at least keep fellow animals with backbones and no more than four legs around, especially the ones with warm blood and fur that nurse their young and have obvious emotions and learning abilities. How did we let matters get to the point where snow leopards, double-humped wild camels, Gobi grizzly bears, polar bears, sloth bears, sun bears, spectacled bears, and a quarter to a third—or more—of all the other big wild vertebrates on the planet are at risk of vanishing, if not during our lifetime then on our children's or grandchildren's watch? These are the kinds of animals whose lives fascinate and inspire us, and have done so since the earliest tales were told. How did efforts to conserve such species in the wild come to be viewed as subsidiary to current economic and social issues? Why is saving wildlife thought of as just one of many special interest causes, a hobby, a nice thing to do if you like that sort of nature stuff? As a position to be supported or opposed depending on which political ideology you identify with? I am so far from being able to understand this kind of reasoning that it gets to be important for me to spend time where I simply don't hear any world news. The Gobi works splendidly for that.

———

THE DIRECTOR AND MOST OF THE RANGERS DEPARTED FOR BAYANTOOROI ON May 6. Pared down to a small enough crew to make the *ger* feel spacious, we had two days left to catch a bear before closing the traps for the year. There was no happy movie ending. Bears were coming in to the sites and sniffing around the closed-off feeders, but they avoided the food in the traps. They may have been previously captured bears that were extra wary of entering any more metal boxes. One bear came two nights in a row. It knocked around the motion-activated camera and auxiliary flashes Joe had set up on a canyon wall next to the most commonly used wildlife trail to the feeder. But the animal kept clear of the trap, refusing to give in to the tempting scents of the sweet treats inside.

Undeterred, Joe salvaged his equipment and deployed it farther up the canyon, anchoring everything to the rock face at a narrow pinch point in the wash. He intended to leave the gear and have Puji collect it a month or two later. We left for UB that afternoon. Two days later, I was watching the

BBC news on a television in our hotel room and learned that the amount of carbon dioxide in the atmosphere measured at an observatory on the summit of Mauna Loa in Hawaii topped 400 parts per million for the first time since scientists began taking measurements there fifty-five years earlier. The reporter said it was also probably the first time such a concentration had been reached in the past three million years.

Since carbon dioxide is the primary greenhouse gas responsible for global warming, exceeding the benchmark of 400 parts per million seemed a bad omen for desert-dwelling people and wildlife. The curious thing about the newscast was that the lengthiest story dealt with three young women kept captive in a man's basement for years. Next came a discussion about capital gains taxes, followed by another news item. This one was about a building collapse.

When you're yelling at the old TV in an Ulaanbaatar hotel room where half the lights don't work and the bedcovers have holes from cigarette burns in them, it's probably time to switch over to one of Mongolia's wrestling channels. Which is what I did. Then I flew home.

In mid-May, I was back in northwest Montana and mowing the lawn (what a concept) and thinking of all the camels and wild asses and *mazaalai* the cuttings could feed. Every year when I return from the Gobi and look up at the thickly forested mountainsides alive with meltwater rivulets and cascading creeks, I say the same thing to myself: Those grizzlies out there have no idea how good they've got it. They take all that soft, lush abundance of vegetation I see on the surrounding mountainsides as their due, just as I usually take the verdant fields around my house for granted. But for every moment of the first week back, I feel as though I've been dropped into the emerald Land of Oz.

Near the end of the month, Harry called with news that the rangers found a dead female bear near Altan Tevsh. It appeared to be one of the young females we caught and collared at that oasis in 2012. The cause of death was unknown. Harry also had more news to pass along. When the rangers got around to systematically examining all the photos from camera traps taken in 2012, they found one from Mukhar Zadgai, where we had trapped Big Bawa this spring. The image appears to be of him, a year younger than when we met. Large and chubby with a white blaze on his shoulder, the male in the picture was mating with a young ear-tagged female. Although she was likely one of the two females we captured that year at Altan Tevsh, the quality of the nighttime image was too poor to permit a positive identification. The union could have produced cubs this year, but if it did, and the female in the photo is the one recently found dead, those cubs will have starved to death by now.

After that call, the story of the dead female turned into something of a *mazaalai* murder mystery. Rangers performed an autopsy, noting that the body had more signs of damage than scavengers would have caused. The female had been in a fight that left her with grave wounds and busted ribs. There was fur—not her own—stuck in her teeth. Some came from wolves. Yet some belonged to another bear. May and June are the breeding period for grizzlies. One possible scenario was that a male attempted to mate with her, things went wrong, she fought her suitor, and he ended up mauling her.

That explanation would make the most sense if she were defending cubs at the time. As with some other carnivores such as lions, male bears may kill the offspring of a breeding age female they meet. The loss causes her to come back into breeding condition sooner than if she were to continue nursing and tending young. The male thus creates an opportunity to impregnate the female and pass on his genes. However, Baboo made a follow-up visit to the carcass and reported that the female's mammary glands were not enlarged and producing milk, which means that she had not given birth to cubs this year. And what about the wolf fur in her mouth? Probably drawn by the scent of blood, a pack might have come upon the injured female and, taking advantage of her weakened state, finished her off. But the wolf hairs among her teeth said she didn't go down easily.

Another unsparing possibility is that the female encountered wolves and fought them off but suffered serious injuries during the battle. A hungry male bear then came upon the wounded female and killed and partially ate her, but, again, it cost the attacker some hide. Around the period of her death, Big Bawa's GPS signal fixed his position as no more than a kilometer (six-tenths of a mile) away. Although some other male bear might have been responsible for the female's death, Big Bawa was the only one in the vicinity with an active radio collar and therefore became the prime suspect. My image of him as an example of *mazaalai* overcoming the challenges of a stingy environment to become stout and strong wasn't shaken. Yet I could no longer picture this male apart from the role he may have played in subtracting a breeding-age female from the population. Objectively, I knew he was just being a bear. My opinion of his behavior didn't mean a thing. Emotionally, I wanted to kick his big fat butt. Of course, that wouldn't do anything except get me mauled, too.

On July 2, Harry e-mailed me a series of photos taken in early May by the automatic camera at Bogt Tsagaan Ders, the oasis with a wide pool and broad field of reeds in the western mountain complex. The nighttime images showed an adult female in the background at the feeding bin and two little baby bears close together in the foreground. Even though photos of older juveniles have provided indisputable visual proof of reproduction in the

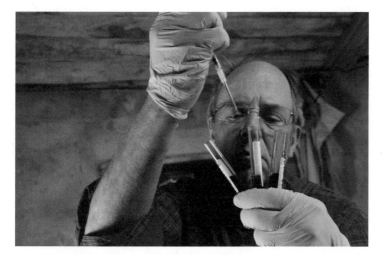

Harry prepares samples of blood drawn from a captured bear. Lab analysis can determine various aspects of the animal's nutritional status, hormonal condition, and general health. Photo: Joe Riis

population over the years, it was a coup to have these images of brand new Gobi bears in 2013. They may have been the first pictures of baby *mazaalai* ever taken.

The rarity of photos of young Gobi bears didn't necessarily reflect a rarity of births. Rather, the researchers believed, mothers were reluctant to bring small offspring to the artificial feeding sites where they risked encountering larger and possibly dangerous bears. This behavior could partially explain the population's unequal sex ratio of fourteen males and just eight females determined by Proctor and Odko's hair-sampling survey. On North America's Pacific coast, grizzly females with newborns are exceptionally wary and defensive around concentrations of grizz at salmon-spawning streams. Some new mothers avoid the fishing areas altogether despite the superabundance of rich food to be had there. This is why the Gobi Bear Project, the conservation group MAMA, and the GGSPA were working together to place more feeding bins at or close to oases. The idea was to make it easier for mothers with young to obtain grain pellets when a larger bear was coming to drink and feed in the area. Having secondary bins available near a water source would benefit newly independent juveniles and subdominant adult bears in the same way.

The babies in the early May photos looked so small and hopelessly cute, anyone who viewed them was bound to be smitten. These were the most hopeful images caught on camera that I'd seen in a long time. More than any other subject, they represented what the Year of Protecting Gobi Bears was supposed to be all about—the promise of new life.

10

To Be Continued

Deep within the southern reaches of the Great Gobi Strictly Protected Area, the oasis named Ulzii Belgech lies hidden among some of the tallest peaks in the central mountain complex. The only way to get there by vehicle from our Shar Khuls base camp was to drive over a couple of lesser ranges toward a break in the main chain and then start following the loops of a wash squeezed between ever-higher cliff walls. That wasn't a rare sort of route for us, but the floor of this particular slot canyon was more gullied and boulder-strewn than most. Even by Gobi standards it was seemingly endless. We made the trip infrequently. I could never tell where we were along the succession of curves until we came to one with time-worn figures of camels, asses, and ibex etched into the rocks on one side. Close at last! Little more than a mile beyond the petrogylphs waited water, trees, a Project feeding bin with barbed wire strung around it, and an automatic camera focused on the location.

From the springs, a short walk would take us within sight of an unusual formation on a ledge above the base of a cliff. It was a hand-built wall meant to serve as a defensive perimeter. Bandits put it in place a century earlier while holed up here between raids. According to our rangers, the leader was a Buddhist lama. But he was much more and much less than that. The most notorious outlaw of his day in all of Mongolia, he was a real twisted blood-and-smoking-skull-lovin' package of loco, and his aim was to rule an empire. I'll let the man introduce himself through some lines he wrote in 1912:

I am a mendicant monk from the Russian Tsar's kingdom, but I am born of the great Mongols. My herds are on the Volga River, my water source is the Irtysh. There are many hero warriors with me, I have many riches. Now I have come to meet with you beggars, you remnants of the Oirats, in the time when the war for power begins. Will you support the enemy? My homeland is Altai, Irtysh, Khobuk-sari, Emil, Bortala, and Alatai. This is the Oirat mother country. By descent I am the great-grandson of Amursana, the reincarnation of Mahakala, owning the horse Maralbashi. I am he whom they call the hero Dambiijantsan. I came to move my pastures back to my own land, to collect my subject households and bondservants, to give favour, and to move freely.

He went by the name of Ja Lama and claimed to be from the southeastern European region of Astrakhan, where the delta of the Volga River empties into the north end of the Caspian Sea. Formerly part of the Mongol empire and then the Ottoman Turk empire, Astrakhan was absorbed by Russia

[Previous Spread] An ancient stone artifact—probably a grinding tool—discovered in a cave in the western mountain complex (and given to a Mongolian university). Photo: Doug Chadwick

Ja Lama. Photo: public domain

during the sixteenth century. When Ja Lama first showed up in Mongolia around 1890 (some say it was later), most of the country was under the sway of China's Qing dynasty. Russia was trying to extend its influence from the north, while various Mongol khans led insurrections against both forms of foreign control. Proclaiming himself the descendant of an Oirat prince as well as the reincarnation of a renowned holy man, Ja Lama gathered followers and focused on agitating against Chinese rule. That got him arrested and deported to Russia—three times.

The Qing claim to Outer Mongolia began to crumble in 1911 under pressure from the forces of the Mongolian Revolution for independence. Suddenly, Ja Lama was back from Russia and raising an army. With a force of 2,000, he joined other Mongol warlords in battles that drove the Chinese from the northern city of Khovd. As he went on to liberate additional territory, his reputation grew. Ja Lama's backstory of being a reborn Buddhist lama was now accompanied by rumors that he was bulletproof and could never be killed. Before long, he was given official recognition as the military governor of a large western segment of the country. It was beginning to look as though his dream of re-establishing an Oirat kingdom might actually play out.

But Ja Lama was gaining a reputation as well for ruthless slaughter. Although some of the many versions of Ja Lama's doings stretch the limits of belief, they all agree on his penchant for cruelty. He was said to inflict tortures that were beyond awful on captured troops and be particularly keen on ripping out still-beating hearts. He put the heads of some enemies on display and turned the heads of others into skull bowls in which he cooked the hearts mixed with the victims' entrails, and.... Let's just agree that this was not the monk you'd choose to teach core Buddhist tenets of peace and compassion. Once he gained a measure of authority over the western region, Ja Lama imposed quirky but fearfully strict codes of moral and religious behavior—even of hygiene. To discourage any of his subjects from even thinking about bending the rules, he would personally gouge out an offender's eyes or beat the person to death in public. Small wonder he only drank from wells he dug himself to be sure that the water hadn't been poisoned.

An early map of east-central Asia. Map: public domain

The region where western Mongolia, China, Russia, and the now-independent Republic of Khazakstan come together holds a complicated mosaic of ethnicities and cultures. Through the second decade of the twentieth century, China tried to reassert its former control over the area while Russia worked to exert its own influence without appearing to threaten the Mongols' newfound sense of autonomy. Uncomfortable with Ja Lama's tyrannical operating style and concerned that he would actually succeed in reviving Oirat and create a separatist state, the Russians orchestrated his arrest by Mongolian officials in 1914. He was imprisoned for a year, then carted off to Siberia. From there he made his way back to Astrakhan. A man who met him there reported that Ja Lama was barely recognizable, having morphed from a furious robed monk with reputed supernatural talents into a dapper Russian gentleman in a tailored suit and top hat who insisted that he wanted nothing more to do with Mongols and battle.

By 1918, however, he had again slipped back into Mongolia. The political scene remained in flux, not to say tumultuous. White Russians still loyal to the Tsar battled pursuing Red Russians representing the Bolshevik Revolution that had dethroned the Romanov dynasty. For their part, the Chinese threatened to absorb more of Outer Mongolia even as the last of the old Qing and Manchu rulers battled revolutionary forces within China itself. Ja Lama kept busy trying to organize a rebellion against the Chinese ensconced in southern Mongolia. He urged temples and monasteries to join his cause of forming an empire whose capital would become renowned as a religious center rivaling Lhasa or Mecca. Though Mongolian officials had no more love for China than Ja Lama did, they issued yet another arrest warrant for the uncontrollably wild and weird monk.

Ja Lama fled to the Gobi with a large band of followers. There, he set about robbing traders along the branch of the Silk Road between Mongolia and Tibet. Conducting raids primarily in the section of the desert under Chinese control, he targeted the richest caravans and once made off with a fabulous shipment of gold. Or so that chapter of his story goes. It might even be true.

The oasis and its surroundings are less than a day's horseback ride from the current border of China. Whenever we wandered around Ulzii Belgech searching for *mazaalai* tracks, I imagined Ja Lama and his ragtag desperadoes returning to bivouac between the crags with fresh plunder. I could shut my eyes and see evening shadows turning to night in the canyon bottom. The poplar grove and tamarisk thickets begin to glow with the light from campfires as the families that some of the monk's followers brought along prepared meals. Fermented mare's milk is passed around, and revelry echoes off the surrounding cliffs, far from the eyes and ears of the world. With his long-barreled rifle always close at hand, Ja Lama is making a careful inventory of the loot. He orders it guarded upon pain of dismemberment and strides off to join the others with an extra bounce in his step. For him, after all, this life on the prowl has nothing to do with common thieving. It's about amassing a fortune large enough to help bring a holy Oirat kingdom into being.

The outlaws made camps at many places in the Gobi while preying on Silk Road commerce. How often they relied on this particular oasis as a hideaway is anyone's guess. There are unconfirmed accounts of Ja Lama's renegades shifting to Shar Khuls for a while after killing a Chinese gang that had moved in and begun growing opium. In the end, Mongolian officials gave up trying to corner the guy and sent a message inviting him to a top-level meeting. Apparently convinced that he was going to be asked to serve as a minister or potentate of some sort, Ja Lama bit at the bait and departed whichever desert mountains hideout he was in for a city in the north. Upon reaching his destination, he was promptly executed. Well, one report has things happening this way. Another has the increasingly influential Russian communists ordering Ja Lama's death. In this variation, a provincial police chief talks his way into the raiders' camp somewhere by posing as a special envoy from Mongolia's government and shoots Ja Lama dead.

Whatever the fatal sequence might have been, all the versions agree that Ja Lama's head was cut off and hung in the main street of Uliastai to dispel any lingering notions about this monk's immortality. From there, the head was taken to Urga (present-day Ulaanbaatar). Next, someone stole the thing and smuggled it to Russia, where it ended up in the Hermitage. This museum, built by Catherine the Great in Saint Petersburg, could hardly be more grand and opulent. You can see Ja Lama's head on display there today inside a glass case. The label below it simply reads: #3394 Head of a Mongolian—an inglorious title for a cranium once afire with dreams of a reign that would live forever in human memory.

———

ONE MORNING IN 2014, A COUPLE DAYS AFTER A RECENT CHECK OF THE OASIS near the bandits' breastwork, I arose at five o'clock and hiked away from the Shar Khuls camp following the beam from my headlamp. It was the sole light in the Gobi landscape. Venus hung above the horizon, the last bright counterpoint in the heavens as the surrounding stars began to fade. Silhouettes of mountains were just starting to emerge from the darkness when I came to a cliff below a ridgeline. I played my light across the face, searching for an easy way to ascend. None appeared. All I met as I angled upward were sharply eroded stone teeth offering uncertain holds. I found myself thinking of Ja Lama, wondering whether or not he believed he was genuinely bulletproof. At the top, I nestled into a cubby out of the wind, looked up, and informed Venus, "Cheated Death again."

The wall wasn't all that forbidding. I was mostly joking about cheating Death. Lots of us mortals do that, sometimes to blow off the tension built up during a risky activity, and sometimes just for the hell of it. It's a way to acknowledge the innate, bone-deep fear of dying we all carry and, by making light of it, dispel some of its sting. Yet this time I heard a voice in my head saying, "Ah, but every day you say you've cheated Death, you are a day older, my friend."

It's been a while since I could call myself young. Death doesn't have to operate through sudden surprise, and it needn't depend on your making a mistake. It only has to wait. Death has all the time in the world on its side. We don't. No creature does. And yet here they were: snow leopards and ibex, jerboas and gerbils, saker falcons and vespertine bats, animating terrain where their kind have continuously claimed a home for tens of thousands of years. Camel spiders and beetles were scuttling along eons before that.

In my Gobi explorations, I came daily upon the desert-shriveled remains of dead animals and plants. Yet every day, I also saw their kind go right on running, burrowing, flying, and flowering in defiance of the passage of time. No, death can't be cheated; not by the individual. But life is the stronger force. Knit together with threads of a miraculous self-perpetuating molecule, DNA, the populations, subspecies, and species to which every individual belongs endure, and, more than that, prevail. The default condition for nearly every part of Earth's surface is being amazingly alive. Cover one place with lava and volcanic ash; it comes back as forest or jungle rustling and singing with animals. Bury another landscape beneath ice sheets; when they melt, lichens, mosses, and then tundra and its fauna soon appear. Take away more and more rainfall from a grassland; it becomes a desert inhabited by flora and fauna adapted to the paucity of water. We don't call Earth the sphere of condensed cosmic material third-closest to the sun. We call it the Living Planet.

When the environment changes, organisms can evolve to change with it. As a rule, species last for half a million to a million years. When one does go extinct, it may be because its predators or competitors evolved superior abilities or because it specialized to take advantage of a particular food or physical setting that disappeared. Where does the subspecies *Ursus arctos gobiensis*—or whatever label scientists ultimately agree on for this unique population—fit within the ongoing dance?

Genetic studies suggest that Gobi bears represent an ancient line of the brown/grizzly bear. We know that that they experienced a marked decline in range and numbers after Soviet-era authorities drilled wells to encourage the expansion of livestock grazing during the latter part of the twentieth century. But what kind of shape were *mazaalai* in before that? Were they already a relict life form on the way out by the time they were officially discovered by science in 1943? Or were they a naturally small and thinly dispersed but nonetheless stable population? No one has much to offer besides conjecture yet. It's probable that *mazaalai* were more widespread and numerous than

Lit by the setting sun, an adult Gobi bear crosses a rocky
outcropping at the base of a cliff. Photo: Joe Riis

anyone bothered to note during the time of the Mongol empire. Then again, that might have been when a swelling human population and flourishing trade along the Great Silk Road started these bears on a downward spiral. Or maybe it was the later spread of firearms that sparked a retreat toward the harshest, least visited reaches of the Gobi.

The amount of time, effort, and money being expended on the three or possibly four dozen Gobi bears left in the world today is not large, but it is appreciable. Such an investment might be better applied toward saving other seriously threatened wildlife present in larger numbers and inhabiting settings with more favorable climate and habitat trends—wildlife with a better chance of pulling through. There is something unsettling about a population of grizzlies, one of the strongest and fiercest of big untamed mammals, being reduced to rummaging for livestock chow in feeding troughs—dependent to some extent on artificial life support now. But then again, this is a new kind of epoch in the Living Planet's history.

In the Anthropocene, as Jon Mooallem observes in his 2013 book *Wild Ones*, "The line between conservation and domestication has blurred." It gets blurrier by the year. "We train condors not to perch on power lines," he writes. "We ship plague vaccine to [*black-footed*] ferrets. We shoot barred owls to make room in the forest for spotted owls. We monitor pygmy rabbits with infrared cameras and military drones. We carry migrating salamanders across the roads in our palms." And before that, people were feeding captive-reared whooping crane chicks with hand puppets and flying ultralight aircraft beside the grown birds to travel south for the winter and north when the weather warms, in effect teaching them to migrate.

Whooping cranes, bald eagles, American bison, white rhinos, great whales, Siberian tigers, gingko trees, and pandas are among the examples of striking life forms that were almost driven to extinction before help arrived. Instead of vanishing, they become prominent symbols of wildlife conservation. People around the globe were rooting for them—and still are. By contrast, if Gobi bears were to disappear once and for all, few people would miss them because the world remains largely unaware that they exist. Just as with better-known creatures, human actions left *mazaalai* critically endangered in the modern world, and it's going to take human actions to reverse their condition. The fastest and least expensive step in that direction will be to introduce them to a far wider audience, taking advantage of social media as well as more traditional outlets.[1] It's also the easiest step. Those that follow will call for more funds, more work, and more political will.

Suppose for a moment that all the steps are taken, and the bear population trend within the GGSPA turns markedly upward. Then what? With its scant vegetation and limited water, the reserve alone, though enormous, can't support a sufficiently large population to ensure the survival of Gobi bears over time. The animals need to expand beyond the reserve. Where? Into any chunks of former desert range they can colonize, as long as they are protected there. And after that? Keep in mind that the Gobi Desert, already half a million square miles big, is expanding as Central Asia warms and dries. As climate change combined with relentless overgrazing transforms more semi-desert habitats into true desert, wildlife adapted to highly arid conditions could conceivably gain rather than lose potential habitat as people abandon more of the area.

We don't understand enough about Gobi bear lives, the practical consequences of global warming, or how the next generations of humans will value wildlife to predict the future for these bears. Keeping *mazaalai* indefinitely confined to a single reserve and dependent on direct human intervention isn't a very desirable goal. Letting this long-lived line of *Ursus arctos* recover enough of its range and numbers to have more of a say about its own destiny is.

1 Shortly before the Project's 2014 spring field season began, *National Geographic*'s editors worked closely with Joe Riis and me in a rush to get a Gobi bear article published, not in the magazine but online. ("Can the World's Rarest Bear Be Saved?" http://news.nationalgeographic.com/news/special-features/2014/04/140417-rarest-bears-world-mongolia-gobi/.) The material included both Joe's powerful photographs and video segments he had put together. It all went up on *National Geographic's* website about the time I was boarding my flight to Mongolia. Although *National Geographic Magazine* has been available in Mongolia in the Mongolian language since 2012, there are not nearly as many subscribers in the country as folks with computers, and practically everyone has a smartphone. As our Project team members traipsed from office to office for meetings with politicians before leaving UB for the desert, it became apparent that the article had instantly made the rounds within Mongolian government circles. At the same time, the story was collecting online comments and Facebook Likes from around the world. The longest of the video segments, which Joe had uploaded to YouTube, was being widely viewed too. (https://www.youtube.com/watch?v=LVFK-0Cj8sxI.) Unfortunately, Joe's flight reservation was misplaced by one of the airlines, and he ended up not being able to fly to Mongolia in time to join the 2014 journey.

BASED AT THE SHAR KHULS OASIS IN THE CENTRAL MOUNTAIN COMPLEX DURING the spring of 2014, the Gobi Bear Project team captured two bears—the ones described in the first chapter. The crew consisted of rangers Ankhaa, Boldoo, Nyamaa, Puji the patroller, and the cook, Gelree, all from Bayantooroi; Odko and Miji's biologist son Boyoko, both from Ulaanbaatar; and Harry and myself. Also with us was the new GGSPA director, Dovchoo (who came to prefer the nickname Dovchin). He had taken over the position after his predecessor, Gotov, unexpectedly fell ill and died.

On May 9, we caught another bear at the Tsagaan Tokhoi oasis, number three of the season. It was a golden-colored male with a large hairless patch on one side of his neck. A good portion of his left ear was missing, possibly bitten off. His claws were worn to stubs. Some of his teeth were ground down nearly to the gums. Yet others showed little wear, leading Harry to estimate that the animal was only about twelve years old. And although he didn't have the long frame of the male we had collared earlier in the season at Tsagaan Burgas, this second male was more solidly muscled. With a thick neck, a fair amount of fat for a springtime bear, and a total weight of 251 pounds, he had come through the winter—and whatever cost him part of an ear—in reasonably good condition.

Our old friend Altan was regularly showing up around the feeder and trap at Khotul Us in the meantime. Although he managed to snitch a little food from the box, he never did go in. But we did make two additional captures at the Tsagaan Burgas oasis before the spring expedition ended. They were both of the same lanky male we had caught there earlier. Like Altan, he couldn't seem to resist coming back for the bait every so often. We could tell from images on the trap camera that on some of his repeat visits, this Burgas bear kept his long body mostly outside the metal box and stretched a front leg wa-a-a-a-ay in to whisk out the closest piles of dried fruit and grain pellets without triggering the door to fall. But on two occasions following his first capture, he went a little too far toward the piles in the back of the trap and temporarily lost his freedom again.

Earlier in the season, Dovchoo had wandered down to the wetlands by Shar Khuls and returned with a chunk of dried bear dung, holding it excitedly out for view. We passed his prize all around, probing and exclaiming before placing it in a plastic bag for later analysis. Another instance of wildlife nerds getting all hopped up over a piece of crap? Yes, though it sounds way better to call it a case of undaunted curiosity. The thing was loaded with long strands of wild camel hair. We started looking around harder and found

[Top] A good-sized adult male captured and radio-collared at Tsagaan Burgas. [Bottom] Unable to resist the bait in the trap during a drought that stifled springtime plant growth, the same bear was captured twice more that season and simply released with everyone's best wishes. Photos: Doug Chadwick

several more droppings like it nearby. Then we came upon a camel carcass with dozens of fur-stuffed scats around it a mile farther up the wash. As the season went on, we turned up droppings containing various kinds of large mammal hairs all across the study area. In other years, such dung had been extremely rare. Now it was almost common.

What caused the change? Was it related to the months of rainless weather that began in the summer of 2013? So far in 2014, most of the shrubs that would normally have been leafing out by now stayed winter-brown and brittle. Golden buttons and wild rhubarb sprouts had yet to make an appearance. It was hard to find a new shoot emerging from the ground anywhere except at oases. Had the reserve's grizzlies been actively hunting the larger animals out of desperation? Possibly, but the likeliest explanation was that more ungulates than usual weakened and died over winter, and the bears turned to scavenging carcasses to compensate for the shortage of new plant growth. Normally, *mazaalai* didn't appear to do much scavenging, but sharing a homeland with varied populations of wild ungulates was beginning to look more and more important to the bears' survival over the long run in an already desertified environment subject to unpredictable spells of drought.

The persistence of the bear we kept catching at Tsagaan Burgas might have been a straightforward sign of how desperate he was for a meal. Yet it might also have meant that he didn't process the experience of being trapped in the same way other *mazaalai* did. Among North American grizzlies, certain individuals, once nabbed, prove almost impossible to lure into a trap again. Others will shy away for months or even years but then suddenly enter a trap once more. Still others get re-captured within days, and a few, which I heard field biologists describe as "trap-happy," do it over and over. While it's hard to guess the psychological cost to any grizz of being confined and handled by humans, the worst physical pain the captive experiences as a rule is simply the jab of a sedative-delivering needle. Whatever is done next happens in the chemical haze of La-La Land as far as the bear is concerned, and by the time the animal is more or less itself again, it is freed. For whatever reasons, the overall experience doesn't seem to register as negative enough for some individuals to outweigh the attraction of another easy meal. The Burgas bear sported an identifying blue tag in each ear but had not yet been given a Mongolian name. So for the time being, I just called him Two Blue. Or Mooch.

On May 10, Puji returned from checking the traps to report another day without sign of fresh bear activity at the oases. I had recently returned to the Shar Khuls camp from a long hike through the hills and mountains leading east, when the wash where we pitched our tents began to turn into a parking lot. The arriving convoy included the Secretary of the Ministry of Environment, Mr. Batbold. He was traveling with an entourage of assistants, a Mongolian film crew, and officials from the nearest big town, Bayanhongor. Adiya Yadamsuren of the Mongolian Academy of Sciences, who had studied wild camels in and around the GGSPA since 2002, had joined the party as well.

The newcomers put up tents and set about preparing meals. After dinner, people built a campfire in the canyon wash that wound past the underground *ger*. People began to gather around the blaze until they formed a large circle. As sure as stars come out to dance in the Mongolian desert night, a vodka glass began its orbit through the company.

Batbold limited himself to a few ceremonial sips and then stood to address the group. He extolled the growing public awareness of *mazaalai* achieved during and since 2013, the Year of the Gobi Bear. Briefly, he reviewed the progress being made toward providing more supplemental food, modifying several springs to ensure a more reliable supply of water, and countering ninja miners. He emphasized the need to safeguard not only the bears but their neighbors too, drawing special attention to value of the reserve in conserving wild camels and snow leopards. I saw Adiya, the camel researcher, smiling and nodding.

Although the speech seemed a tad formal for a setting this remote, Batbold, a tall, imposing figure in his forties, gave the words the weight of sincerity. Odko sat next to Harry and translated, while Boyoko did the same for me. Soon, it was Harry's turn to grin and nod—the Secretary declared, "Allowing commercial mining in this reserve? THAT IS NEVER GOING TO HAPPEN!" He was referring to a recent proposal by Mongolian politicians to open a big bloc of the mountainous southern reaches of the reserve to gold mining. It was a sentiment shared by all. Earlier in the season, Ankhaa had declared, "If that happens, I will not work here." Harry felt the same way, but Ankhaa's steadfastness was far more significant, for walking away from the Gobi would mean giving up the job he both loved and depended on to make his living. Both Ankhaa and Harry knew that the rugged southern portion of the GGSPA holds the reserve's richest wildlife. If it were opened to development, the bears, wild camels, wild ass, and other big mammals would be on their way out.

Batbold described how pressures from a growing human population were making Mongolia's native animals more scarce almost everywhere except within fully protected areas. Hunting and trapping traditions were strong, game laws were weak, and illegal killing continued virtually unchecked. Batbold favored establishing hunting reserves with well-enforced limits on harvests as a step toward improving conservation. At the same time, he wanted to start a nationwide campaign "to change our way of thinking about wildlife from the gun to the camera." With that, he sat down. Someone walked to the circle's center and began a round of traditional storytelling. Singing followed, and the unusually warm night air carried the choruses far out into the darkness.

Secretary Batbold retired early. Most everyone else did the same. It had been a good evening, a hopeful evening. The next morning proved more encouraging still after the group fired up their vehicles and set out to view the oasis trap sites. From the moment Puji rolled up to the traveling convoy on his motorbike to report a bear in the box at Tsagaan Burgas, I knew it was Two Blue. I also knew the Project would soon owe a round of thanks to our troublesome bait junkie male, for he was going to be first *mazaalai* that the Secretary and most of the other new arrivals had ever seen in their lives.

Once everyone had made it to the setting and taken up a good viewing position, the door of the trap was raised. And the only thing that happened was that Two Blue stayed completely hidden inside the dark recesses of the box. Thirty seconds passed, and thirty more. The newcomers were starting to look at each other. They shifted their feet and fiddled with camera dials. Another half-minute went by. People were exchanging shrugs when this big, long bulk of bear exploded from the opening, all humped shoulders, bunched hindquarters, burly butt, churning legs, and flying fur, racing in a straight line past the SUVs and trucks and Russian vans while still cameras clicked, video cameras hummed, and wide-eyed people gaped and gasped. Seconds later, Two Blue plowed into a willow thicket and was gone, as if the hairy blur raising geysers of dust from its paws had been a dervish or djinn conjured from the dry desert air. Harry and the crew turned away and calmly set about re-baiting the trap, leaving the visitors staring in the direction the creature had chosen, hoping in vain for a last glimpse.

Inspired by Two Blue's short-lived but overpowering sprint across the oasis, the crowd returned to camp in a merry mood. Batbold had already provided the GGSPA with the funds to hire more staff, continue improving springs, and set up small cloud-seeding machines in a couple of sites.[2] Now, the secretary was telling us that new Chinese motorbikes were on the way to improve transportation for the rangers.

When the visitors en route to Tsagaan Burgas passed the feeder at Tsagaan Tokhoi earlier in the day, we made sure they understood that the rangers had poured around 800 pounds of pelletized grain into that bin at the start of springtime. It was now empty. Hungry bears had gobbled every last

2 The effectiveness of ground-based cloud-seeding is debatable. But there is enough circumstantial evidence of its success in increasing precipitation by at least a modest amount that a number of countries in Asia and elsewhere employ the technique at times.

scrap even before we showed up to start trapping three weeks earlier. This made an impression on Batbold. Back at camp, he was now talking enthusiastically about further increasing the supply of food pellets, which Tumen planned to upgrade with corn and peanuts in order to add protein and fat.

It looked as though Two Blue deserved not only our thanks for boosting the conservation work underway here but also special thanks from the GGSPA bears as a whole. If the boost in supplemental food came as promised, more *mazaalai* bellies were going to stay full for longer during the early spring and fall pre-hibernation periods in the future.

Batbold was making ready to depart the Shar Khuls camp. In getting to know him a bit, we had a better appreciation of the compromises this ecologist had to make in his role as a government officer with administrative responsibilities and political considerations reaching far beyond this dusty outback. Yet his commitment to supporting the reserve and its shaggy bears was genuine, and it definitely seemed strengthened by this trip to observe the Project's field operations firsthand. Sensing this, Harry asked Batbold if he might be interested in attending the annual meeting of the International Association for Bear Research and Management (IBA), which was to be held in Greece that fall. He could present a key talk on Mongolia's efforts to conserve Gobi bears, Harry suggested, offering to make the necessary arrangements with IBA. Batbold was intrigued. Recognizing a prime opportunity to generate more interest and support from other countries, he said he would look into finding time to attend.

To me, these sounded like the sort of polite and well-intentioned promises that busy people tend to make before parting, but rarely follow up on. However, by the summer of 2014, the GGSPA rangers were speeding over the desert floor astride new motorcycles delivered by Batbold. When he traveled to a meeting in China to discuss Gobi bears, he took two longtime Project personnel, Odko and Bayasa, with him. And when October rolled around, Batbold did go to Greece, where he gave a presentation about *mazaalai* and their needs to a room full of bear experts from scores of nations. Before and after the talk, he, Harry, and Project member Michael Proctor, an IBA vice president now, kept busy passing along more information about Mongolia's desert grizzlies informally.

During a portion of our 2014 expedition, students from the University of Mongolia passed through the reserve to collect images from the scores of automatic cameras they'd set up the previous year under the supervision of University of Mongolia ecologist Dr. R. Samiya. While poring through the results, they discovered a springtime photo of a mother with a new cub at a feeder in the western mountain complex. This marked the second consecutive year with undeniable visual proof of ongoing reproduction in this critically endangered grizzly population. Odko e-mailed news that the summer of 2014 finally brought a series of good rains to the Gobi. They heralded a favorable supply of natural food into the fall—and a better-than-average chance of survival for the youngest Gobi bears. The P.S. to her e-mail mentioned that two different Mongolian companies marketing consumer goods were interested in using Gobi Bear as a brand name. Gobi Bear bread? Why not?

Harry went straight from the fall IBA meeting in Greece to Mongolia for his standard fall survey of bear activities in the GGSPA. He found that the generous summer rains had nourished a bumper crop of *Nitraria* berries. A great many of the bear droppings Harry found around the feeders at oases were purple from all the remains of sugar-rich nitre bush fruits in them.

Odko completed her analyses of hair samples collected in the reserve during 2013 and the spring of 2014. They showed that the absolute minimum number of individual *mazaalai* was no longer twenty-two but twenty-seven. Although the change was only five animals, that represented an increase of almost 23 percent. The new upper estimate for the actual number of bears in the population was raised accordingly from thirty-one to between thirty-six and forty. This was not absolute proof that the population was increasing, but the probability that it was looking better. Poring over all the camera trap photos GGSPA field staff collected through fall, ranger-biologist Nyamaa counted what he thought to be thirty-six distinct individuals. Professor Samiya's university students scrutinized the pictures their automatic cameras collected throughout the reserve and came up with a total of forty individuals. Because of poor image quality in low light, variation in the positions of bodies relative to the camera, and the subjective nature of people's interpretations of size and color, counts based on apparent differences between photo subjects are not considered highly reliable. Just the same, the similarity of both photo sampling results to the upper estimate for the population size based on Odko's genetic sampling was striking.

The Gobi Bear team hadn't yet come up with a way to more accurately gauge the percentage of animals staying away from the feeders due to wariness around unfamiliar objects, human scent, or the presence of dominant bears. Meanwhile, it was all we could do to reach known oases within the three mountain complexes with some regularity. As a result, we couldn't say with confidence that a minor enclave of grizz wasn't holed up like Ja Lama's band somewhere near waterholes no one knew about. And what about mountains on the Chinese side of the Gobi? Reports of a bear there came in so rarely

An automatic camera photo in 2014 was evidence that this critically endangered
species with a very small number of breeding females is still reproducing—the best kind
of research result possible. Photo: Courtesy of the Gobi Bear Project

that we were inclined to believe that any *mazaalai* spotted in China these
days was a wanderer from the core population in the GGSPA rather than part
of a small resident Chinese group. Maybe we were right. But were we fully
factoring in how much the near-absence of sightings in China reflected the
enormous scale of the desert there and the scarcity of humans who might
chance upon a bear?

What we knew for sure was this: The GGSPA held most, if not all, of the
remaining Gobi bears in the world. All our indicators pointed to this population being at least stable and, by some measures, growing. Support from
the Ministry of Environment was improving. The government, academic,
and conservation parties working on the bears' behalf were cooperating
more closely. The gold mining bill that so concerned Batbold, Ankhaa, and
the rest of us on the Gobi bear team failed to pass in Parliament, pushing
the threat away to simmer on the back burner. And *mazaalai* were drawing
more attention from the public in Mongolia and elsewhere.

At this stage in the march of the Anthropocene, with humanity swarming
across the planet and vacuuming resources from its last wild corners, hope
for saving imperiled wild creatures can be such a fragile thing that I'm almost
afraid to hold it tightly. But for the first time since joining the Project, I sensed
that enough things were going in the right direction for Gobi bears that the
animals might be on the way to a comeback, and I carried that hope with me

after I returned to the States. A Buddhist nun once counseled me about the struggle that people who feel real empathy for living creatures face in these days of global species declines. The Great Grief, she called it and said—better than I can paraphrase here—that acknowledging it is part of the practice of compassion. Then you go on and keep doing as much good as you can.

———

IT WAS MID-APRIL OF 2015 WHEN I ARRIVED FOR THE FIFTH STRAIGHT SPRING in Ulaanbaatar, where more than half the population of Mongolia had now crowded in. Partially built high rises capped by construction cranes dominated more of the urban skyline than I remembered. New suburbs mixed with shantytowns and encampments of *gers* continued spilling outward from the edges faster and farther than anyone ever expected. Despite recently imposed rules that allow only automobiles with even-numbered license plates on the roads one day and odd-numbered plates the next, the traffic was still jammed up most of the day. UB symbolizes Mongolia's transition from a largely self-sufficient traditional pastoral culture to a modern culture more focused on industrial development. This is generally viewed as progress, but it means being increasingly tied to the global economy, which is periodically subject to the financial equivalent of dust storms.

Mongolia's main customer for its products is China. Trade between the two nations totaled $324 million in 2006. By 2013, the figure was $6 billion. Most of that rise reflected expanding sales by Mongolia of its coal, gold, copper, and other minerals, a huge portion of them coming from lodes in the Gobi Desert. By late 2011, Mongolia led the world—by far—with a GDP of more than 17 percent.[3] This measure of the nation's economic activity stayed aloft the next year but then began a decline that brought it to 7.8 percent by 2014. The slide continued into 2015, falling to under 3 percent. Mongolia's currency, the tugrik, lost 12 percent of its value in 2013 and 24 percent in the first part of 2015. In the meantime, the inflation rate was running at an average of more than 12 percent annually.

When the mining boom first hit, Mongolia gave extremely generous deals to foreign corporations developing the deposits, accepting modest royalty payments in return for the country's mineral wealth. Even so, the country's treasury swelled. With rising prosperity came rising expectations. Citizens looking to the government to do more to improve the country's outdated infrastructure and address problems of poverty were disappointed. Elections were called, a different administration took over in 2012, and new people

---

3 Gross Domestic Product is the total market value of all
final goods and services produced in a country during
the year. For comparison, the GDP for the United States
averages 2.5 to 3 percent.

were appointed to run government departments. One of them was Batbold in the Ministry of Environment.

Mongolia's Parliament voted to place limits on foreign ownership of mining operations and raised royalty payments on the resources extracted. Where foreign investors had been waiting in line to do business in "Minegolia," they now began to turn skittish. But the chief cause of the country's economic downturn was its huge neighbor to the south: China. Through the start of the twenty-first century, its economy grew to rival that of the United States. Then, as financial writers would say, China caught a cold. Inflationary forces rose, and the country's exports fell. Its industries contracted, consuming fewer raw materials. The contagion spread. Before long, prices for commodities from coal, iron ore, and gypsum (for concrete) to precious metals were sinking worldwide.

The discovery in Mongolia's Gobi of the world's largest (some say second-largest) known reserve of coal had been celebrated years earlier as the foundation for a new era of wealth for the nation. Suddenly, demand for the black fuel started to slide. China needed less of the stuff as manufacturing slowed. The country, which had become the biggest source of carbon emissions on the globe, was also under international pressures to slow climate change. Mongolia's income from commodities continued to dwindle. With every cut in government budgets for public works and social services, more of the citizenry became disenchanted. Yet another election was held; yet another administration took over.

Harry and I went to the Ministry of Environment in mid-April of 2015 for a pre-expedition visit with the secretary, which Odko had arranged. Except that Batbold, our Gobi champion, was gone. The more heavyset man who replaced him began our meeting by explaining that nature reserves including the GGSPA would be receiving less government funding this year. In fact, he asked Harry if the Gobi Bear Project could buy new batteries for the remote radio repeater stations in the GGSPA. Installed during Batbold's tenure to improve communications in the far-flung reserve, the system hadn't been working lately because the batteries had died. Harry and I exchanged glances and a resigned shrug. "Yes," he told the new secretary. "We'll do that."

Walking aimlessly around the streets of UB after the meeting, I thought about how many more elements of unnatural history go into equations for conserving wild lives in the twenty-first century. I wondered how biologists were supposed to keep factoring in biosphere-changing forces like unchecked population growth and global warming that had whole societies scrambling for answers. We were pretty clearly in over our heads. But we were all there

Project team members search the edge of the thick Shar Khuls oasis reedbeds for tracks, droppings, and other signs of wildlife. Photo: Doug Chadwick

together, and maybe that was telling us to look harder for common ways out. For my part, perhaps I ought to be focusing less on just what Gobi bears needed and think more about what kinds of actions could benefit *mazaalai* and Mongolians alike.

Diversifying the production of goods in the country should help stabilize the economy by reducing the present heavy reliance on minerals, which have comprised as much as 80 percent of Mongolia's total exports. One nonconsumptive industry with potential for major growth was tourism featuring the country's grand landscapes, traditional cultures, and native wildlife. The passage of laws permanently protecting special strongholds of nature like the GGSPA would be a relief for the bears and the rest of the wildlife community. Whatever encouraged these animals to flourish inside core reserves and begin to replenish areas outside them would be an endowment for natural history tour companies and all kinds of other businesses associated with travel and outdoor adventure.

But those were all idealistic notions, and I had almost no idea of how to turn them into practical economic realities. Within days, I'd be bouncing in a Russian van along stony tracks farther and farther from everybody else in the world. Once deep in the reserve's desert mountains, I'd be busy trying to help catch thirsty, long-eared grizz and collecting another season of data about the natural history of their kind. This was something I know how to do.

I FORGOT TO MENTION ONE OTHER CHANGE SINCE 2014. WE HAD BEEN TOLD that members of Parliament—the State Great Khural (or Hural) as the national legislative body is also known—were lobbying anew for opening the reserve to gold mining. It never ends, does it, the push to get at the gleaming treasure that can transform an ordinary human into a powerful lord, a thief, or a fool? This time, the mining interests were once again focused on the southwestern section of the GGSPA. The new head of the Ministry of Environment—not the current secretary we met but his boss, the minister himself—had publicly stated his support for allowing gold mining in the western GGSPA. That happened to be where were going to set up our base camp and begin trapping this spring.

The western mountain complex and its surroundings are the driest portion of the GGSPA—the starkest desert within the giant reserve. It appeared to hold fewer bears than the other two mountain complexes. But we needed to confirm that impression because Project members hadn't spent as much time in the western complex as elsewhere. This was partly because the oases there are widely separated from one another, making it difficult to reach more than a couple in a day when trapping. Despite the challenges, Harry wanted to spend the spring trying to catch bears in the west so we could build a more detailed picture of the role the area plays in the population's overall use of the reserve.

The renewed mining threat reminded me of the never-ending proposals in the United States for oil development on the coastal plain of the Arctic National Wildlife Refuge, where the North Slope of Alaska's Brooks Range tapers down toward the edge of the Beaufort Sea. One of my first *National Geographic* assignments was to go there in the midst of a ramped-up campaign by big energy companies and their political allies to bulldoze in roads and start drilling the place. What happened then is what keeps happening over and over: Conservationists campaign against the proposal. Pleas and accusations escalate. Members of Congress fly over the area so they can say they took a look at the vast, pristine landscape for themselves. They fly back to Washington thinking about what all that means to Americans who love nature, wild places, new automobiles, and inexpensive gasoline. Then the politicians vote. The ayes in favor of drilling aren't quite enough. And then, sooner or later, the price of oil spikes. Or an election brings a new batch of legislators into office or yields a pro-development administration, and the pressure to open up the refuge builds again.

On the way to the GGSPA headquarters from UB, we stopped in Bayankhongor, the capital of the province, or *aimag*, that includes the eastern half of the reserve. A center for regional mineral companies, the town itself ran on locally mined coal. Thick smoke poured out of power plant stacks in the heart of Bayankhongor, and the wind currents swirled streamers of soot and ash over the buildings and streets. You can see similar scenes in cities and towns all over Mongolia. I read a thick government document outlining strategies for meeting future energy needs. The plan for the country's tomorrows dwelled almost exclusively on repeating its dirty yesterdays—building more coal-fueled power plants. Solar and wind power were scarcely mentioned. For a nation that experiences an average of 257 cloudless days per year, a still higher number of days with sunshine, and very few days without strong winds, this report was useful mainly as an example of fossilized thought.

Not too surprisingly, Bayankhongor's political representatives had been favorable toward earlier proposals for opening the reserve to mining. Since then, a charismatic young lama from the temple on the hillside above town had formed a nature club for schoolkids, an outgrowth of the Gobi Bear Club that Harry established with the help of local teachers years before. Attitudes began changing. A recreation area was built along the central avenue with playground equipment for children and sculpted versions of native fauna. The city named it Gobi Bear Park. Some tourism takes place in the desert mountains to the south, and opportunities for attracting more visitors are being discussed. Although the GGSPA is off-limits to the public, people understood that wildlife in adjoining parts of the province could become a special attraction if allowed to flourish there.

Soon after reaching Bayantooroi, we took a tour of our own, driving a short distance from the reserve headquarters to the Hunter Hall Wild Camel Breeding Center, a 150-acre fenced compound established in 2004 for the captive breeding of this critically endangered species. In the fall of 2013, rangers trucked two young males from this facility south into the western mountain complex and released them at the Bogt Tsagaan Ders oasis (loosely translated as Grove of Plants). Eighteen others from the breeding center had previously been released in other GGSPA sites. Named Naran and Jolan, the pair of young males were satellite-collared to monitor their movements. By the time the winter breeding season got underway a few months later, Naran had gathered a harem of five wild females and looked to be adjusting to life without fences just fine. Yet before the year was out, he had walked 200 miles back to the Breeding Center. Jolan showed up at the same place not long afterward. The best guess is that the extra-dry conditions of 2013, which carried over into the first half of 2014 (and had us collecting all kinds of hair-filled *mazaalai* scat in the central mountain complex) shriveled water sources and made new forage growth so scarce that Naran and Jolan opted to trek all the way back to the compound where they remembered life being more bountiful.

The Bogt Tsagaan Ders oasis was the water source closest to the site where we would be setting up a base camp. I learned this as we were driving that direction through tremendous stretches of desert pavement and hills virtually free of vegetation. At times, the strong sunlight glinting off the gravel's glossy desert patina made it seem as though we were wandering a world made of glass. If you looked over that world during some of the breaks during our drive, you would have seen the figures of the two largest Mongolian rangers, Ankhaa and Nyamaa, out on the flats raising dust from one of their wrestling matches. Nyamaa seldom won these battles of the titans, but he never refused an invitation for another go-round. Watching the fierce determination in Ankhaa's face when he was at risk of being thrown, you would never know that when Harry and I parted company with him and the other

GGSPA members of the Gobi Bear Project after a spring field season together, the big man's eyes leaked tears.

Night fell before the two vans and two motorcycles that made up our little caravan finally crawled up a canyon and stopped at the camp spot. The *ger* that the rangers said was waiting there for us turned out to be a small aluminum-sided trailer plonked down in the open on stones at the base of a hill. Good enough. Although the word *ger* is used to describe the traditional round dwelling more widely called a yurt, it broadest meaning is "home."

We were between the western end of the Inges (Female Wild Camel) Range and the eastern end of the Atas (Male Wild Camel) Range, the two tallest sets of mountains in the reserve. The ranges trend east-west. This gap we were in runs north-south, and our camp sat more or less at its high point amid clusters of lesser peaks and foothills named the Botgos (Baby Camel) Mountains. Like much of the country we came through, our surroundings were mostly barren slopes, gravel-plated swales, and lighter-colored mineral playas. And like usual, wherever we ended up pitching tents in the reserve, it was dark and we were fighting a cold wind that wanted to snatch everything and sail it away over the countryside. As each tent was assembled, two or three people had to hold the fabric in place long enough for someone to anchor the sides and corners with long spikes driven into the gravel and then pile rocks atop the spikes so they wouldn't pull loose in a real gale.

Home; for the next three weeks, it would be my tent and the *ger* on the rocks, in the wind, under the sun and the stars. We were the only people inhabiting this arc of Asia and could have been the last ones on the planet, for all we could tell. Before the sun rose, I climbed the hillocks around camp and from the top of each looked out over hundreds more—all the baby camels made of stone marching away toward the feet of their mother and father, the massive Inges and Atas. Reverting to the habit that probably had most of the crew secretly referring to me as Annoying Guy, I burst in the trailer door and gave a thumbs-up sign with my news-that's-never-news: "Guess what, gang? It looks like it's going to be clear and sunny today!" The gang rolled their eyes and resumed making ready to set off and open traps at two oases.

The first water source, Bogt Tsagaan Ders, had two feeders now, each with a nearby box trap. The bins were separated by nearly a half-mile of *Phragmites* reed beds. I knew that their roots spread down into sodden ground or these plants wouldn't have been here, but the ground between clumps of the tall, feathery-topped grasses was covered with powdery alkaline dust. Enough pieces of camel, wild ass, and gazelle skeletons lay scattered across the surface to make the description "bone-dry" more meaningful the farther

I walked. Desiccated dung, trails, and hoofprints were everywhere. They intersected the distinctive double trails of *mazaalai*. The most heavily used of those parallel footpaths ran between the two feeders and the only open water, a pool near the southwestern corner of the great swath of reeds.

Although the pool was fairly wide and deep compared to most other open water in the reserve, GGSPA staff had brought in a backhoe and dug a trench across thirty yards of bare ground and on into one edge of the pool. The idea was to drain more subsurface water into the natural reservoir. Since the trench had water trickling along its bottom, this also offered more room for arriving animals to drink. Pallas's sandgrouse loved the place. Fast-flying squadrons passed overhead almost constantly, calling out to one another as they came to sip. The extra amounts of water these birds require help digest a diet of dried seeds. Soon, the males would also take care to soak their chests and then carry the water absorbed by the breast-feathers back to chicks in distant nests.

Odko collected bear fur from the barbed wire around the first trap we readied for capture. The metal box was dented and rusted to the color of the brown rock outcrops on the nearest hill but still in good working order. The second trap looked the same. By contrast, the feeder next to it, recently put in place with support from Tumen's organization, MAMA, stood out as a novelty with its smooth sides and bright green coat of paint. The automatic camera set on a post there showed two bears arriving just two days earlier. Rangers had transferred food pellets from the feeder into the trap earlier this spring to get bears used to finding food there. That worked. One of the bears had just left a track in the middle of the fodder pile. We added the usual smorgasbord of treats inside, slid the trapdoor into its slots, raised it in place to fall, and arranged the triggering mechanism. I could feel the odds for a capture rising by the minute, but I wouldn't have bet on a *mazaalai* being the first creature caught.

While wolves had left their pawprints across the oasis, it looked as though the most regular visitors to the trap sites were their smaller relatives: foxes. We found one fresh fox dropping inside the second trap and another conspicuously deposited on a big stone just outside. A third scat rested atop a pile of bear dung at the site. That was a fox making a statement. Whether it was an announcement to other foxes with territories in the area or an opinion about bears is hard to say.

During the afternoon, we moved on toward the Khukh Khuls oasis, where the crumbling old fort and parade grounds stood next to the wash with a series of pools. Though it took the better part of an hour to drive there, it was only about seven miles away, and pawprints along the old four-wheel-drive vehicle route suggested that the area's *mazaalai* were commuting between the two sites pretty regularly. Khukh Khuls also had two feeders. Once again, MAMA had helped provide the second metal bin, installed a good distance from the first, to address the Project's concern that dominant bears might be monopolizing the supplemental food at oases with a single feeder. Only the old feeder, the original one, had a trap next to it and food pellets piled inside. The automatic camera's photos included several of an adult bear repeatedly going in and out of the metal box. When? Yesterday. I was liking our chances of catching grizz during this year's expedition more all the time.

Mandakh, one of the motorcycle patrol rangers for the western third of the reserve, returned from a run to the oases the next morning to say a fox had cleaned out the goodies we arranged inside the second trap at Bogt Tsagaan Ders. The raider also chewed apart the trigger cord and somehow set off the trap without getting caught. But there were no bears. Either they were away foraging for natural foods or they got spooked by the unfamiliar scents at the traps—our stink from yesterday. Okay. It would fade a bit. Aside from a No Peeing at an Oasis rule, we didn't make a diligent effort to avoid leaving any scent when we set up traps or carried out follow-up inspections. Bears using the area tended to continue making visits. The question was always when one would have become sufficiently habituated to our smells or simply hungry enough to venture inside the trap the next time it arrived.

We used what was left of the day for making a run to distant Baruuntooroi, where I had seen my first free-roaming Gobi bear in 2011. The oasis had a solar panel array at one edge now. It was built to power a pump that brings subsurface water up into a concrete-lined pool. Without a doubt, this was an improvement over the tiny, shallow natural pool available earlier. Except the pump wasn't working, so the volume of flow was no stronger than in the past. We couldn't detect a big shift in use by the bears; their tracks and droppings were common as ever. The old feeding bin was empty, but Baruuntooroi had a new MAMA feeder a couple hundred yards away. As at the other oases, rangers had closed the bin off after transferring a share of the food pellets into the open box trap close by. We readied the trap for action. And now it was time for this season's team to split up.

Ankhaa, Amgaa, and moto-ranger Mandakh, would stay at the Baruuntooroi *ger* up in the hills to monitor this oasis. The other moto-ranger for this portion of the reserve, Altanshagai (Shagai) Nanzad, would return to the Baby Camel *ger* with Odko, Harry, the van driver Dondogdorj (Donduk) Ramjin, myself, and Khosbayar (Khosoo) Munkhjargal. A single mother from Bayantooroi, Khosoo was also a strong, lean amateur athlete. Given the opportunity to run and hike in new country and see its wild animals, she had left her young son temporarily in the care of family and hired on as the expedition cook. Baruuntooroi is so far removed from other oases that this trap was the only one the smaller team would tend to. The rest of us would be driving to tend the three other traps and explore some of the terrain farther to the southwest. Since we'd be burning the most gas, we siphoned a share from the barrel in Ankhaa's van into our fuel containers. Then the Baruuntooroi crew took off up the steep ravine toward the *ger*, and we headed back to base camp, where Nyamaa was waiting to meet us. He had stayed to re-bait and re-set the foxed trap.

————

IN THEORY, I APPRECIATE BIOLOGICAL DIVERSITY IN ALL ITS MULTITUDE OF forms. But personally, I've always disliked camel ticks. For one thing, the little bastards track and hunt you relentlessly, and they're fast. Also, they make the poplar groves so unwelcoming that you'd rather stumble across the hot rocks of a steep hillside than sit for a moment in the green shade of an oasis. Finally, it made me sorry for the bears and camels just to think about how many ticks were hiding under those thick woolen coats. That was my attitude up through 2014. It's different now. Now I really deeply hate everything about these eight-legged nanobot blood-harvesters' lives.

You try waking up in your tent and stumbling out to take a leak only to find a big camel tick with its head drilled into the tip of your penis, as if the creature had studied psychology to fix on the ultimate spot for panicking and demoralizing a male human. I'll skip further details except to say that trying to exert a controlled gentle pull to get the beast out was making for the worst morning wake-up I'd ever had. Harry greeted me with a "How's it going?" later on. I told him exactly how. Instead of reacting, he nodded and said that he had to deal with a dick tick of his own that morning—another memento from our previous day at Baruuntooroi, where the ticks were two or three times as thick as I remembered from earlier visits.

Over the next couple of days, the camera by the second trap at Bogt Tsagaan Ders captured 183 photos. A handful were of birds. All the rest were of foxes. They kept snitching the jam and raisins and dried apricots among the grain pellets; we kept replacing the treats, inadvertently carrying out bear research and a deli dessert program for midsize canines at the same time. It wasn't just *Vulpes vulpes*, the widespread common (or red) fox taking advantage. From the photos, it looked as though the lighter-colored, slightly smaller corsac fox, *Vulpes corsac*, closely tied to Central Asia's steppe and arid habitats, was a full participant too.

We usually encountered wild asses among the hills while traveling to the oases. Black-tailed gazelles appeared as singles or pairs on the flatter stretches, and we saw more camels than we ever had while working in the central or eastern mountain complexes. But in relation to the expanses of terrain within view, the hoofed mammals were still very few and far between. Like the vegetation they depend on. Like the water that plants need to grow. It's the Gobi.

During a walkabout at Khukh Khuls, I had just proudly added hoopoes and fork-tailed swifts to my list of local birds when Odko and Nyamaa waved me over to look at a tamarisk shrub in the center of a dry wash leading toward the springs. Then Nyamaa leaned down and disappeared through a hole in this bush's tangle of branches. Peering in, I could only see him from the waist up, displaying his ready grin. He was squatting in a hole dug by a bear in the sandy silt of the wash. It was about five feet long and more than two feet deep, a perfect fit for an adult. It also had the well-rubbed look of long use. This could have been a grizzly day bed, but I'd never seen one of this size and depth. I think the crew had found a *mazaalai* winter den. Most of the sleeping animal would have been in contact with insulating ground, while the upper part of the body exposed to the air was partially sheltered by the canopy of interlacing branches. As a place to spend the frozen months, this pit couldn't compare with the underground den grizzlies elsewhere typically excavate. But the floor of the wash presented as good an opportunity to burrow into soil as this stony desert offers, and the result was surely no worse than a bed on the floor of a cliffside cave.

Whatever purpose the digging served, it was as near as we came to a bear until one went into the first trap at Bogt Tsagaan Ders on April 29. The captive was a male weighing 202 pounds, with a white blaze running from his right shoulder partway down his front leg. He appeared to be just three to four years old. A fit and feisty example of recent reproduction and successful early survival, he was the nineteenth different member of the GGSPA *mazaalai* population captured during the Project. (Repeat captures of individuals aren't counted.) Three days later at Kukh Khuls, we caught Number 20, another three- or four-year-old male. Though weighing just 155 pounds, the animal wasn't noticeably thin. He was merely a smaller-framed bear than the first male and probably his brother. The two of them were most likely the pair of youngsters recorded by an automatic camera at Baruuntooroi in 2014.

THE SECOND YOUNG MALE WAS THE LAST CAPTURE OF THE SEASON. WE RAN the traps for another week without success. Even the foxes seem to have turned their attention elsewhere, perhaps because more vegetation was starting to leaf out, and the rodents were more active as May got underway. Farther west in Baruuntooroi, the other team had no luck at all. Our last satellite phone call to that crew was to tell them to come back to the Baby Camel camp. We made an expedition together to survey a reported water source south of the Atas Range and found the spring in a wash. At the moment, it offered only one pool with a bucket's worth of liquid. Yet, as we had come to expect wherever even the stingiest flow of water surfaced, the whole area was webbed with trails, stamped with tracks, and littered with bones. Next to the spring was a hill formed entirely of white quartz—a single, perfect crystalline cone of a peak set against the backdrop of the looming Atas Range, radiating light like a lamp.

Now that I'd been on the Project for five seasons, climbing that hill of bright crystal, as much as catching another bear, had become the kind of experience that would stand out in my memory, the kind that answered the question I so often asked myself about what I was really doing out here. This wasn't the middle of nowhere. It was no less the center of the things going on in the world than any other part of Earth. What took place here happened with fewer drops of liquid and fewer people but with every bit as much meaning and no end of wonder.

Now that we were leaving the core of the desert behind, making the long drive back north toward the reserve headquarters and then on to UB, I found myself mentally thumbing through the season's memories. Not all the strongest ones glowed. I could too easily recollect Harry's tick bite becoming infected, discomforting him for days. I remembered Khosoo jogging downhill from camp, bound for a long ramble in the break between Atas and Inges, but then unexpectedly sprinting back waving her arms and shouting two words over and over. Someone translated: "Big wind! Big wind!" I looked northwest to see a titanic black cloud racing toward us over the Atas Range like the breaking front wave of a tsunami. Within moments, it swallowed the afternoon sun, and we were scrambling through the sudden darkness to take down tent poles and heap rocks onto the loose fabric while temperatures plummeted and grit began to pepper our faces.

But I remembered as well a party inside the *ger* to celebrate a combination of the season's first bear capture and Khosoo's birthday. Odko made a cake from bread dough, cookies, and scoops of Nutella, while Khosoo wore a paper crown decorated with drawings of *mazaalai* made by Shagai, the artist in the group. We shared a little vodka and a lot of singing that drowned out the winds causing the trailer to tremble. The storm of cold air that had rolled down from the Altai Range, sweeping the Gobi's dust before it, wasn't quite done with us yet.

I could readily call to mind another scene in the *ger* with Odko disinfecting and rewrapping wounds on Shagai's arm. They were deep gouges made by the teeth of a rutting male camel back at the Bayantooroi breeding compound. On a different day, when Shagai took off his undershirt while Odko bathed those wounds, I noticed an older, healed wound near his shoulder socket. That one, I learned, came from the bullet of a ninja miner when Shagai and another ranger walked in to roust an illegal camp. The man was later arrested. I asked what happened next. Shagai shrugged. "Nothing; maybe a minor fine," he replied through Odko. "The miner probably knew somebody"—a relative in the local police force perhaps, or a judge. Or else he was in the pay of a big businessman who knew the police and judges. I'd now heard enough similar stories from other rangers to understand that this is how such matters often play out.

I never heard Shagai complain. For that matter, I'm not sure I heard any of the Mongolians ever gripe about pain, much less about the occasional aggravations of Gobi camp life and travel. Rather, my brain was more likely to bring up an image of Shagai, Nyamaa, and Donduk lying together on the *ger's* linoleum floor with their heads propped up on gunny sacks or on someone's shoulder and their laughter making the bare-bones trailer a luxurious place.

The memories that came most often to mind and still do are from my solitary hikes. I took them almost every morning and evening and sometimes, when Shagai or Nyamaa scouted the traps by motorbike and returned early with no bear news, through the better part of the day. Roaming the Botgos hills, the lower slopes of the Atas and Inges Mountains, and mile after mile of the break between them was different from winding my way through the endlessly dividing, crag-topped canyons of the other mountain complexes. Every direction I chose for walking from the Baby Camel *ger* led through more obliging country. I felt a continuous opening, a sense of being drawn outward, of anticipation without having to be constantly alert. It was still the Gobi, but less ragged, less exacting in terms of the need to pick a route carefully and avoid getting lost. And if I did get disoriented among the proliferation of hills, I could always get to the top of one from which I could place myself in relation to the two great ranges east and west, see a way to more open ground—and see a way back.

I'm not sure I'm explaining this well. I'm trying to say that I felt invited to walk and keep walking as never before and explore as I pleased, on my own, far from my Gobi Project colleagues, farther yet from anyone else, without worries and without limits. Here within ready reach was a greater freedom than I had ever experienced in a lifetime of hikes. The feeling of being so completely unfettered was what made me begin to think of that freedom, in itself as my reason for being there. It didn't matter why I was walking or what anyone thought about it. Or even what I thought about it. It didn't matter who I was. Every step simply made me glad to be in the place where I was stepping. Sitting and waiting made me glad to be where I sat and waited. I would be crossing a low ridge and see a band of wild asses on a path below and stand there noting the details of their behavior, not rushing to interpret them, not making any judgments about their meaning, just absorbing, as long as they stayed in view. In the break between the tall ranges, I once knelt behind a stone and watched a solitary camel that I first mistook for a distant tree because it stood so tall above the distant gravels and brush. I continued watching for an hour as the camel came closer and passed near and then strode onward until it became too small for me to make out anymore.

Another afternoon, I was following animal trails in the terrain not all that far from camp when I looked up at the hill behind me to see a huge pair of eyes watching from the top. They were the openings to two caves in a block of off-white granite positioned like a head atop the light brown strata of the hill. I couldn't help feeling watched from on high by a portentous presence. At the same time, I knew that I would have to go up and peer into those eyes. The caves weren't deep, but the floor of one extended far enough into the granite that if I found myself in a hard Gobi rainstorm here—I remember smiling to myself while trying to imagine that—I could stretch out inside and stay totally dry. A sand-like layer of granite chips eroded from the sides and ceiling covered that floor, forming a smooth bed, with one exception: In the center, part of a stone showed slightly above the chips. Unlike the granite and unlike all the rock lower on the hill, this stone was dark and looked very smooth—oddly so. The cold winds roaring across the slopes outside didn't reach inside as I inspected the cave. I doubted they had shaped the contours of this stone. Something made me reach out and begin digging gently around the edge to expose more of the rock. A short time later, I gently lifted up a prehistoric tool.

It looked like a grinding stone—a classic pestle with a bulbous, slightly chipped bottom and tapering handle that perfectly fit my hand. The heft of the stone felt just right as well, for it was heavy—heavier than any of the rocks in the countryside I had encountered. Whoever used this tool brought

[Top] Odko points to the cave where the author found the ancient tool.
[Bottom] Thousands of years ago, more plant life flourished across the Gobi. Humans probably used tools like this to grind wild grains or other vegetation. Photos: Doug Chadwick

it from somewhere else, possibly a long distance away. I replaced the stone in the depression on the cave floor exactly as I had found it and started looking more carefully, first inside the two caves, then all around the granite cap and on up to its very top, squinting into every nook and cranny. I found no scrapers, no spear or arrow points, not so much as a flake of worked stone, only crumbling granite. Then I searched downslope from the granite cap, making ever-widening circles. Nothing. Returning to the cave, I sat and contemplated the artifact, imagining myself in the place of the owner who left it here ... what? Ten thousand years ago, 20,000? Before that?

Did someone who came to this part of the Gobi seasonally, perhaps after summer's thunderstorms stimulated a burst of new plant growth, stash the tool here to use when he or she returned? It would have been a heavy item to carry on long journeys afoot to other seasonal hunting and foraging grounds. Perhaps the owner only camped here a while out of the wind with a fine view over the break between Atas and Inges, where camels and asses and gazelles would be easy to keep in sight, and intended to take the tool with him or her upon leaving. A day or two later, many miles away, that traveler abruptly stopped short and muttered the Stone Age equivalent of, "Awww SHIT! I forgot the grinder!" Until I finally developed better habits, I used to accidentally leave behind the likes of binoculars, knives, clothes hung on a branch to dry overnight, and so on. Sometimes I went back; sometimes I just kept on cussing and going.

Up on the granite cap whose eerie-eyed stare led to all these questions, I carefully photographed the tool in place, photographed it exposed on the cave floor, stepped away from the cave to take pictures of it and the granite formation against the terrain in the background, recorded the GPS coordinates, and described details of the setting in my notebook. Then I took the ancient tool so I could bring it to the reserve headquarters. For the rest of our stay in the western mountain complex, I made a point of exploring other caves I noticed during my hikes. In the entryways, I found bird nests and wildflowers I hadn't seen before; deeper inside, I discovered mostly spiders and rodent droppings, never another artifact. But I didn't stop making detours up the sides of hills and mountains for a look.

AT HEADQUARTERS, DIRECTOR DOVCHOO SAID, "NO, I HAVE NOT HEARD ABOUT stone tools found in the reserve. Nothing like this or any other kind. People sometimes find old rifle shells or army equipment some places, but not things from long ago." I asked his permission to pass the grinder along to someone in a university paleontology department in Ulaanbaatar so we might all learn more about its origins. (I'm still waiting to hear the results.)

Getting to UB required some pushing and digging, because we fought heavy snow and icy roads from the Gobi-Altai Range all the way north. Dodging cars that were skidding toward us and big rigs mired in drifts, we made it to our meeting with Damdin Tsogtbaatar, a former Minister of the Environment, former Minister of Foreign Affairs, and, as of 2015, Minister of Construction and Urban Development. Though that title made it seem that he might have moved away from the wildlife sphere, he was still dedicated to its protection.

"The government," Mr. Tsogtbaatar told us, "is committed to conservation but unreliable in the financial support it provides from one administration to the next. Therefore, what is required is an independent body that can keep raising capital." He is working to form one—a nongovernment Mongolian conservation group able to meet the challenge of protecting the Gobi bears, camels, and snow leopards. Tsogtbaatar considered these Mongolia's Big Three—the equals of elephants, tigers, and other big mammals with the kind of charisma that can inspire people around the world to safeguard them and, in doing so, shore up entire natural communities.

Of *mazaalai*, Tsogtbaatar had this to say: "Saving this animal is really a priority not only for conservationists but for every Mongolian. There is no other bear like it because it lives in such an extreme environment.... We cannot lose this animal without saying we did everything we could to keep it." Those of us with the Project had all said much the same thing over the years, but it was heartening to hear the words coming from an impressively bright, dynamic, and experienced politician highly placed in the government, especially in 2015. Tsogtbaatar was intent on finding ways to garner more international support for the Big Three. He invited the Gobi Bear Project to coordinate with the independent Mongolian group he envisioned, and Harry agreed that this seemed like a natural alliance and a promising one.

———

I FLEW HOME TO THE UNITED STATES IN MID-MAY. AT THE START OF JULY, HARRY began telephoning and e-mailing me about the smaller of the two young *mazaalai* brothers we had captured that spring. Number 20 had left GGSPA and was in China heading more or less due west. Next, he was deeper in China, crossing stretches of grim-looking desert toward some stringers of uplands in the direction of the Tian Shan Mountains. Essentially, he was doing what a great many young male carnivores do—dispersing from the

A warmer, drier climate in the Gobi is not what the world's last desert-dwelling grizzlies need. Still, if this frighteningly small, virtually unknown group of survivors can win more attention and guaranteed protection, they could stand a chance at carrying on their ancient line. The best evidence from the Gobi Bear Project suggests that the population is holding its own and just possibly beginning to grow. Photo: Joe Riis

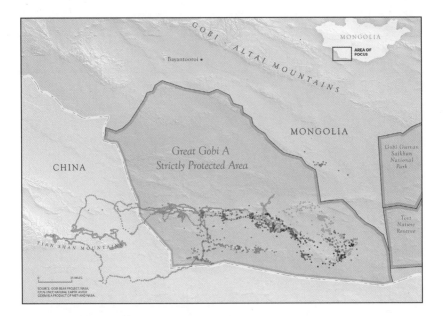

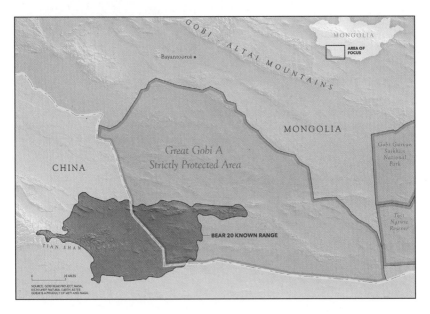

[Top] Each point represents the recorded location of one of the Gobi bears radio-collared from 2005 through 2015. Each color represents a different bear. [Bottom] In 2015, bear Number 20, a young male, wandered more than a hundred miles into China, reaching heights of 12,000 feet in the Tian Shan Mountains He returned to GGSPA after a couple months, but the hope is that other *mazaalai* will continue to explore previously occupied habitats and re-establish healthy populations there.

countryside he grew up in and looking for a home range of his own. I began spending a fair amount of time scrolling this way and that on my computer screen, flying over the region via Google Earth to try and trace his route. By July 8, less than a week after Harry's first news about Number 20, the young male had traveled more than 110 miles from where we captured him and was above 12,700 feet in the Chinese mountains. The conifer forests that defined the habitat at that elevation were visible on the satellite images as phalanxes of pointed shadows.

This tendency to disperse long distances into unfamiliar habitats is a major reason why young male bears tend to suffer higher rates of death than other age and sex classes. They suffer accidents, starvation in marginal environments, and encounters with other large carnivores or humans. Even if this first radioed *mazaalai* known to have moved beyond the reserve's boundaries survived in the new area, we were going to have to count Number 20 as a loss from the GGSPA population unless he returned.

Which is exactly what he did. The signal from his satellite radio collar put his location back in the reserve's western mountain complex at Baruuntooroi later in the summer. He'd just gone on walkabout, a Chinese mountain adventure, and then headed homeward to familiar surroundings.

Knowing that a bear left the reserve and traveled that far to a different realm may only tell us that we happened to document a rare exception to the life history of *mazaalai* today. But one bear is 5 percent of a sample of twenty radio collared *mazaalai*. If over the years, 5 percent of the population is making those kinds of journeys, perhaps talking about the world's rarest bear reclaiming a portion of its former range and numbers is not so much wishful thinking as it is a realistic expectation. Reasonable. Doable. What it really tells us is something we already knew: how much we have yet to learn about Gobi grizzly bears. Or I could say: how much of one of the world's wildest places there is yet to explore.

And save.

Acknowledgments

Thanks, Harry Reynolds and Michael Proctor, for inviting me to join the Gobi Bear Project, for your companionship out there in the vast drylands, and for passing along your considerable knowledge all the while. Thank you, Amgalan Luvsanjamba, for sharing the biological information you accumulated over decades throughout much of Mongolia. To Odbayar Tumendemberel and Bayasgalan Amgalan, my thanks for interpreting the Mongolian language and explaining so many situations and concepts I had scant hope of understanding on my own.

I am grateful to Ankhbayar Buyankhishig, Nyambayar Yanjin, Purevdorj Narangerel, Nasanjargal Battushig, Enkhbold Erdenekhuu, Nyamdavaa Davaadagva, Altanshagai Nanzad, and their fellow Great Gobi Strictly Protected Area (GGSPA) rangers for pointing out how the desert's wild communities work, on scales both grand and intricate, and for showing me ways to cope with the Gobi environment myself. I'm equally grateful for the support and guidance provided to the Gobi Bear Project by the reserve's former director, Batmunkh Mijiddorj, by its current one, Dovchindorj Ganbold, and by the Ministry of Environment that oversees GGSPA.

Thank you, N. Tumenjargal, a private citizen and founder of MAMA, for helping the reserve improve the bears' food security year by year. And extra thanks to Daniel J. Miller, whom I first met ages ago in Kathmandu. During my 2015 visit to Mongolia, he was acting chief of the USAID office in Ulaanbaatar. He let Harry and me stay in his quarters while in the city, took a special interest in the Gobi Bear Project, provided historical information about the Gobi Desert, and later read over my manuscript and offered valuable suggestions.

Of course, I'm very glad for the chance to also pay my respects to the Patagonia Books team—in particular, Karla Olson, John Dutton, Jane Sievert, and Scott Massey. Their commitment to saving wild places and lives, enthusiasm for adventure and exploration, and generous patience with my shortcomings brought this volume to life.

Finally, Abraham Streep, a freelance editor working under contract with Patagonia, played an invaluable role in helping me revise the first draft of this book. This is my chance to repeat what I said so often, only now for all to hear: "Okay, Abe, I get it. You were right. Thank you."

As Harry, who found this skull of an argali ram, might tell you: Sometimes when you're feeling overwhelmed by the strangeness of the Gobi, the best thing to do is join it. Photo: Doug Chadwick

HOW TO HELP

For more information and a chance to contribute to the effort described in this book, please have a look at the website gobibearproject.com. The project has no offices, formal staff, or salaries to pay. Donations will go straight to research, conservation, and the training of Mongolians working for the future survival of *mazaalai* and the wild community to which those rarest of bears belong.

[Opposite] Boldbayar (Boyoko) Mijiddorj holds a wolf pup rescued after villagers killed the mother and other pups in a den outside the reserve. GGSPA is one of the few places wolves are safe from persecution in livestock-focused Mongolia. Photo: Doug Chadwick [Above] The 2011 expedition crew (from left to right): (upper row) Odko, Hunter Causey, Puji, a driver, Ankhaa, Unuruu (a translator), Ariunbold, a driver, Michael; (lower row) Harry, the author, Nasaa (lying down), a driver, Amgaa, Bayasa, Cori, Geerlee. Photo: Joe Riis

Michael taking the classic tourist photo of a reserve's entrance sign—except that tourists aren't allowed within Great Gobi Strictly (also called Special) Protected Area. Photo: Joe Riis